Dear Barbra .
Lots of Love
Carolann .

Jordon's
Pathway

by
**Carolann Frankie and
Roland Bush-Cavell**

© 2014 Carolann Frankie and Roland Bush-Cavell
ISBN Number 978-0-9576596-4-3

Published by Mind Body Soul Development Organisation Limited

For more information on our work, please visit:
www.jordonspathway.co.uk
Or email: info@carolannspathway.co.uk

Dedication

Jordon's Pathway is dedicated to Jordon, Lauren, Lisa and Brian and to autistic children, their parents, families and carers, all over the world. We hope that sharing our story will help increase the understanding and support given to all those diagnosed with autism and those who care for them, for we know that so many of you face your challenges alone.

We would like to thank Lisa and Brian for sharing in the writing of this book and for helping to bring Jordon's story to the world. A big thank you to Natalie who has helped us in our editing and to all our readers who have shown so much support. You know who you are!

All events in this book are true to our memory of them, as we look back over the 16 years of Jordon's life. Some names have been changed and other names omitted to respect individual privacy. This is Jordon's story...

Table of Contents

About the Authors

About Carolann Frankie

A devoted mother and grandmother, Carolann was inspired to write Jordon's Pathway, her third book collaboration, to help bring her grandson's story to the world, provide an insight into autism and to help parents who are facing the challenges of an autistic diagnosis. She lives in London, England.

About Roland Bush-Cavell

Roland's great love is writing and when he is not working as a fundraiser for charities, he pours his creativity into books. Jordon's Pathway is the first 'true-life' story Roland has written and his third collaboration with his friend, Carolann Frankie. He lives in London, England.

Introduction

It is springtime and I am walking on a woodland pathway just a few steps behind my two beautiful grandchildren, overcome by a mixture of thought and overwhelming emotions. Most affecting is the realisation of the immensity of the journey they are taking and the love I have for them both. Seeing them hand in hand as they walk together, respecting the gap that exists between us and them, I well up with tears of emotion at the thought of how far we have come together. For, both my grandchildren have been diagnosed with autism, a disorder that affects not just them but the whole family, a family that spends every waking moment dealing with the ramifications. With the diagnosis of autism spectrum disorder on the increase, there are even wider-reaching consequences arising from my grandchildren's stories, for the issues that autism raises affect us all, challenging us on every level and bringing with it the potential for a world full of emotional pain. I walk behind these two innocents who will never be able to deal with the world without our help, wondering what future my darling grandchildren might hope for and indeed what the future holds for us all.

Being the grandmother of an autistic grandson has been one of the most heart-wrenching, testing and endearing learning experiences of my life. We have lived through years of hard work, anxiety, sacrifice, huge demands upon our patience and even fear for Jordon's life; an uphill climb through a forest of uncertainty where I have even worried that my daughter might be lost to the overwhelming impact that autism has had on her young life. For autism has far wider ramifications than affecting just the person who is diagnosed; it impacts on all those who have to continually adjust and learn to deal with it. My own worry is not that Jordon will be affected by autism, for he already has been, but that my daughter Lisa and her partner Brian might be robbed of their own lives by the demands it places upon them.

Jordon's journey is the subject of this book, yet we recently had our worst fears confirmed, when my four year old granddaughter Lauren was diagnosed. She is also autistic; something we suspected but did not dare face nor admit to ourselves. For now Lisa and Brian face the same trying journey they have endured with Jordon, long years of challenges ahead of them once more. Where with Jordon, we faced the unknown, now we know what to expect and the nature of what will be demanded of us all in the years ahead.

Having seen just how little the world knows of autism and the huge impact that comes with it, I wanted to share Jordon's story and the life we live together as a family; how Lisa, Brian and I have had to work together to cope every day of our lives, to bring the best to Jordon and to help him walk a pathway that, while it is for him more isolated than any life we could ever imagine, also casts his parents into a role of solitary confinement, excluded in many ways from the non-autistic world that surrounds them, held at bay by this disorder.

Lauren's journey will be of equal impact and importance to us as a family and yet her life has just begun. Here I wish to bring to you the story we have been living through for sixteen years, the story of Jordon, a joy to us all who has been a focus for this little family for so long, the tale of an autistic boy who is fast growing into a wholesome young man in his own right.

Jordon is a darling child and he is one of the best teachers I have ever had. His position on the autistic spectrum demands that we learn patience, it also demands that we learn to give freely without expectation of an emotional reward. For, every single thing he learns in his life takes him an age to accept and this means that every new behaviour may take months, or even years, for him to develop. Every time we see him take on a new idea it is a revelation to all of us and the rewards of seeing him achieve progress on his pathway are immense, not least because they are so hard won.

Autism is a lifelong developmental disability that affects how a person communicates with and relates to other people. Autism also affects how a person makes sense of the world around them. This means that the last sixteen years of our family life have been totally dominated by the need to care for Jordon and find ways of helping him to learn and move forwards. I have seen my daughter take upon herself every element of this full time job and together, along the way, we have developed an understanding of what autism means for Jordon, the impact it has on his thought processes and our family life.

The nature of the syndrome means that it is a full-time demand on the parents' time. 24 hours a day, seven days a week, they help their child develop, called upon to be the bridge between their offspring's mind and the outside world. Caring for an autistic child is a vocation and a duty that is never asked for and once embarked upon, continues for the rest of the parents' lives. It comes with a daily commitment to deal with a child that baffles you at every turn, perhaps taking years before they show you even the smallest outward display of love.

It is my sincere wish that Jordon's story, the life we have lived with him so far, brings to you our understanding of autism and what the word means, seen first-hand through the eyes of a grandmother who has followed every step he has taken on his pathway. Bearing witness to his painful growth, as he matured into the vibrant young man he is today, means he has a very special place in my heart. I feel it to be essential that others might benefit from sharing what we have discovered along the way; because the lessons learned in loving children that are so alienated from the world are valuable to all of us, whether we have an autistic child in our family or not.

Autism is incredibly difficult to relate to. Despite there being increasing coverage and presence on television and in the press, many people still have no idea what it actually means for those who are autistic.

We see children who behave strangely, making weird noises, acting unusually but appearing physically untouched. We see parents who are burdened with the additional responsibilities and even though we can appreciate how difficult it must be, our understanding may go no further.

Yet, as with all behaviours, there is a reason that autistic children are the way they are, there is a reason that they act so strangely and why they can react in such seemingly odd ways to the world around them. From their perspective, everything they do is normal, they are responding to a world that they only partially see, from a point of view that is hampered and so very different from our own. For them to adjust with their limited understanding is so very hard. So, the burden falls upon their nearest and dearest and those who have the will to care. Those of us who are here and can see what is happening have every faculty we need to help. Yet we see families who are worn down by the pressure and the burden of these special children who are born to them. Yes, they bring unique gifts with them, but as with all things of value, the lessons we learn from autistic children are hard fought for and can come at the cost of what would be considered a normal life.

Autistic children are constantly vulnerable; it might take years for them to learn not to run into traffic or to keep their hands away from fire or not to eat what is harmful and even when they do learn, it may only be because we have conditioned them, not because they understand. They are essentially naïve to this world and they do not connect the physical harms within it with their own well-being. An autistic child may be told thousands of times not to eat dirt or insects, not to bite the furniture, not to push their fingers into a door-frame or an electrical plug socket, or to climb and pull a shelving unit on top of themselves or to eat foul things, but even after years of coaching might inadvertently harm themselves, as though they had never heard a single warning.

So parents of autistic children can become long-term carers for their offspring. They devote their lives to helping them cope with the world, caring for their needs, helping them avoid harming themselves and slowly, inexorably encouraging that child to a higher level of understanding. Yet, emotionally, these parents are servants to much more. An autistic child immerses you in a world that focuses on them, often to the exclusion of all else. Fulfilling this need for constant attention, with sometimes scant emotional reward, brings the danger of becoming lost to feelings of hopelessness. Parents of autistic children can, quite rightly, feel abandoned by society, slaves to their situations, lost in a solitary emotional environment, adrift in an autistic world which closes in until they feel trapped and unable to escape.

Yet, despite our perception of an autistic child's behaviour being the cause of much hardship, rarely do they intentionally do wrong. Blaming an autistic child for being the way they are, for ignoring us, for being so scared of life that they scream, for lashing out, is as much use as blaming a bird for flying out of our grasp. We see these children become so frustrated with a world that does not meet their needs that they throw themselves into fits, that they hit and shout and scream and stamp and do these same things over and over and over again. Autistic children are not naughty, they are not bad; they are lost in the space we have created around them. If it is difficult for an autistic child to learn, then how much harder is it for us to appreciate that love and patience are the only remedies that will help and that our own negative reactions demonstrate not their limitations but our own.

Yet there is hope, for as much as caring for an autistic child is seemingly a physical struggle; managing their everyday needs, ensuring they are safe, dealing with the tiredness of coping, in fact, the greatest struggle is with the huge emotional lessons they confront us with; the burden of the unfairness, the seemingly random nature of this lifelong imprisonment to caring, the lack of love, the lack of support, the racking fear of spending the rest of your life caring for another who is almost completely blocked with little prospect of emotional reward. All these burdening feelings are half of the journey with an autistic child. The good news is that there is hope for every single one of these. For, once you find out what autism is and gain an understanding, it is far easier to deal with. Every single fear and emotional burden has both an explanation and a remedy and gaining an insight into autism offers hope for every parent and every autistic child.

Perhaps one of the biggest mistakes anyone who cares for an autistic child can make and the most common assumption for those that do not know, is to expect that there is a way to get an autistic child to obey you. The sad fact is that there is no way of compelling an autistic child to do what you say or of imposing your will upon him or her. They simply cannot relate to an order or someone telling them what to do.

An autistic child does not battle your will, rather they live in a world they do not understand, where everything remains alien and strange. They cannot relate to the world they perceive, let alone appreciate why we would compel them to follow our lead within it. They are not seeking to do things their way, through willfulness or obstinacy, rather they are trapped in an intellectual hall of mirrors where they relate everything they see to their own needs and find it hugely difficult to appreciate our understanding of the world. As their guides, we can only gently lead them by the hand, attempting to relate to the causes of their feelings and explain to them the effects of their actions. When we understand, in turn, how distorted everything appears to an autistic child, it can educate us as to why they can become so frustrated and even angry with the world.

Therefore, the ways we have of relating to an autistic child are far narrower than when dealing with children who do not have this disorder. The only way to relate to your autistic child is through cooperation, applying patience and learning to communicate in a way that you both relate to. For, it is only by relating as much as is possible to their behaviours, by endeavouring to understand their thinking, that one can identify where the problems and frustrations originate. Taking this understanding approach can help unlock the doorway between the autistic child's brain and the outside world. Once you have widened your own understanding, then headway can be made. While this is an enormous task and one that often costs the parents dearly, there is no other route available.

Parents of autistic children are called upon to extend levels of patience and emotional fortitude that very few of us ever encounter. As much as an autistic child helps us learn about the value of extending love and friendship, so the parents of autistic children can be angels to their offspring, while from the outside, the day to day traumas seem to offer an emotional purgatory.

Only love, patience and understanding affords any means of escape from otherwise hellish situations, in just the same way as caring for an autistic child can actually open our eyes to the things in life that are so important. We are all very lucky in that we are equipped to help these children, in just the same way that loving them can show us all our very human limitations.

I felt called upon to share the approach we took, the ways we found of helping Jordon deal with the situations he encountered in his everyday life. Our hope is that sharing our experiences might help people in coping with autism in their own offspring and, for those who have no connection with autism, to understand more about those whose lives it touches. For, along the way, we gained many valuable insights, all of which have helped us to encourage Jordon to develop positively and to move on with his life.

This is Jordon's story.

Chapter One - A Difficult Birth

Sixteen years ago, I stood in a white-walled delivery room in our local hospital, watching my second grandson Jordon being born into this world. At the time, little did we know the future trials my daughter Lisa and her partner Brian would be facing and how difficult the years ahead would be for us all. Nor did I suspect the wonderful voyage of discovery and fulfilment that would accompany Jordon's arrival, this perfectly formed and beautiful healthy-looking baby, who came into life with what would later be diagnosed as autism spectrum disorder.

Jordon was Lisa and Brian's firstborn and the fulfilment of all their wishes to start their own family. Even now, when I look back at the heart-breaking situations we went through to bring Jordon to this stage in life, now he is sixteen years old, heartache wells up inside me and the emotional pain moves me to tears. Yet, what has come with him has been a world of love, teaching us how to see life through the eyes of an autistic child and how to respect and understand someone who sees reality in a totally different way to us all.

Several hours prior to my arrival in the hospital, I sat at home, just three miles away, pondering the fact that Lisa was being induced sometime in the next 24 hours, three days before her due date. Waiting for the phone call to say that her labour had commenced was a nerve wracking time.

As it was Lisa's first child, despite being induced, the feeling amongst the medical staff was that it would still take some while before Jordon was born. Yet, once the procedure was carried out, Lisa went into labour almost immediately and by the time I received a phone call, she was in the second stage. The phone rang and I was asked to come to the hospital immediately if I was to be in time for the birth of my grandson. This was shocking news, I had no idea it would be so quick. She had been in labour for only four hours and everything was moving far more swiftly than anyone had suspected. I had to move very quickly if I was to be with Brian by Lisa's side in time for the birth.

Thankfully, I was prepared and my front door slammed behind me as I hurried along the pathway to my car. With no other thought in my head other than to be there for Jordon's arrival into the world, I drove to the hospital. Lisa wanted me to be there for her and Brian and so I could not afford to be late. Fortunately, with the hospital in such close proximity, it was a mere 15 minutes before I arrived, thinking I would still have adequate time before the actual event. Thankfully, I found a parking space immediately, parked the car and hurried into the hospital's main entrance.

Brian was waiting for me at the door to the delivery suite. He was hurrying me in, waving his hand and, all of a sudden, everything became very urgent. Cool, calm and collected, he stood and ushered me in with the words, quietly spoken, "she's starting to push" as I rushed into the delivery room. There Lisa lay, all by herself in bed, dressed in only a white hospital gown, covered with a thin white sheet. Red-faced and in obvious pain, she was clutching at the mask that delivered pain-relieving gas and air, desperate to bring her child into the world. Everything had happened so quickly that the hospital staff had not had the opportunity to give her a pain-relieving injection and no one was in the room at this point, other than myself, Lisa and Brian.

Brian stood next to Lisa's bed, holding her hand, while I looked on waiting for my grandson to arrive. At that moment, my attention was drawn to the bleep of the baby's heartbeat monitor.

Something was wrong.

Turning to Brian, I asked him to call the nurse in urgently, while I took Lisa's hand in mine.

What should have been a regular, steady beep, was interspersed with long uneven pauses, each one causing my own heart to skip a beat. The whole scene held an almost surreal dreamlike quality to it. Seemingly moving in slow motion, Brian returned with the nurse, but in fact arrived almost immediately. The nurse was all swift, precise movements and intense concentration as she first studied the monitor, then turned to Lisa, staring directly into her face. She seemed to come to an instant decision and, turning swiftly on her heel, she left the room, leaving all three of us there, somehow frozen in time, waiting for each of the long silences to be replaced with the reprieve of yet another irregular bleep.

Clutching Lisa tightly, I could feel the pulse in her hand, urging her to breathe, living the moment with her, I was aware of a doctor suddenly entering the room. He was clothed head to toe in green; a green overall, green headwear and a green mask, all I could see was his eyes and they held the same intense focus that I had seen in the nurse's face. In his gloved hands he held a gleaming silver tray full of large metallic medical instruments that clanked in his hands as he neared Lisa's bed. I could see cold hard edges and the reflection of the overhead lighting on polished steel. Turning my own gaze away from this frightening array of implements I saw the doctor's eyes focusing on Lisa, appraising her as he neared the bed.

A shudder ran through me, gripped by anxiety, wondering what was to come next. I looked into Lisa's face, as the doctor began the procedure to bring Jordon into this world.

Lisa's eyelids were closed tight against the hurt and moments later, her cry of pain filled me with anguish, its silent echo ran right through me. I was dimly aware of holding my breath, waiting, hoping, until, after what seemed like an age, the silence was broken by my baby grandson's first ragged cry.

A wave of joy and relief for my daughter came over me, holding back the tears, I wanted to reach out and hold her. Brian was there at her side but all I could do was to stroke her hair and praise her, as I found myself repeating over and over, "he is here, he is here."

Lisa's face was a strained mask, drained of all colour, her skin almost completely white. I kissed her on the forehead as the nurse passed her beautiful baby into her arms for the very first time.

Brian's eyes filled with tears as Lisa gently passed him the tiny form of their baby. The doctor had seemingly vanished from the room, leaving almost silently as the three of us shared this unique moment. Jordon, the new centre of our little family, now held our full attention.

On 18th April 1997 at 1:18pm, weighing 7lb 10oz, Jordon was born into the world.

I marvelled that, at that point, Brian, a man who is normally quite guarded with his emotions, was openly crying, as he clutched Jordon's tiny form to his chest and gazed at his newborn son. I also wondered, because Brian too had suffered quite serious health issues recently, whether he had truly believed he would survive to see this moment.

The air that I breathe

The months up until Jordon's birth had not been easy; both Lisa and Brian had suffered quite worrying medical problems, making the latter stages of the pregnancy difficult and sometimes traumatic. I had watched them both go through some troubling times.

In the later stages of the pregnancy, Lisa had begun to feel increasingly unwell. She had complained of troubling spots in her vision, headaches and giddiness that made her feel like she was ready to faint. Her body had begun to swell up and her hands and feet had ballooned. At that time, she became increasingly dependent on Brian, who was doing marvellously well, despite having a full time job he was very supportive and I couldn't help but admire him for diligently providing Lisa with all the help he could.

But this situation was soon to end in a way that was both surprising and, as it seems even now, incredibly unfair to them both.

One night, when Lisa was seven months pregnant, poor Brian woke up with pains in his chest. At first he ignored it, but he was soon in agony, fighting for each and every breath. Lisa woke up, in the middle of the night to the sight of him silhouetted beside her, bathed in sweat, his face grey and gasping for air.

After a flurry of desperate phone calls, the paramedics arrived and minutes later, Brian was in an ambulance, being rushed to hospital with what was later diagnosed as a collapsed lung. Lisa and I could not work it out. Lisa said Brian had been absolutely fine when he went to bed and he was a fit and healthy young man, it didn't make any sense.

In hospital, after some chaotic activity and many attempts, the medical team managed to re-inflate Brian's lung and he was kept in for observation. But, this meant their roles were now reversed; while Brian recovered, it was Lisa who was providing support, travelling to visit him while she herself was unwell.

Soon, though, Brian was discharged and he returned to work, but his recovery was short lived; once more his lung suddenly collapsed and again he found himself in an ambulance being rushed to hospital. There, five attempts were made to re-inflate his lung, puncturing his chest each time, but it just wasn't working. The doctors had to make a decision and to ensure his lung did not collapse again, Brian was admitted for what was quite a major operation.

You can imagine my feelings while we readied ourselves for the surgery, my mind roamed, imagining the very worst of scenarios, yet clinging to the hope that all would go smoothly and Brian would emerge fit and well.

Thankfully, Brian's operation was successful and to this day he bears a souvenir of that time, a scar eighteen inches long, from his left shoulder blade, to his lowest rib and, clustered around it, the puncture marks where they attempted so many times to re-inflate his lung.

So, once more, Brian found himself recovering in hospital, while Lisa's own ill health meant that she had to leave her job as a nursery assistant two weeks ahead of schedule. Yet, she insisted on visiting Brian every day in hospital, taking the train to central London so she could be at his bedside.

I was a frequent visitor and one day, I remember walking into the ward and stopping dead in my tracks. There was Brian wrapped in bandages and still in obvious pain from the surgery, Lisa holding his hand, her head hanging with tiredness, dark circles under her eyes and her feet so swollen that she had no laces in her trainers. They both looked so sad, I couldn't help but wonder just how long they would be able to cope like this. I made up my mind and I asked them both to come stay with me, to rest while they recovered and they agreed they would, just until Brian felt better and Lisa's swelling had come down.

One endearing side effect of the pregnancy was that Lisa had an absolute obsession for oranges and little piles of orange peel began to appear on my kitchen table.

But her stay with me was short-lived. A few days after they both moved in with me, Lisa had a regular appointment at the health clinic and there she received a diagnosis of her own. Her blood pressure was dangerously high and her symptoms were getting worse. The doctor was quick to act, Lisa had pre-eclampsia, not an uncommon condition, but one that left untreated can prove to be fatal.

So it was for less than a week that Brian and Lisa stayed with me, before it was Lisa's turn to be admitted to hospital for observation and there she remained for nearly two weeks prior to the birth, until she was near enough to her term date to induce. Our roles were reversed; instead of sitting beside Lisa while Brian lay in the hospital bed, it was Brian sat beside me while Lisa lay ill and awaiting the birth.

We became regular visitors, trying to cheer her up and talking about the impending happy day, trying to paint a positive picture of the future ahead. I brought baby clothes to the bedside and a daily replenishment for Lisa's constant supply of oranges! Feeling very sad each time I left the ward, Lisa's unhappy face remained with me each time I left her behind.

It struck me for a moment how awful and how sad that this young healthy couple should suddenly be flung into this situation, both of them dealing with illnesses that came with no clue or warning. We were spending so long in hospitals that the cold vinyl covered floors, fluorescent lighting and plastic chairs seemed like they were all part of our second home. Yet, how glad I am to say that they both came through the experience.

All these worrying events were the prelude to 18th April, when dear little Jordon was born into the world. Yet, even after the birth, there was no escape from hospital beds; Lisa remained so that her blood pressure could be monitored and because Jordon was losing weight, the medical team wanted to keep an eye on him also. It was such a disappointment, but they had to stay for a further week under the hospital's care before returning home. At least Lisa had complete bed-rest, while Brian and I kept up the bedside chat, giving us time to cuddle Jordon and to discuss their plans for bringing him home.

The good news was that Jordon remained in his cot next to Lisa's bed so that she could show him a mother's love and begin to bond. But, even at this stage, Jordon would prove very difficult to feed. We took the pressure off of Lisa by taking turns in helping and reassured each other by saying it would be fine when we got him home.

Despite these difficulties, eventually the hospital were satisfied with Lisa and Jordon's state of health and allowed them to leave, her blood pressure levels reduced and Jordon having taken enough milk to regain a little weight.

So, we began settling Jordon into his new home. I remember seeing him in his cot, standing there looking down at his miraculous tiny form, wanting to stroke his face and cradle his tiny hands in my own. The same feelings arose as when Lisa was giving birth and I wanted to reach out to Jordon, to tell him it was ok, to take away his pain at being born into the world and to reassure him that all would be well. Our problems were now seemingly over and we could get on with a normal life once more.

Yet for some reason a troubling thought echoed in my mind "Time will tell. Time will tell".

Chapter Two - Problem Parents

Now, we all expect babies to cry every now and again. After all, it is one of the ways they let us know that they are in discomfort, hungry or in pain and it lets us know it is time to provide for their needs.

This intermittent crying was not what we experienced with Jordon. In fact, after we got him home and the second day had passed, from the moment he awoke to the moment he went to sleep all he seemed to do was cry or wriggle in discomfort. It was really quite alarming. I have raised three children and had never seen anything like it before. He would arch his back, go completely rigid, stiffening his arms and legs, writhing in his cot, or in our arms, without cease. At their invitation, I was an increasingly frequent visitor to Lisa and Brian's home, there to help Lisa and so, I was witness to all of Jordon's behaviour. Not at any time of day did he lie quietly with his eyes open and we could not work out what it was that was leading him to be constantly distressed. It was heart-breaking for, all the while, we were desperately trying to identify what was wrong, to find an answer that would fit these worrying symptoms, but at that time all we knew was that all was not as it should be and Jordon was suffering.

When he was awake, which was most of the time, his eyes appeared glazed and dull and the only reliable way of getting him to sleep was to continuously rock him backwards and forwards on your shoulder or in your arms. Jordon's behaviour became progressively more unsettling for us all. There was no let-up in the noise or the movement, nor any signs to indicate the source of the obvious distress he was experiencing and it would continue night and day. While his crying was initially merely disquieting, we all became increasingly concerned as we struggled to find ways to help Jordon find some peace.

Usually, to get a baby to sleep, you merely cradle them in your arms and, with a bit of tender encouragement they will nod off. In Jordon's case, we learned that the rocking had to be constant, repetitive and continuous. If we maintained the same monotonous rhythm, then we would have some hope of his eyes closing. Any deviation from this rule, any failure to keep up this regular rocking motion and he would almost instantly wake up. Even when we were able, eventually and after much patience, to get him to sleep, he would often wake up the moment we put him into his cot and we would have to start all over again.

This was not normal behaviour; not what you would expect from the average baby. Inevitably, he would, sometime later, wake up screaming and continue unabated until we persuaded him to sleep once more. Often, the only way we actually succeeded in getting him back to sleep again was by waiting until he nodded off through sheer exhaustion. This meant that we were all soon spending the majority of our many waking hours, walking up and down, holding on to an anguished baby that was screaming so loudly we knew he was suffering some form of horrendous discomfort. His little face was heartbroken and I would talk gently to him, stroking his tiny head and kissing away the tears that ran down his cheeks, his eyes screwed shut, confined to a world of misery.

This cycle of crying, rocking and waking would continue all day and all night for three or four rounds over a period of hours before he would settle down and even so, the longest we could ever get him to settle was about two and a half hours and what a relief it was for all of us when he did! Because when Jordon was awake he would not be put down, it meant you needed at least two adults on hand to cater for him; one to walk around the room with Jordon in their arms and the other to make a bottle in an attempt to pacify him.

The effect this was having on us all was appalling. Our arms would ache from the demands of maintaining the constant rocking and we were groggy from sleep deprivation.

Brian would regularly take a turn and, on the occasions he was successful in getting Jordon to sleep, could be seen dozing off in a chair with his son's tiny form on his chest. Taking turns, working together in this way allowed all of us just a couple of hours sleep each night so that we were ready for the cycle to begin the next day and each morning we woke and prayed fervently that this would be a better day for everyone.

Even though the situation was potentially overwhelming, I still wanted to know the origin of his sleeping problems. In an effort to understand, I would stand by Jordon's cot, putting my mind to his behaviour and observing his distress. With him being so dear to me, it was like emotional torture to see him crying, arching his back and writhing as if tormented. There was no outward sign as to what was wrong, we had quickly gone to consult with the medical professionals, but initially they had no suggestions and neither did Lisa, Brian or I, none of us were doctors. So, Jordon's behaviour continued relentlessly, with no clues as to what the underlying problem might be.

Nil by mouth

As you would expect, as his concerned family, we tried everything we could to settle Jordon down into a normal pattern of behaviour, for his crying and inability to sleep was not the full extent of the problems we faced in the early weeks with this little lad. Try as we might, the feeding problems he had experienced since birth failed to improve. We tried everything that we could think of and whatever was suggested to us.

No matter what we tried, it was almost impossible to get him to take milk down.

While it was obvious this was not normal, we were later to discover there was an underlying problem. No one would have suspected at this stage, but as an autistic child, Jordon simply did not realise that he needed to suck to gain sustenance. His thought process did not make the connection between sucking to draw in milk or as we later discovered, even swallowing food, to alleviate his own hunger. Things that are second nature to the rest of us were, to him, incomprehensible. He could not make the link between his feelings of hunger and the physical action necessary to alleviate them.

Of course, we continued our regular visits to the doctor's surgery to elicit their help and consulted with the health visitor whenever they came on their scheduled visits. Then we tried everything the medical professionals recommended, special feeding bottles designed to overcome colic, changing the size of the teats he used on his normal feeding bottles and even giving him a dummy to offer him some measure of the comfort he so obviously needed.

We listened to friends and we tried every option, however, no matter what we attempted, a typical night for Jordon was for him to constantly wake up. As the days progressed and the weeks turned into months, every moment he was awake, he would be squirming or screaming, crying continuously and making us all very unhappy in our concern for his situation.

Overanxious parents

By this time, we were all exhausted and increasingly desperate to find out what was troubling Jordon. At our wits' end, we continued what was by now a campaign to get an answer from the medical profession.

I knew that none of Jordon's behaviour was normal. There was obviously something quite dreadfully wrong and yet none of the medical professionals with whom we spoke and shared our concerns seemed to appreciate just how bad his situation was and it was months before we were to finally gain some insight into the cause of at least some of the difficulties Jordon was experiencing.

We were, by now, very regular visitors to the doctor's surgery, seeking any kind of help they might offer, anything that might cast light upon the situation. It was on one such visit that we were sat in the surgery with a new health visitor who had been assigned to us. We described the extreme nature of Jordon's behaviour and took pains to put it in perspective, detailing the length of time he would lie awake and the inexplicable nature of his distress. We thought we had done a pretty good job of explaining all the trouble we had been experiencing so as to identify the source of the problem.

Having listened intently, the health visitor then promptly told us that Jordon was probably crying because he was picking up on our anxiety. She seemed to have gained the impression that we were paranoid and imagining things. Now I can imagine why she might have thought this; we were being driven to distraction with something so obviously amiss with Jordon and we probably did look very worried. However, she seemed to think it was a severe case of colic coupled with overanxious parents who were exacerbating the problem.

I could not agree, I had seen colic first hand and it just did not fit Jordon's behaviour. Yet, here we were, hearing how this was typical and more, that we must be imagining things or the cause of it ourselves. I had never heard anything like it; here we were trying everything we could to find out the root cause of the problems, only to be told that it was our own worry causing this tiny baby to be constantly distressed. It felt like we were being patronised and the comments seemed somehow ill-informed and even ridiculous. We knew that something was wrong, but it didn't seem we were being listened to and we felt let down, disappointed and helpless. We were doing everything we could, detailing our situation, Jordon's behaviour and the effect it was having on him and the family and the only answer we received was that this was somehow a psychological problem and that we were causing it ourselves.

There didn't seem anywhere else to turn, we were already talking to the medical professionals, what could we possibly do next? I remember feeling drained and confused by the fact that those who should help us were suggesting we were the problem.

The most bitter irony was that we were the opposite of what we were being accused of. We spent hours each day calmly talking to Jordon, soothing and relaxing him in any way we could. Being told our own anxiety was the root cause by people who are trained to know best was a depressing state of affairs.

So, despite our best efforts, the situation continued unabated and as we tried all the suggestions put to us, an unfortunate and dramatic turn of events was to ensure the health professionals took notice at last.

One day, at two and a half months of age, very soon after we were suggested as being the cause of his problems, Jordon developed an extremely high temperature. Lisa was at home with him when she noticed he had suddenly gone quiet, the colour draining from his face and his eyes blank and unfocused. Ashen faced, Lisa picked him up from his cot. By now, he was a marbled grey and white and his whole body was as limp as a rag doll, hanging in Lisa's arms as if he was unconscious or worse. She tried lifting his arms and they flopped like dead weights, completely unresponsive. On the verge of hysteria, without stopping to think, she rushed him to the car and drove to the nearest hospital, the place of Jordon's birth.

Of course, I didn't hear about this until very soon afterwards, but I can imagine Lisa must have been quite a sight as she arrived in the Accident and Emergency ward. She told me that her face was nearly as white as Jordon's as she ran to the reception desk nearly demented with fear, clutching his tiny limp form in her arms. Jordon was still completely unresponsive and as limp as if his body were made of cloth and inside all Lisa could do was to repeat to herself, "let him be alright. Let him be alright. Please let him come through this" over and over to hold the panic at bay.

The receptionist had taken one look at Jordon and didn't speak, instead she called out immediately for a nurse who brought with her a whirlwind of action. Jordon was instantly surrounded by a medical team and whisked off to be examined. All the while, Lisa answered a barrage of questions, as they tried to determine what was wrong.

As soon as I was told, Lisa's voice, breathless with anxiety, on the phone, I felt as if the culmination of all our concerns were falling upon us in that very moment. The worries, the unspoken fear that had shadowed us, that something was very seriously wrong with Jordon seemed to have finally delivered their answer. After weathering the storm of the weeks and months that were now behind us, this first lightning strike shocked us all.

By the time we spoke, Lisa now knew Jordon's diagnosis and it was obvious that the verdict we had tried so hard to obtain for all this time was upon us. In the pause while I waited for her to tell me the news, I could not help but wish that it should not have come to this. I wished the health professionals had spotted this first. Instead, events had come to a head and our answer had fallen upon us in the worst way possible and I also wished with every bone in my body that it should not have to come in this way. My poor Jordon!

Lisa had been told Jordon had a condition called kidney reflux which, we were to subsequently learn, is one of the most common problems associated with children's kidneys.

Lisa asked them why this had not been diagnosed before and even as I heard the news, my frustrations threatened to turn into anger. For two months the entire family had been through an immense ordeal and it had taken the collapse of a tiny baby to get a diagnosis that was obviously quite readily accessible. There was only one conclusion I could draw, having not witnessed the symptoms for themselves; our concerns had not been taken seriously. Had they been, we would have been referred to the hospital for the necessary tests. What was frustrating was that all the hospital staff around Lisa knew nothing of what she had been through, or how hard she had tried to get the answer they so easily provided.

I was ready to pay a visit to our health centre and confront them, to tell them exactly what I thought. Our desperation had moved us, pushed us to do everything we could, yet the answers we were given were worse than meaningless and the end result was a great risk to Jordon's health and well-being. My anger was curbed by the fact that at least we now had an answer and even though it revealed a problem with Jordon's kidney, my intense exasperation was finally being salved with relief. This didn't stop me, however. Sometime later, I confronted the doctor at the health clinic and let her know that Jordon had faced a serious risk to his health. I received a very guarded response and a thought that "It must have just happened".

Still, knowing the cause of the problem at last meant we knew what we were dealing with.

The medical explanation was that a valve in Jordon's bladder was not working properly and urine was flowing back up the ureter to the kidney. As a result, Jordon was suffering considerable pain and undiagnosed infections.

A Year of Pain

So we had, or so we thought, a clue as to some of the reasons for Jordon's unusual behaviour and constant distress. The nursing staff told Lisa that his condition meant that passing water was extremely difficult and painful. Quite simply, Jordon had been in constant pain since the time of his birth up until now, over two months later.

There was now hope on the horizon and the prospect of a long term solution. Over the coming nine months there were to be many repeat prescriptions of antibiotics and in the meantime, we began to understand how his symptoms could have contributed to his extreme behaviour.

Yet, deep down, I knew that something was still not quite right. My intuition and the physical signs said that things just didn't add up. Having kidney reflux did not explain all of the symptoms Jordon was displaying. There was no force behind his urination at all, intermittently he would still be in great pain and all the while, the problems we experienced with his feeding continued.

So, we returned to the hospital, but they had no suggestions, we visited the doctor's surgery once more and spoke with the health visitor. Despite now being a lot more attentive and willing to listen to us, they were as much in the dark as we were and no suggestions were forthcoming.

Eventually, as the problems continued to worsen, a decision was made to investigate further. Something wasn't right. So, Jordon was referred to a hospital in central London, where he would be x-rayed to determine why his condition was not improving.

On the allotted day, we travelled there by train and London Underground, before walking the final few hundred yards to the imposing hospital entrance.

There, the staff took very good care of us. We were led into an x-ray room and Jordon was laid down, but he had no concept of what was going on, from the moment he was laid on the table he struggled and became increasingly distressed. The medical staff were obviously surprised and concerned by the volume and frequency of his frantic ear-piercing screams and we all tried our best to calm him down, but he continued, holding himself rigid and screaming with all his might.

We were gently ushered out of the room, retreating behind the protective wall while Brian remained, clothed in a heavy protective apron, tasked with holding his son still, immobilising him while the x-ray was completed. Watching through the thick glass window, Lisa and I began to cry. It was heart wrenching to see Jordon struggle and Brian having to restrain him against his will, his tiny arms and legs seemingly lost amidst all the cold-looking medical equipment. The metal table and its iron sides made it seem as if he were tethered in a cage and there Brian stood, immobile, fixing Jordon to the table, his face a mask, as he dealt with the pain of watching his son in such anguish.

Eventually, the x-ray was complete and we returned to Jordon's side. By now, his face was distraught, red and covered in tears and as he was let up, he became totally uncontrollable. Once more, Brian struggled to hold him, eventually having to secure his writhing form in his push chair as we settled down to await the results.

Our turn came and, in his office, the doctor patiently explained what we were looking at. I stared at the glowing picture in disbelief and a cold shudder ran through me. Jordon's right kidney looked nothing at all like the healthy left kidney beside it; instead it was a tiny shrunken walnut encompassed by a vague sack shape, a baggy balloon of accumulated fluid and his ureter, which should have been a clear tube, looked very much like a flattened straw. I gasped and turned to Lisa, whose eyes were boring into the image. I could see the shock and sadness wash over her. We were both stunned, no wonder Jordon had been behaving the way he had. He must have been in agony and at last we knew the true source of all his pain.

When he was writhing and arching his back, it wasn't just discomfort, it was the bruising pain of the unrelenting pressure of this sack of fluid applied directly to his kidney. It must have been as if it were locked in the tightening jaws of a vice for weeks on end and his crying had been an agonised cry for help! My poor Jordon. Lisa's face showed what we all felt, complete anguish that he should have borne such a painful burden for so long and borne it alone.

Jordon's kidney and ureter were not formed or functioning properly and so severe was the problem, they would have to be surgically removed. The three of us looked at Jordon as he sat white-faced, exhausted, sad and lonely in his pushchair, not knowing that he was to face the further pain of an operation. Our hearts went out to him.

The need to operate was urgent and the surgeon felt far more comfortable arranging an appointment for surgery after Jordon's first birthday, which, while to him was a significant date, was thankfully in just ten days' time.

The sense of shock we all shared, the sense of disappointment to have come this far with him and be told that surgery was the only solution rendered us mute and lost in our own thoughts for much of the way back home, as we allowed the awful news to sink in.

Just a few days later, Lisa and Brian received a letter. Disappointingly, Jordon's surgery was to be on the actual day of his first birthday, meaning that when we should be celebrating, he would be in the operating theatre.

So we sat-out the remaining time in apprehension of what would come next. At this time, a change came over Lisa and she seemed to strengthen, to take control, her maternal instincts driving her to see the operation as a positive thing with a positive outcome. By contrast, I was feeling weak, the sadness I felt for Jordon and his situation had overwhelmed me and I couldn't help but question why one so young had to face all of this so early in his life.

When the time of the operation was upon us, Lisa and Brian found themselves sat once more in a ward directly beside Jordon who was in a hospital cot, holding on to a toy that had flashing lights. Lisa told me just how unusual it was to see him getting involved, interacting and pushing buttons on any toy. Watching closely, for a moment it took her mind off of the situation, for usually it was very difficult to interest him in anything of this nature and she wondered why on today of all days, this should change.

The time of the operation came and two nurses came to where they sat. Lisa was asked to bring Jordon to the operating theatre, where she could hold him while the anaesthetic was administered. Then she would be asked to leave before the surgery began.

So it was that Brian sat watching as Lisa gently lifted Jordon's tiny form up out of the hospital cot and carried him across the ward and through the doors to the corridor beyond. As the doors swung shut behind her, he got one final glimpse of his tiny son cradled in her arms.

Brian was deeply immersed in his own thoughts, trying to appear brave for Lisa and to be positive that Jordon would be alright. Yet, they both held on tight to their emotions throughout that wait, for there was little to be said, they wanted nothing more than the operation to be over and for Jordon to come through without complications.

All throughout that period, both before and after the operation, I believe we were all drawing strength from the courage Lisa was showing; she had this air of implacable determination about her, as if the threat to her child had galvanised her to stand against all the emotions that would surely otherwise sweep her away. So, it was from her strength that I drew my own, admiring her example and how well she was facing the situation.

Lisa told me afterwards just how sad she felt at having to carry Jordon into the operating theatre. For a whole year she and Brian had been robbed of the opportunity to see their son enjoying life, laughing and gurgling and being a simple pleasure to himself and the family. Instead, his pain was a source of concern to everyone. Having to hold her son, watching as he was injected and observing him slide slowly into unconsciousness as the sedative took effect, this compounded the sense of loss and injustice. You would expect your child to be glowing in happiness on their first birthday, surrounded by presents and the smiles of a happy family, not laid out on an operating table. For Lisa, having to leave Jordon, knowing that as soon as the doors to the theatre closed they would begin the procedure and operate on her baby boy, was yet one more emotional wound to heal.

Lisa returned and then came the wait. She and Brian went to the cafeteria, going through the motions of ordering a meal that neither of them would eat. Brian had gazed at Lisa across the table, a look of despair on his face, saying quietly, almost whispering "I want my child back". When I heard this, I felt my heart swell with emotion, because Brian, who was normally so restrained, had voiced what we all so desperately wanted, for Jordon to be back in our arms and safe once more.

There they were to remain, nervously watching the clock, and very much aware of their own helplessness. If you have never been in the situation of waiting for a loved one to return from surgery then you are fortunate. The feeling of helplessness is almost overwhelming and compounded when it is one so young, when all your feelings of love and protectiveness are heightened. It is like they are on the other side of a barrier you cannot penetrate with their life held in the balance and in someone else's hands. The cold whiteness of the hospital environment adds to the surreal quality of that waiting time and there is no small talk, with nothing to do but watch the hands of the clock as the minutes tick by. All the while Lisa and Brian were looking to each other for support while they lived out their hopes and fears in their minds, desperately wishing the time away and praying for the wait to be over.

Eventually, their food untouched, they left the cafeteria, returned to the ward and continued their vigil. After what seemed like a lifetime, the ward doors opened and the medical staff wheeled in a trolley, in the middle of which lay Jordon, almost lost in what seemed like a tangle of bandages, surgical tape, wires and tubes.

The surgeon who performed the operation had witnessed some of Jordon's surprising behaviour and made a point of discussing it with them both. Usually after an operation of this magnitude, a child so young would be expected to remain lying down in recovery. Instead, Jordon stood up almost immediately it was over and the anaesthetic had worn off and he had to quickly be sedated again. The surgeon could barely believe it and his obvious shock at Jordon's behaviour reinforced suspicions in my mind that there was more to his medical problems than we realised at the time.

With hindsight, we now know that this was a very early clue that Jordon did not easily relate to what was going on with his body. This is a typical disconnect in autistic children, they can overreact or underreact to pain because they can feel it, but do not understand it. It means that they have the same sensation we all experience, but they have no way of knowing what they should do about it or how to express themselves. So, their reactions can manifest in ways that seem totally bizarre to the rest of us.

After this initial reaction, for the next four days, Jordon was laid out in the hospital cot to allow him time to heal. He looked so forlorn with a drip feeding into the back of his bandaged hand and the whole time he was recovering, the only physical contact we could manage was to reach into the cot so that he could stroke our fingers. All the while, the hospital staff brought food that, while it would have been suitable for many other one year olds, simply wasn't right for Jordon. The hospital staff tried to understand and accommodate us, but it was frustrating to have to explain why a one year old boy could not chew, for in truth we didn't know ourselves, we just knew that it was so. So we mashed the food the staff brought to entice him to eat and after a day or so I took to bringing in home-made food as a way around it, as Lisa and Brian simply would not leave his bedside.

After four days Jordon was discharged and all three of us walked out of the entrance and on to the pavement outside the hospital. The noise of the London traffic that greeted us was in no way able to drown out the sense of relief I was feeling, knowing that the future was a lot brighter than the past and that there was hope on the horizon for my grandson. The emotional pain and sleepless nights were behind us and we could move on as a family.

This sense of euphoria lasted for about three minutes as, all of a sudden, Jordon began to vomit. At once he was violently retching, which prompted him to start crying again.

With a sense of foreboding we rushed back into the hospital knowing that once more, something was wrong. The staff was obviously concerned, but felt his condition was stable enough for him to go home. Jordon's bed had already been taken by another child in need and we were told if we remained concerned to go to our local hospital. So, we travelled home on the train, but Jordon continued to vomit all the way, while we took turns rocking him gently in an effort to soothe him. As it transpired, we did not have time to go home, with Jordon's condition deteriorating, we went straight to our local hospital, where he was immediately admitted into an isolation room in a children's ward.

It seemed surreal; we had gone from one hospital to another in a matter of hours and there we watched Jordon have tubes inserted into him all over again. We learned that he had developed gastroenteritis and would have to remain in quarantine. We too, as visitors, were quarantined in the isolation unit. So, our trials continued and for the next four days we found ourselves sitting and sleeping on hard plastic seats just to be beside him. We were confined away from the rest of the hospital, alongside Jordon's cot, in chairs that did not offer the prospect of a decent night's sleep. As he was a short-term patient, the rules said that we did not warrant blankets and pillows. So, Lisa and Brian stayed overnight with their coats covering them to keep warm, patiently waiting while they looked for signs of Jordon's recovery.

I cannot begin to say how sad I felt and how hard the feelings of despair were hitting us. We were all tired and yet unable to complain as we did not want to be anywhere else than at Jordon's side.

Compared to the previous hardships, this brief bout in hospital was, by comparison, not so huge a worry. For, eventually, Jordon recovered, was given the all clear and released to go home and get on with what we were hoping, would be some kind of normality.

Things are still not what they seem

A few weeks after the operation, Lisa and Jordon came to see me. It was a lovely sunny day and knowing that they would soon arrive, I looked out of the window to see them walking down the pathway towards me, Jordon clutching his mother's hand.

Despite this being a time of great relief for us all, the look on Jordon's face as he walked towards the house sent alarm bells ringing in my mind once more. We had, up until this point, ascribed all of his behaviour to the pain of the physical medical problems we had subsequently identified, which had now been dealt with by the operation. But the look on Jordon's face still contained this unusual quality to it, one that I had previously written-off as being the result of all the pain he had endured.

Despite the success of his operation and now being pain free, he still had this air of distraction, as though he wasn't fully aware of his surroundings and was instead disassociated, in his own little world and undisturbed by what was going on around him. Now, with no obvious reasons for his behaviour, it seemed very odd indeed.

All through this time, the feeling that all was not well and something else was wrong would not leave me. Yet I shied away from telling Lisa. If I brought this news so soon after all the previous trials, that there was yet another problem that was affecting Jordon, I wasn't sure what her reaction would be. She had been through so much already, I barely had the heart to raise yet another problem with her son. But the worry had already begun to work away inside me and I knew that at some point we would have to talk once more about Jordon's state of health and see if we could figure out just what was affecting him.

Chapter Three - First Contact

So, at last, the operation was behind us, the kidney was removed and yet Jordon continued to be a very difficult child to bring up and none of us knew the reason why. Right up until this point, everything about his behaviour could be blamed on his unseen medical condition and the problems with his kidney. With the kidney's removal, we knew that all should be well again, but at the same time it was not and this did not make sense.

It wasn't merely that he had a strange look upon his face, up until the operation we had quite often remarked that he would be "...alright once he has had his operation." "Once the operation is over, we can move on." It wasn't that we ignored his symptoms, rather we excused them because we imagined that they were side effects, results of all the pain and discomfort he was experiencing.

As Jordon was Lisa's firstborn, she had no direct comparisons to make. Granted, Jordon was a very difficult child and having worked in a nursery Lisa knew she was experiencing more severe problems than other young mothers, but it was difficult for her to gain perspective. So, it was mainly my knowledge gained through raising my three children that meant I had a greater insight into how worrying some of these signs actually were. Also, I was well accustomed to my intuition aiding my insight and I could not shake off this feeling that there was yet more news to come.

Jordon's feeding was still very problematic and as the months went by, he was developing some additional unusual behaviours. In retrospect, these are very obvious clues, but because we had no diagnosis of autism until much later, we took them as isolated problems to deal with until we could ascertain their cause. Amongst the signs was the fact that Jordon would not respond to his name or questions. He remained seemingly oblivious or aloof. Neither would he point at any object when in fact, it is quite common for children of this age to point at what they want.

Instead, if he wanted something, like a drink for instance, he would indicate his need by grabbing Lisa, Brian or I by the hand or the arm and pulling us to what it was he wanted. He seemed to only be able to make the connection between us and the object in this way.

In fact, these are quite obvious signs of autism, but not knowing anything about it at the time, neither Lisa, Brian, nor I, had any clue as to the root cause of these worrying behaviours. Jordon was simply unable to ask for anything he wanted and he was not able to learn to do so until he was many years older.

So, there was a long period when Jordon would be wanting something and not be able to communicate it to us, which would lead to more frustration and problems. We usually had to guess what he wanted and if we could not work it out, then Jordon would cry, become very cross with us and if we could not help him, then eventually he began to hit his own head with his fists. If you have ever seen a child do this to themselves, then you know that it is like feeling each blow as a punch to the heart. You feel so inadequate that you cannot help your child and that they are in such anguish that they will physically harm themselves. For any parent, self-harm, if it continues, can be the beginning of experiencing true despair. You feel so useless to your child as a parent, that they are so distraught, that they would rather damage themselves than relate to your seemingly useless attempts to help. This is just one of the emotional burdens parents of children with autism learn to live with, a bar on the doorway between your world and that of your child. No matter what you do, it will never be good enough to enjoy full communication and understanding with your own offspring. You will always communicate through a veil of misunderstanding and you can work for your whole life, knowing that this will never truly be overcome, because it remains beyond your power to control and their ability to give.

It became a priority to work around this communication block as much as we could. We did not want him hurting himself and so we made sure that everyday things Jordon frequently wanted, like a drink, were readily available all the time. That way, Jordon could reach for it himself when he was thirsty.

When we were unable to interpret his pulling at us, which was often, he would inevitably dissolve into frustration and screaming. So this now became part of our everyday life, dealing with a child that was unable to communicate and constantly throwing tantrums.

Don't come near me

Once he was no longer a very young baby, throughout his early childhood, picking Jordon up remained a difficult task. It was obvious that the close physical contact made him very anxious and as soon as any one of us picked him up, he would begin to throw himself about, reacting so violently that he was very difficult to hold onto. We knew therefore that he needed reassuring and the only way we could gently introduce physical contact and familiarise him with it, was by gently stroking his arms and his hands. In retrospect, I realise by approaching it in this way we were employing the right method and we were to later learn that a trademark sign of autism for many children is a child totally rejecting physical touch. Yet, we did not know at the time that we were witnessing the effects of autism, we just knew that something was driving Jordon to push away human contact.

Shop till you drop!

Even now, looking back, every waking moment in the early years seemed like a battle, all part of a lengthening campaign to meet Jordon's needs. We were trying anything we could to bring some happiness to him, all the while having no idea where his distress originated nor, try as we might, how to deal with it. So our lives became a process of trial and error, causing big frustrations for us all. We used to sit and discuss how we might help Jordon and deal with each new block we found on his pathway and these conversations went on and on, because there was seemingly no end to his problems.

Certain situations were particularly trying, to the extent they became ordeals for us all. Trips to the shops became something we learned to dread and eventually began to avoid at all costs. On a typical trip to the supermarket, Jordon would begin to scream as soon as we entered and from the age of one year onwards, when he was just learning to walk, whenever we walked into a supermarket, he would either throw himself on the floor or run off. In fact, it was nigh on impossible to get Jordon to walk with you. We tried walking reins but he viewed these as a constraint on his freedom and they would also trigger a tantrum.

I now know that all of Jordon's reactions were born from the frustration of not understanding the situations he found himself in. For Jordon and any autistic child, the world is a very frightening place, with no reference points or clues as to why we as adults want their involvement in it. Typically with children, toys or sweets can be used as an incentive or reward, but with Jordon's eating difficulties and little understanding of how to play with toys, at that early stage, even the promise of something he liked as a reward for good behaviour was not an option. On the occasions when we did find something that Jordon could relate to as a reward, be it a toy or a game, anything that would please him momentarily, there was no guarantee that it would work a second time around. Nine times out of ten, yesterday's pleasing distraction would be today's irrelevancy and therefore at that time, even bribery would not work.

We were getting used to people who had not encountered Jordon's behaviour, failing to comprehend the severity of it. Many people simply could not believe that it was as bad as we said. In a way, like many of the situations in Jordon's life, it would have been funny if it wasn't so strikingly sad. There was one particular occasion when Jordon was around two years old, Lisa and her friend Jennie went to the supermarket. Jennie and Lisa have been very good friends ever since they went to school together. So they know each other well and while Jennie is now more than familiar with Jordon, at that young age she had not experienced the full extent of his behavioural problems. At that stage, Jordon remained undiagnosed and yet Lisa had already begun, whenever possible, to avoid taking Jordon anywhere near a supermarket and instead she would go by herself, while I minded Jordon at home. Even so, Lisa did not like to leave Jordon with me for too long, because she knew just how demanding he could be.

Up until that point, Jennie had no experience of just how bad Jordon could be and with the very best of intentions, she offered to help Lisa with her next trip to the shops, "it'll be fine, we can cope with him!"

Most people would reasonably imagine that all it would take was a positive attitude and a firm resolve, but Jordon wasn't in the habit of playing by our rules.

That day, he was dressed in track suit bottoms, a T-shirt and trainers, this was what he found most comfortable and because he was otherwise so difficult to clothe, it was a typical outfit for him to wear.

Jennie, Jordon and Lisa set off, Lisa knowing full well what was to come. After a drive to the supermarket, parking the car and readying themselves with a trolley, they walked Jordon into the supermarket entrance.

This was as far as they got and, from beginning to end, their trip to the store lasted a grand total of five minutes.

No sooner had they crossed the threshold, when Jordon threw himself down on the floor and started screaming at the top of his lungs. There was little prelude, he reacted the moment he found himself in that alien environment, quickly escalating into a tantrum that could be heard halfway round the supermarket and no matter what they did, as usual, there was no consoling him. Lisa tried her usual tactics of talking softly to Jordon, trying to cuddle him and offering reassurance, but to no avail. It was a fruitless pursuit when he was in this state and it was impossible to be heard above the constant screaming.

Many of the other shoppers stared at Lisa as though she was the worst parent in the world and had a very naughty child. Of course Lisa was used to this happening on virtually every occasion she went out with Jordon, but when he went stiff as a board, as happened when he had his worst outbursts, she knew this was a particularly bad episode. So after several minutes of trying to deal with him, the only remedy was removal.

Taking an arm each, Jennie and Lisa had to physically lift Jordon up while he continued to scream and march him back to the car, abandoning their supermarket trolley and leaving it behind them.

Jennie wasn't shocked at Jordon's behaviour, but was definitely surprised and annoyed having born witness to the reactions he and Lisa received from bystanders and all she knew of Lisa's world began to make more sense. I remember her remarking how she was incensed at how rude and judgemental some of the onlookers were, making comments alongside the usual staring. While the people around her were shocked by Jordon's behaviour, Jennie was more shocked at their lack of sympathy and support.

While Jennie had her revelation as to what we were facing, this was a regular occurrence for Lisa, Brian and me. Over the years we became quite used to abandoning trolleys in supermarkets and leaving shopping behind, as it was the only option for us to maintain our sanity and care for Jordon during his regular outbursts.

It wasn't merely the intensity of the outbursts that was difficult to deal with, unfortunately, once Jordon had started screaming, he would not stop and typically it was only sheer exhaustion that would wear him down enough that he would sleep. So, while the only option whenever this occurred was to get him back into the car and drive home, it wouldn't stop there. This was the situation Lisa and Jennie had found themselves in as they drove Jordon back home with him in the baby seat. Even when he was taken from the supermarket and all should have been well, for some considerable time afterwards, Jordon was still screaming at the top of his lungs and sobbing his heart out. Eventually of course he did quieten down; Jennie had her ordeal by fire and lived to tell the tale!

The real shame of these episodes was how stressful they were for all involved. People would look at Lisa as though she was a terrible person, staring daggers at Jordon for his seemingly naughty behaviour and this would in turn, compound the very real dread Lisa began to feel at the thought of taking Jordon out to any kind of public place, especially when she knew there would be a lot of people present.

Happily, later on in life, with our gentle encouragement Jordon was more able to cope with supermarkets, but when we reached this point, the next shopping-related behaviour we had to deal with was Jordon attempting to monopolise the shopping trolley. At first, we tried many ways to get Jordon comfortable with shopping. We tried putting him in the trolley seat, but Jordon was not having any of it; he would insist on remaining standing up, which was unsafe and meant we had to then take him out. Then we tried to get him to walk alongside the trolley, but again he was having none of it. The only way he would walk with us was if we allowed him to be the one pushing the trolley; letting him have his way was our only option, for if we tried to interfere, he would become very aggravated. So, we became his followers, gingerly stepping behind an out of control young boy who was pushing a trolley far too big for him to handle. Even then we actually felt we had achieved something because we had found a way of getting him to walk around a supermarket!

So, our supermarket shopping continued. We would walk around, gathering the items on our shopping list, but here we encountered a further obstacle, to Jordon's mind, the trolley was his and the only thing allowed in it were the items he wanted, which were a particular brand of fizzy drink and crisps. Any attempt to put anything else in the trolley, even the food for his meals, would result in yet another tantrum. The only remedy was to carry the items we wanted in our arms and proceed around the supermarket with a virtually empty trolley, sometimes with only two items in it! What a sight we must have been, with our arms full and an empty trolley, under the orders of a young boy who was by now making unusual noises and acting very strangely indeed.

Queues were another matter entirely and if, when we had finished our shopping, there was a line of people ahead of us at the till point, our hearts would sink. Jordon did not understand queues or the concept of queuing and waiting was not something he related to at all. If we attempted to join a queue, Jordon would immediately begin to push the people in front of us out of the way, all the time making what to them would be very strange noises indeed. He was not at all shy of trying to push his way to the front, grabbing at whatever was nearest to hand.

Even when we managed to join the queue, and Jordon wasn't jostling his way to the front, he would then proceed to try and arrange the people in the queue into an orderly and perfectly straight line. This was yet another symptom of his autism, this need for symmetry and order. So the people in the queue would suddenly find a small child shoving at their legs, shunting them out of the way, tugging at their trousers or skirts or worse. We did everything we could to hold him back, but even at that age, he was a force to be reckoned with. It was incredibly embarrassing for us. Any attempt to curtail his activities, say if we tried to take hold of his arm, would be met by him immediately dropping to the floor like a dead weight. So we had to try and gently usher him back to our trolley, otherwise he would go into his tantrum and be an absolute nightmare to deal with.

All the more testing was that shouting or becoming angry with Jordon simply did not work. If you lost your temper with him at that age, he would only get worse and it would also look very bad in the eyes of the people around us. Some bystanders did seem to understand, but the majority were judgemental of us as a family and our seeming inability to deal with a naughty child. So we could not do anything other than sound positive and calm and controlled while he created mayhem.

Eventually we learned that as soon as any sign of tantrum presented itself, there was only one real plan to viably pursue, one person would take Jordon back to the car while the other person carried on with quickly finishing the shopping. As a result, going out with Jordon demanded at least two adults, one to get on with the shopping or whatever was the task in hand and one to devote all their time to keeping him in his pushchair or to keep a tight hold on him. All the time, Lisa's patience and self-control amazed me, she always showed such calm and love for Jordon. On more than one occasion I remember observing how patient she could be and welling up with maternal pride.

This was one of the few times a bribe had a hope of success, the promise of the melt in the mouth type of crisps Jordon enjoyed and lemonade would persuade him into a supermarket. We then had to convince him to allow items that were not crisps and lemonade into the trolley! For all the while he would not let anything other than crisps and lemonade be put in the trolley, we were still being governed by his limitations rather than helping him adjust to life.

So we adopted a strategy, every trip we made, we would introduce one new item to the trolley, gradually, trip by trip adding to what Jordon would accept. Initially, each new item that went into that trolley was a battle. For each one, we had to give Jordon a reason as to why that item should be there. At that age, the only explanation that Jordon would accept was that it was an item he could eat. So we gently told him that milk was for his drink, bread was for sandwiches and so on. Eventually, after a long period of time, constant repetition and many visits we reached a level where there were so many 'approved' items that we could put what we wanted in the trolley without individual battles. Even so, the trips had to be extremely quick, for Jordon would otherwise be dragging the trolley and us with it, straight to the checkout. Too long spent in the supermarket and we would be back to square one, the shopping trip would have to be abandoned and we were driving back home with only half our shopping bought, if we were lucky!

The supermarket tsunami of fear

Part of the reason that shopping was so affecting for Jordon was the sheer scale of input to his senses. Autistic children tend to share a love of order, and you can see this when they place their toys in neat lines, or in Jordon's case when he would return to a room and replace a cup we had moved to the exact same spot where he had last seen it resting. Routines, patterns of behaviour that won't change, the need for things to be the same in every detail, no matter how it comes out in the child, are a trademark of autism. So, when Jordon walked into a shopping centre, any large store or supermarket, for him it was like walking into a chaotic world of colour and confusion, where the only constant was a lack of coherent order and quiet. Dozens of people walking in seemingly random directions in a vast space, announcements over the loudspeaker system, conversations overheard, rows and rows of different coloured products, stacks and heaps of vegetables, cooked foods, the clank of a trolley hitting a shelf, tills bleeping, children shouting, cold rows of refrigerated products, the smell of the fish counter, of baking bread, the insistent glare and rapid flicker of fluorescent lighting, this is all overwhelming sensory input and mayhem to the autistic mind. To us, it would be the sensory equivalent of walking into a tornado or jumping into a whirlpool, the sheer enormity of it all would frighten us to death. This is why supermarkets, to Jordon, were a source of fear and confusion and why we would face a denial to enter, a refusal to bear the experience and a tantrum, all born out of the autistic brain's inability to deal with the seemingly confused world we inhabit.

Other people's pain

One of the behavioural trends that became apparent from the age of seven or eight onwards, was Jordon's reaction to other people in distress. While Jordon has made enormous leaps in his development, even now, while he cannot really relate to the pain or suffering of others, he does not like to see people unhappy. From an early age, it became clear that if someone was visibly upset, Jordon would find it difficult to bear and as he became increasingly able to express himself, it was obvious that he always found other people's unhappiness disturbing. This was especially true of young children. If he saw another child crying, even before he was able to talk, it would make Jordon uneasy and he would show signs of agitation, flapping his hands and making strange groaning noises, rocking on his feet from one leg to another in the way that he did when he wanted to express strong emotions.

Whenever this happened, we tried to reassure Jordon, to put the other person's pain into context, to help him to understand the reason they were crying or upset. With babies and young children, we explained that they had to cry to let people know that they needed something or were in distress. So that he could understand distress, we had to refer to things such as 'wanting a drink' or 'having a tummy ache' as being the cause, otherwise he wouldn't have understood. Yet still he would shout and scream if a child's crying was not controlled by their parents or an adult.

Even with our intervention, by the time he was around seven or eight years old, he still found crying so worrying that he would do anything he could to make it stop. Typically, he would try and intervene, reassuring whoever was in distress by placing a hand on their shoulder. Heavily, clumsily, he would pat them with his palm, an awkward gesture that he had learned signified a wish to help. Then, when he was old enough and had developed some language skills, he started saying "No!", the only way he had of verbalising that he wanted it to stop. This of course was not a strategy that worked particularly well. The first a crying child might know of Jordon's arrival would be the sound of his robotic sounding voice saying loudly, "No! No!" Then the awkward hand placed woodenly on their shoulders. The tall autistic boy, waving his arms and intent on getting them to calm down could be quite disturbing for whatever small child Jordon was trying to reassure. Frequently their crying might cease momentarily, shocked by Jordon's surprising presence, but then once their initial surprise was overcome, the strangeness of his behaviour would sometimes add to their woes, perhaps intimidating or shocking them and making the situation worse. Then the crying would begin again in earnest and Jordon would become even more concerned and agitated himself. When it reached this stage, we would have no option but to remove Jordon from wherever he was to get him away from the situation before he became really distressed. He would usually recover quickly if we were able to do this, but if we were in a shop or supermarket, it was yet another reason for us to abandon a shopping trip unexpectedly.

Even today, Jordon does not fully understand the reasons why any of us cry. His autism is the impenetrable barrier that prevents him from relating to emotions. To him, crying is merely a noise he does not like and because he does not have an insight into human emotion, he does not recognise that crying is a result of distress; all he wants is for the noise to stop. His own lack of understanding of someone else's pain, in turn, causes him emotional pain and he cannot relate to either.

Knowing that this hurdle is too large for Jordon to overcome, that he does not understand nor comprehend the emotional side of life, we have taught him now that he is to ask any person who is crying if they are alright and to politely ask them not to cry, a much more socially acceptable strategy. Yet despite all we have achieved, if he hears someone crying, he will sometimes revert to his original behaviour and he begins groaning and flapping his hands in distress, which is our cue to console and reassure him as much as we are able or make a hasty retreat.

Making the right noises

It is worth pointing out that in just the same way that Jordon likes set patterns and conformity in his life, whenever we need to reassure him, we have learnt that repeating the same phrase can help. Therefore, the phrase, "it's ok!" Is one of our most effective measures. Since he was little, if he was experiencing any form of disquiet, we would approach him and take him by the upper arms to attract his eye contact. We would then say, "look at me, Jordon" and once we had his attention to let him know that everything is alright we would say, "it's ok". We would always smile at Jordon when we did this as he has learned that a smile is a sign that everything is well with the world.

Once we have used this phrase, Jordon will begin to calm down. Now that he has language skills often he will repeat the phrase back to us, "It's OK, Nan, Baby Has A Tummy Ache!" and he may do this several times or more to compound the reassurance. If he remains uncertain, then he will continue to repeat the phrase again and again and we will be called upon to answer him, smiling into his face and offering consolation until he is ready to move on

"It's ok Jordon. It's ok!" Is a mantra we often repeat, so that we are as much programmed to respond in this way as he is.

Round and round in circles

Jordon started to walk at around one year of age, which is around about the time you would expect any average baby to take their first steps and become a toddler.

As his walking improved we noticed that he would quite often spend his time walking in circles around the room or round tables and furniture. As time progressed, it happened more often, until we found that anything he could continuously walk around, he did.

If Jordon wasn't walking around the furniture in repetitive loops, then he would often spin round and round on the spot, his eyes rolled back in his head and looking up into the corners of his eyelids.

Spinning round and round isn't strange behaviour for a child, but with Jordon, it was the eye-rolling, the frequency and the length of time he would do it for that was concerning. He would just go on and on spinning or walking round in circles, far more than seemed usual and yet he seemed quite happy at the time, engaged in his own little world.

We learned later that this behaviour is typical of an autistic child. One of the theories to explain why autistic children behave in this way is that all the while they are spinning, they are totally absorbed in the sensations of their body and it serves to block out the confusion of a world they do not understand. While the repetition of any behaviour is reassuring in itself, spinning can also induce feelings of euphoria, so it serves a dual purpose, providing reassurance and good feelings. From the outside, at a time when we had no context, it merely appeared strange. We used to try and understand and would ask each other why, but in those days, we did not know the reason and none of us could find an answer.

Of course, we did intervene, the repetitive behaviour was disturbing, so we tried to distract and interest Jordon in what was going on around him. I always worried he might fall and as soon as the spinning started, I would race to stop him and come up with any kind of distraction that would take his mind off of it. I would call to him and try and interest him in something else, because if we did not interrupt his behaviour then, he would happily continue, without stopping, for hours on end. Thankfully, as he grew up, he learned to stop certain behaviours himself, as he did with spinning, which lessened and gradually died out as he learned to talk.

While we all recognised it as unusual, only my innermost feelings said that this behaviour was an indication of something far more worrying. Something was definitely wrong.

Like talking to a brick wall

Even up until the age of two years, Jordon remained unresponsive to any verbal contact. You could call his name and he would not respond nor turn around. If you were trying to tell him something, he would typically ignore you and walk away. If you tried to involve him or interest him with a toy then he would simply pay no attention. The exception were toys that were animated, made noises or had flashing lights and these would sometimes hold his interest if you were lucky.

Because of this behaviour; his seeming obliviousness to what was going on around him, there was initially a question mark in our minds as to whether Jordon might be hard of hearing or deaf. It was the only thing that we could think of at the time that went some way to explaining why he would ignore us so blatantly. Yet my intuition told me this was not the answer and even though it was suggested that his hearing might be the cause, we all knew that it could not really be the problem, as whenever Jordon's favourite television programme came on and the theme tune could be heard, he would run like the wind to the television. If it was deafness, then it was very selective!

So we knew for sure that he could hear. We also knew that he was able to observe and grasp certain things, to copy them; Jordon learned how to turn up the volume on the television by himself, so we also knew that he could relate to the outside world, to observe it and take in information.

However, even now, having come on such a long journey with Jordon, we know he still has immense difficulty in relating to his own feelings and in relating to other people. It is this disconnection between himself and others where his true 'deafness' lies, as Jordon cannot hear or see life in the same way we do. The fault lies deep within his brain and nowhere as obvious as his ears or eyes.

I have learned to trust my feelings and to let them be my guide and so I started to look more deeply into his situation, to explore what it might be that was preventing him from relating to his surroundings, to the input he ignored and why he remained oblivious to so much of what went on in the world around him.

Change is not good

Because the outside world is so difficult for an autistic child to understand and it is so difficult for them to reason, nothing has perspective. The smallest change in an autistic child's environment, especially when they are young and new to the world, can give rise to fear. To an autistic child, sitting in a different seat to the one you normally occupy means that their whole world is now different. Because they have no context to inform them, the effect of any change, no matter how small, is unknown. Jordon was a typical autistic child in this respect.

As a consequence of this world view, that has huge difficulty in placing change in perspective, Jordon, as a young child, could spend all day in a room with me and not touch anything at all. He did not know what ramifications would come with changing this outside world, nor what relevance it would have to him and as a consequence, he left it alone. Unlike other children his age, who would have been roaming around and examining whatever was around them, he seemed to have absolutely no inquisitiveness in his nature. It was quite odd to see this little boy, with a seeming lack of the normal expected responses and some increasingly strange behaviours manifesting.

Jordon was not interested in ornaments or the usual things in your home that arouse a child's interest and they reach out for, be it a magazine on a coffee table or your finest bone china ornaments! He could, however, relate to those things that offered a function that served him in some way or interested him. So, he would play with the switch on a lamp to see the light go on and off and he soon learned to switch on the television because television programmes diverted him, but if he did not know the function of an object, if it could not of itself offer something to him, then it held no interest. So he would sit, seemingly disinterested and oblivious as to what was going on around him, waving his hands and rocking, completely ignoring whatever I placed in front of him.

And so, for us to attract his attention, it meant that we had to find things with a purpose that he could relate to. A picture held no interest, because it was inanimate, but a toy that had buttons that triggered flashing lights and noises offered a response he could relate to.

The tactic of showing him that he could influence and control interactive electric toys helped us to develop his memory. He still did not imitate us, instead he learned to operate these responsive toys because he was interested in them and this then stimulated him to recall how they were operated. If we tried to show him how to push the buttons, he generally ignored us, but give him the toy and he would find out how to do it for himself. This is a subtle difference, but a very important one if you are to understand the autistic mind.

In this way, we discovered that direct cause and effect actions were something Jordon could grasp, gradually learning to associate buttons on the remote control with their effect on the television, altering the volume and changing the channels. However, if we tried to force him to make an association in his mind, it generally failed. For instance, we tried to show him the covers of video tape boxes so that he could recognise they contained his favourite programmes. He did not make this simple association and instead, he began to place the boxes in an orderly line, pushing us away when we attempted to intrude. Autism stood in our way once more and Jordon could not grasp that the cartoon characters on the video tape boxes were the same as on the programmes he loved to watch.

I lick what I see and I see what I lick

It is not unusual for a child to put things in their mouth when they are very young. It is all part of growing up for them to experience teething pain or to explore an object and, as a consequence, bite or lick anything that is to hand. However, this behaviour tends to stop when they are around three years old.

Jordon, from the time he was old enough to hold something in his hand, would be prone to put it in his mouth. While this is not in any way unusual, in Jordon's case this behaviour did not cease, rather it increased to a point where it became very clear there was an issue and eventually, if an object was within his reach, he would put it in his mouth or lick it.

The licking behaviour was eventually applied to everything in Jordon's environment and it became a constant activity for him. Wherever he was, no object was safe, walls, carpets, spoons, shoes, tables, windows, you name it, Jordon would lick it as a way of identifying with this world. It was obviously something we wanted to stop, because it appeared so very odd and it also meant Jordon was putting himself at risk of infection from unclean surfaces.

We surmised that licking was a way for Jordon to communicate with an object, to gain familiarity, identify with it and attempt to gain perspective. His other senses were not able to provide him with the insight into the world he perceived and so, he attempted to get to know more by using the only other sense available.

The licking, despite our best efforts, continued as a behaviour pattern right up until he was around three, or perhaps four years old, before we were able to finally wean him off of this stage of his life. It was a particularly difficult thing to achieve, because with Jordon, the world was one great big unknown quantity whose language he did not speak. Licking added another level of communication between him and whatever object held his attention at that time. As the licking had become a set behaviour pattern, something familiar that seemed to add to his life, it took a long time to persuade him to abandon it. To get him to eventually stop, we used a mammoth amount of gentle persuasion over a very long period of time.

Whenever we were teaching Jordon to alter his behaviour, the tone of voice we used was extremely important to him. So we would gently but firmly say "no" and either remove him from whatever he was licking, such as the pavement, a wall, a shop door, a supermarket trolley or take away the offending item, such as shoes, mud, twigs, leaves; anything that had caught his attention and he had got hold of. Generally, he would be upset if we took the object away from him, but we had little choice and it was not unusual for it to provoke another tantrum.

Luckily, Jordon had always accepted a dummy, something we deliberately used to comfort him with during our attempts to settle him down. This actually turned out to be very useful to us because we could use the dummy as an alternative when he decided to lick something he shouldn't, which was just about everything in sight! However, as with very many behaviour patterns in autism, the dummy then became a problem for us. For some while, it was the only reliable method we had of ensuring he did not become upset; quite literally a pacifier, removing the licking behaviour and often calming him if he began to cry. However, it stuck, which meant we were unable to wean Jordon off of his dummy until he was five or six years old. I had become convinced at the time that if we did not wean him off, he would be sucking a dummy forever. However, it wasn't us who persuaded him; Jordon surprised us and decided that he would let go of this particular unwanted behaviour by himself. By then, he was between three and four year's old and it was a great relief to see that phase pass.

This was also a landmark in his life. It showed me he could let go, that he could move on and release the need for the things on which he was dependant. I could appreciate the significance of this seemingly small change. It meant that he could develop. I also learned that changes such as this could only take place when Jordon was ready, for he had to remain in control and had to be, in these small things, the master of his own world.

Further feeding difficulties

Long before Jordon gave up his dummy, the feeding difficulties continued, as did our constant struggle to understand and deal with his behaviours. Naturally, we would discuss every day, as a family, what we could do to help him and improve his quality of life.

It was obvious he was desperately unhappy and as we later learned, confused about the world and his place within it. Any autistic child demands a lot of attention and is a focus for their family; Jordon was no exception.

The pressure to meet his needs, long before the diagnosis of autism was given became unrelenting and I could see the strain it placed on Lisa's relationship with Brian. In the early days, their lives were a constant struggle to cope and keep up.

Jordon was screaming in pain at every feed and despite being able to suck on a dummy, still had great difficulty swallowing milk from a bottle. I know Lisa and Brian were worried out of their minds.

We later learned that it is common for an autistic child to have difficulty in coordinating biting, chewing and swallowing, even to the extent that they aspirate food or drink and it enters the airways, causing them to choke.

We were all at our wits end, typically it could take an hour to get an ounce or so of milk into Jordon, far less than he should be taking in at the time. It sometimes felt as though we were feeding him all the time he was awake, a constant nightmare, bringing with it a real risk of malnourishment. Often, it was Brian who had the most success in getting him to take in milk.

So, as a way of trying to get nutrition into him, we would try anything and earlier than we would normally have contemplated, we began to introduce just a little watered down solid baby food into his diet. It was the only way we could get Jordon to accept food, putting it in his mouth without the need for him to suck from a teat. We started him on porridges, custards, rice; anything that was easy to swallow, feeding him small amounts from a baby spoon. Once the food was in his mouth, he would take it down as if he were merely swallowing his own saliva. And it worked; while his feeding remained problematic, at last he was taking some nourishment. We began to see improvement and Jordon actually started to settle down a little.

This was such a great relief, we continued with the solid food, gradually thickening the consistency and finding, as a result that he would remain satisfied for longer periods of time and neither he nor we had to work so hard to get him to feed. We also ensured during this weaning time that we continued feeding him baby formula from a bottle.

The solid food satisfied him more than the meagre amount of milk he had been taking and it meant he was not constantly famished. At last we now had a much happier baby in this respect.

Music and numbers

Our labours to encourage Jordon to eat continued and when he was around two or three years old, we found that he loved the theme tune to the film Titanic. It had been released in the cinema the year after he was born and whenever it was played, he would seem more peaceful and pliant.

Whenever we wanted him to eat, we started playing this tune on a video tape, beautifully sung by Celine Dion. At every meal time, Jordon would sit in a small chair in front of the television, with Celine Dion singing away. As soon as the music was heard, he would be ready to eat. The first few bars of the tune would play, his mouth would spring open and in would go the nourishing, mashed up, homemade food. Feeding could continue until the track finished, then it would have to go on again if we were to have any hope of him continuing to eat. The moment the music ended his mouth would close. We tried so hard to make it relaxed and fun for him, to get him fed, but it was an incredibly stressful situation nonetheless.

He also loved to flick through the pages of the telephone book, leafing through the uniform listings of addresses and numbers that looked so neat and orderly on the page. Jordon found the book fascinating, he looked as though he was actually reading it, so intently would he pore over the lines. So, we would put the book beside him at every mealtime.

However, once this pattern was established, if you then took the phone book away, or stopped the music, he would immediately stop eating. It was associated behaviour. We had created a routine and for a very long time we could not vary it for breakfast, lunch, nor dinner.

He sounds hungry

Before we arrived at the point where we were giving Jordon solid food, the noises from his stomach would provide quite poignant reminders as to how little he was taking in. Whenever we were successful in getting him to feed, his stomach would start making quite surreal gurgling noises, the loudest I have heard from any baby and a reflection of the fact that his digestive system was craving sustenance. You could actually hear the food enter his empty stomach, it sounded like a drum being hit and then a riot of churning, grumbling and growling noises would ensue.

Hard to swallow

Even today, at the age of sixteen, the problems with food and eating continue, as do issues with the types of food Jordon is prepared to eat. Every new item on the menu is a battle and he can be quite adamant about what he will and will not entertain. Just last week we tried to entice him into eating a doughnut and only after a lot of persuasion, asking him half a dozen times if he would try it, did he finally succumb.

Nowadays, the only way we can hope to get him to try new things when he is totally against it is to appeal to him, to ask him to do it for his 'mum' or his 'nan' and then we may have some hope of success. However, he remains extremely selective. When Jordon stays with me, his evening meal is always followed by a chocolate mousse. He will not accept any other dessert and if I do not have a chocolate mousse to hand, he will perhaps be satisfied with a dry biscuit or the one type of crisps that he will eat, yet nothing else other than these will do.

Up until a few years ago, if a chocolate mousse was not available, Jordon would quickly become distressed. There he would be sat, forlornly staring at the table, his face reddening, screwing up as if he were about to burst into tears. Hating seeing him this way, we felt totally inadequate. We couldn't get him to understand that we were not wilfully withholding the mousse. The only way to avoid a tantrum in this situation was to promise that there would be mousse tomorrow and explain that the shop had sold out or had been closed when we arrived.

Even now, when Jordon is eating, sometimes he views food in his mouth as something to be got rid of and whether he has chewed it or not, he will attempt to swallow far more than is comfortable. He will fill his mouth, be it with food or drink and despite our protestations and encouragement to take smaller mouthfuls, will swallow it whole.

When Jordon eats, it can appear very strange, almost to the point of being comical. When we sit down as a family to eat, I have seen him shovel whatever is on his plate; chunks of food we have cut up for him, of whatever size, directly into his mouth. He will do this until it is stuffed full and then, with his eyes wide open and his cheeks bulging, puffed out as if he were afraid the food were going to be taken from him, he will attempt to swallow everything at once. He will do this with something as large as half a slice of bread at once and despite daily reminders, it is not uncommon to see him attempt to swallow half a sausage whole.

For this reason, up until he was fourteen, we would ensure that nothing went on his plate that was big enough that it could choke him if swallowed whole. So, as if we were catering for a toddler, every single mealtime, his food would be finely chopped before it was presented to him. Finally, at the age of fifteen, after we had spent every day showing and schooling Jordon in how to hold a knife and fork, he learned to hold them in his hand. So, while he has learned this skill, albeit reluctantly (and he is by no means using them properly) he is now able to tear the food, somewhat clumsily, between his knife and fork.

Even with this skill learned, we do still keep an eye on him. Jordon still harbours a tendency to overdo it and on occasion he has been known to heave or retch at the amount of food he has attempted to swallow, his face almost comically expressionless all the while he is choking.

Sitting with him at a recent mealtime, I noticed each mouthful is chewed to the absolute minimum, an accompanying habit he has picked up somewhere and that seems to have stuck, yet the effort he then has to put into swallowing would be enough to make you or I wince. He visibly strains, arching his neck, although his face rarely shows the slightest sign of the effort he is obviously making. Obviously we encourage more chewing, yet it takes constant reminders before he will chew anything like the number of times that is healthy.

The example of chewing is one of the very valuable clues as to how Jordon's mind works and the extent of the communication and associative difficulties he has; the connection is not yet made that he should be chewing more and filling his mouth less to overcome the subsequent discomfort. It is actually very sad to think that what, to most of us, is a natural reflex, something we do not even think about, is still a challenge to Jordon after 16 years of encouragement and coaching. A very poignant reminder as to just how difficult it is to move an autistic child on to the next stage in their development.

When we first began to train Jordon in the use of a fork, we separated the food on his plate to avoid bringing him too many sensations and flavours at once. If we mixed them up, he did not know what he was presented with and could become confused. In his mind the association was then made that food must be presented and kept separate on a plate. If it is mixed together, then even today he will protest and perhaps refuse to eat it, but he is now flexible enough to be persuaded if need be. However, ever mindful of the need for flexibility, we always presented mashed potato and beans mixed together and this is the one food he will happily accept as a mixture. In fact, Jordon now calls this a "Fusion!" and it is one of his favourites.

Even today, we do not dare give Jordon a hot drink. On the very rare occasion that he will drink a cup of tea, he can only be given it lukewarm. The way he thinks means that if a drink feels hot in his mouth, he must get rid of that sensation and the quickest way to do so is to swallow. He would not think to wait until it was cooler or to spit it out, instead if you gave him a very hot cup of tea, he would soon have a scalded mouth and throat.

One of the most ironic, sad, funny facts about autism is that often it casts you into situations where it is like the blind leading the blind. Jordon often adopts behaviours because he cannot understand the world and we avidly watch for these behaviours as they are signs of what is going on in his world, so that we can react to them for him. Tea is a classic example of this, for inadvertently, Jordon has made a connection between tea and ill health!

Jordon will only ever drink tea if he feels unwell. We have surmised it was because several years ago when he had a sore throat, Lisa gave him weak, lukewarm tea to soothe it and as with so many things, the connection between feeling unwell and receiving tea was firmly made in his mind. This is quite useful, because even today, Jordon will not tell us if he is ill. However, if he asks for a beaker of tea, then we know he is poorly. He will always drink tea in one go, emptying the beaker and thanking us, "I Feel Better Now." His response is learned by rote and he will say it whether he feels better or not.

The moment he does really feel better, he won't touch a drop of tea. It is funny, in one way, that we have to interpret his state of health by what he will drink, but even he could not tell you why he does so.

Over the years of teaching Jordon how to eat and drink, there have been many small milestones in his development, each of which can represent the culmination of years of effort by Lisa, Brian and myself. Discussing Jordon's problems has helped us all feel that they were shared, that by working as a team, we could come up with ideas that would help us cope, that there was some hope of control and that none of us were alone.

Jordon's autism meant that in his earlier years, left to his own devices he would not eat, because he did not directly associate hunger with food, with the added complication that if he got a pain in his stomach from being overly hungry, he would not eat because his stomach hurt. The fact that he had to be instructed and reminded how to chew food and that any form of gluten made him hyperactive meant that mealtimes were interesting, to say the least!

One memorable eating-related achievement was at the age of three when we succeeded in getting Jordon to bite and chew Rich Tea biscuits. It may sound pathetic, but the elation we felt made this a time for celebrations all round! Even so, we would not dare risk handing him a whole biscuit because the entire thing would instantly be pushed into his mouth and he was then only a few seconds away from choking. Instead, we would break off very small bits and hand them to him one at a time.

When he first actually took a bite I halfway expected the heavens to open up - 'Hallelujah!' was all I could think at the time, but there was still a long road ahead.

So strange is autism that, once he had got over his initial hyperactive reaction to gluten, while Jordon would chew Rich Tea biscuits, he would not chew any other type of food. Even up until the age of eight we had to ensure that every meal had been mashed up for him and that we fed him ourselves. After that point, things became easier when we finally got across to Jordon how to use a spoon to put food into his mouth and how to chew.

In the meantime, all of Jordon's food had to be mashed up to exactly the right consistency for him to swallow. It had to be wet enough so that he could swallow it (too dry and he would choke) and we took great pains to mash everything up with a knife and fork. He needed some kind of bulk in his stomach so we avoided running his meals through a food processor, in case they were too liquid. Also, we could not guarantee the right consistency. If the texture wasn't 'right' then, despite all our efforts, Jordon would refuse to eat. People used to tell us that he would eat when he was hungry, but that was not the case.

Part of our training of Jordon was to show him how to chew by example. While we were still giving him his mashed up food, whoever was feeding him would mimic chewing. When we eventually started to attempt whole foods for him to chew, there was a period when he would take food into his mouth, say some vegetables or a small piece of sausage, we would encourage him to chew and gradually he learned to do so. However, initially, he would not necessarily chew the actual food, he would make the chewing motions while the food remained untouched either at the side of his mouth or on his tongue. This was a poignant sight to see, because it was plain he was trying to work with us but it revealed the extent to which he found it impossible to relate to why we were asking him to chew. It was sad the lengths we had to go to. We would sit there in front of him, chewing imaginary food and swallowing to demonstrate how it should be done. We would then feed him and he would mimic the action of chewing without actually chewing the food; and then he would promptly swallow it whole.

If you had walked into the room you would have seen a small child surrounded by a table full of potential lunatics. You would note the oblivious look on his face as around him, seemingly mad adults sat with lips pursed, cheeks blown out, making loud "nnumm nnumm" noises. Our mouths would gape open, our jaws would work, we would mimic constant surprise at how delicious the mouthful of nothingness was. We were making such hard work of swallowing, "mmmm" we would nod in agreement with each other at how lovely our food was, even though we had nothing in our mouths. Eyebrows raised and smiling, it was like the worst acting class, a desperate eating audition judged by a young autistic boy who had no clue whatsoever as to what we were doing or why.

We were desperate to ensure Jordon received the right nutrition, especially after the removal of his kidney which meant our worry was compounded. Not only did we have a small boy who had lost a kidney, but his eating problems meant it was all the more difficult to ensure he had what he needed in his diet. We took pains to make sure everything he received was wholesome, home-made and freshly cooked each and every day. His early years were populated with the best food, but we were still limited, the list of items Jordon would not eat, then and today, is a long one. Today he will eat most things we present on a dinner plate, and he will eat chocolate biscuits and one type of crisps! However, he will rarely eat chocolate by itself, he will not eat crisps that are not his favoured square-shaped brand, or ice cream or bananas, or any form of pudding (other than chocolate mousse). He will not eat apples, pears or peaches, strawberries or most types of soft fruit and, if we encourage him and he is actually willing to make an attempt, he pulls the most ridiculous facial expressions and won't take more than the very smallest piece.

Yet, as he has grown and we seek to add variety to his diet, we have found he will eat pizzas, Chinese and curried food, provided it is presented to him on his usual dinner plate. Building a firm routine has been a very effective approach and his day is punctuated by breakfast, lunch and dinner. He will not listen to any other description of these meal times, other than those three words. Therefore, if I wrongly describe lunch as dinner time, which I often do, he will quite promptly put me in my place and will not eat until the 'right' word is used! I have to apologise profusely and promise not to do it again before Jordon will sit down to eat!

Spoons are for swallowing and forks are for chewing

Chewing was perhaps the biggest eating issue we faced. We tried absolutely everything we could, every strategy and every tactic, but to no avail.

The breakthrough first came when Jordon was eight years old and we were first introducing him to a fork, but still feeding him ourselves. By then, we were learning how fixed his associations could become and the solution was actually a very simple one. I said to Lisa, that we had to create and separate two distinct concepts. So, at mealtimes, I would hold up a spoon and show Jordon that you swallowed what was on it. Lisa would hold up a fork and show that you chewed what was on it. We repeated the process over and over again over a period of time while the school he attended endeavoured to help us.

When, eventually, Jordon began to copy, to get the idea, it was like a miracle had occurred. Sat down at the table, Jordon took the food we offered him from a fork and promptly began to chew for the very first time. You cannot quite imagine the look on our faces. Normally, when you put the food in his mouth there was always a pause as we waited to see if he would choke. This time, his jaw began to calmly move up and down as if he had been chewing all his life, while both our mouths hung wide open in amazement!

Glass! Handle with care!

Eating wasn't the only problem that feeding presented. Handing Jordon a glass, at any age, either at home or anywhere we were visiting, brought with it a risk that he would bite into it.

We learned this the hard way and our anxiety is well-founded; we did once give Jordon a glass and he duly bit clean through it. Shattering in his mouth, it littered the floor with broken fragments that clung to his clothes. Immediately, we checked him for blood, looking inside his mouth for pieces, which was no easy task as Jordon was likely to bite our fingers. Then, Lisa and I went to work as if we were a police forensics team, gathering up the fragments and piecing the glass back together, painstakingly reconstructing the shattered pieces into the whole. Eventually, we were successful, by some miracle not one piece was missing, Jordon had not cut himself and we knew he had not swallowed any of the glass. Panic turned to relief and we vowed not to give him a glass to drink from ever again. At home, he has a plastic beaker and even today, if we are eating out and a glass is given to Jordon, we have to insist he is also given a straw and we will then supervise him closely because he is still quite likely to bite into, or even through, any receptacle he is drinking from.

Before and after we discovered the true extent and nature of Jordon's problems, not a moment went by that we weren't discussing and dealing with his difficulties or watching him with the same love, attention and vigilance that one shows a very young child. Yet, we took pains to treat Jordon's challenges as merely a part of everyday life and did not act around him as if anything he did was unusual. For, if we had labelled the way he acted as 'wrong' or 'bad' then we would have placed extra stress upon him, by making a drama out of what, to him, was perfectly normal behaviour. If we had made a big issue of it, then this would have added to his problems, so we did not.

Chapter Four - A Clinical Diagnosis

With all the problems we had encountered with Jordon since the day of his birth, our focus had been on the day-to-day trials of caring for him, something that had absorbed our attention around the clock. We were so immersed in merely coping and addressing his medical issues, that it was only when he was a year old and his operation was behind him, that we started to address a growing suspicion that all was not well and that there was some other underlying cause for the behaviour we were witnessing.

At the same time, we hoped and thought his problems were over, after all, the constant screaming and crying abated and he was far more settled in himself. But with these behaviours reducing, it became apparent that Jordon was not responsive and more and more obvious that something was amiss.

Other signs were appearing; he would not respond to his name and he would not make eye contact, or point to objects as other children might. Brian was working both during the day and several nights a week to ensure his family was supported and all the while, Lisa was busy trying to cope with the demands of a son that needed constant attention. Doing everything we could for Jordon and giving him the care he needed, meant a huge strain on all our lives, with a twenty four hour struggle to meet his needs.

There were emotional strains too for Brian and Lisa; and as a grandmother your instinct is to comfort a crying child, yet when Jordon cried and we attempted to cuddle or hug him, he would struggle against the physical contact. We later learned that this aversion to physical contact is common to many autistic children. For Jordon, in particular, it was uncomfortable, a seeming invasion of his privacy that he could not relate to. He did not understand the concept of a hug or a cuddle, or even a handshake. It had no meaning for him, because he could not relate to his own emotions. He perceived no need within himself to have the kind of closeness a hug conveys and he did not relate to it as a display of affection, because affection was initially alien to his world.

Nowadays, we have progressed and Jordon can relate to the word 'love' and accommodates our need by hugging Lisa or Brian or me, because he knows it pleases us. Over the years, we have built trust with Jordon, never lying to him or making empty promises as these things are very important in his world. In recent months, this has developed more and I believe Jordon truly has an awareness and a level of comprehension of our love and loyalty for him.

When Jordon was young, awareness of autism was much less widespread than it is today. At that time, I was not even familiar with the word 'autism', nor knew what it meant and as a result, we had nothing to inform us other than knowing that all was not well. We were busy coping, Lisa and Brian were trying to make a life for themselves and we all had to put our aspirations on hold while we put all our effort into helping Jordon.

It was my having taken the time to observe Jordon that convinced me there was something more to his behaviour. There was quite obviously a lack of response to outside stimuli; he would not respond to his name or any request, such as asking him to pick up a toy - no interaction at all. I raised this with Lisa and we agreed that something had to be done. Spurred on by our intuition and worried by the abnormalities; that his development was not progressing as it should, we went to the doctor and thereafter to a series of health professionals looking for answers.

Initially, it was suggested that Jordon might have hearing difficulties, but after a series of tests, we had not heard anything conclusive, other than that Jordon's hearing was perfectly ok, but that he did not always respond. In one particular test, a very loud bang made behind his head elicited no response nor curiosity on his part. Yet, a very small bell rung behind him made him immediately turn around, because something about the noise interested him; perhaps it reminded him of a toy tambourine we often shook for him at home. In any event, we knew he could hear, but that sometimes he ignored what he heard.

An autistic child's senses are wide open and yet, at the same time, the child is not always responsive. This is why you could literally shout right behind Jordon's head and not receive a flicker of recognition. He would hear you, but what he was hearing was so totally irrelevant to his mind that there would not be a glimmer of a reaction.

Gradually, at the same time as we put away suspicions of an underlying issue with Jordon's hearing, I still knew that Jordon's behaviour did not match up to any child of mine or of friends that I knew. Something was most definitely wrong and again I had a certainty within me that there was something else, an underlying cause for his unusual behaviour. I knew we had to continue to push for medical advice if we were to find the root cause.

Throughout the following year we took Jordon to see various health professionals. Each of them agreed that there were indications of an underlying issue, but at that point, none of them could tell us what that issue was.

Finally, after just over 12 months full of tests and assessments, when Jordon was two years and four months old, Lisa and I drove, in my car, to the local Child Development Centre. Brian, who dearly wanted to be with us, had no option other than to be at work that day. I can remember it was a clear morning and there was a feeling of dread. We did not know what we might hear and so Lisa and I were very quiet, respecting each other's feelings and nervous of what lay ahead.

We did not know the potential outcome, we had no clue as to what it might be, but we were also trying not to think the worst. We had some thoughts that perhaps he was slightly delayed in his development, possibly because of the kidney problems, yet we truly had no idea and at that stage, neither of us had even heard of autism. We weren't in denial, but it was a very tempting prospect to imagine that his problems all originated from the kidney abnormalities. We were desperately hoping that there were no more health issues and nothing mentally wrong with him.

So, we drove to the clean, well-kept Centre, parked and walked as a little trio into the reception area, myself and Lisa either side of Jordon with his hand gripped firmly in hers to ensure he did not run away. Once there, our route was clear, there were no other children or parents waiting and I distinctly remember there being no queue because I felt a strong sense of relief, as having to queue or spend too long standing still would trigger the usual frustrations from Jordon.

We were guided by the staff into a very large, clean room and we sat in neat little plastic chairs and waited with Jordon at a table. It was obviously a room designed for children as we were surrounded by brightly coloured toys and activity games. The whole place was full of them.

The doctor walked into the room and greeted us politely. I can remember to this day what a lovely manner she had and how she was so obviously a very kind and caring lady as she tried her best to put us at ease. At that moment, I was so very glad that I had accompanied my daughter, knowing that the close relationship and love we have for each other would help her to withstand whatever news we were to hear and that together we were strong enough to deal with the doctor's diagnosis, whatever it might be.

We discussed a few preliminary issues with the doctor and all the while Jordon was busying himself with licking the walls of the room, oblivious to our conversation and to just about everything else going on around him. At that moment, I was praying he could act normally, not to act strangely in front of the doctor, otherwise it might somehow adversely influence her diagnosis. Of course I knew that it was too late for anything of the kind. It was merely that Lisa had already suffered enough pain and I desperately wished that she had no more in her life, so I prayed.

There was a pause in the conversation. The doctor had obviously taken the time to read Jordon's notes before we arrived and there was this moment when she gave Jordon a long appraising gaze. My heart was thumping in my chest, I wanted to take Lisa's hand and to take all emotional pain from her, to make everything ok, but I myself was overcome. I sat there on the verge of crying, because I knew this was a life-changing moment.

The doctor looked directly at us both in turn, a deep penetrating stare and my life stood still as she rose from her chair. With some deliberation, she walked to a cupboard that covered the entire wall. My eyes followed her every movement. At the time, I was beginning to feel the very first signs of panic inside. Reaching into the shelves, I thought she was going to get some kind of test, some medical device that would aid her investigation or perhaps worse, a book that told us just what was wrong with Jordon, detailing the nature of his problems. Instead, she returned to where we sat, holding in her hand a very large box of man-size tissues. Again, she met my gaze and I was filled with dread and fear as all I could see in her features was tremendous concern.

She sat down with a very serious demeanour and I could tell that we were in for some devastating news. The situation was becoming surreal; at some level I could tell the Doctor had been trying to gauge whether we were emotionally strong enough to cope with the news she had to impart. She remained earnest, but extremely kind and sympathetic and I could see that she found it very difficult to tell us what she knew. My instinct was to run, to flee the room and not come back.

I can remember her next words to this day. "I am sorry to have to tell you that Jordon has Autism Spectrum Disorder...and that we do not yet know the severity of his problem."

The news washed over us like a wave, but even when it engulfed us, we still had no idea of its importance. I did not know what autism was and neither did Lisa.

Of course, we were full of questions. What is autism? We asked what it would mean for Jordon's future and how we could deal with it. The answer from the doctor was clear; autism would be with Jordon for the rest of his life. Its very nature was such that, although she could not say exactly how much he could develop, he would always be limited in what he achieved. The nature of his special needs and his position on the autistic spectrum meant that he would always be dependent upon others and that he had little hope of living a 'so called' normal life as we understood it. There was no magic wand that could be waved, just the promise of a future full of autism.

At last we had our answer, the wave had broken upon us and even though it had passed, we still did not truly know what it meant. The doctor had delivered the diagnosis as though she was dropping a cannonball at our feet, one that Lisa and I were to lift and carry out of the room with us. We were both stunned and felt as though the weight of the world had fallen upon our shoulders.

There had been no indication from the medical profession up until this time that autism was what we were dealing with. While we now knew what was causing his problems, we were both at once devastated and confused. We did not know what happened next or what we should be doing. Emotionally numbed by the fear of facing an uncertain future, Lisa and I gathered up Jordon and the reading material we had been given and left the Centre knowing that our lives had now officially changed forever.

In one way, I believe our bemusement was partly because, no matter what the diagnosis, in this day and age, we all expect there to be at least some form of treatment or therapy that holds the answers. Subconsciously, I feel we were waiting for the doctor to outline a course, a treatment plan or anything that offered us a glimmer of hope. The absence of any of this, alongside what was very clearly genuine concern, made it worse. We could tell the doctor was a deeply caring person, but the fact that she could still offer no help or answers meant that they probably did not exist. So instead of being an illumination of our problems, a clue as to what to do next, the diagnosis fell like a sentence upon our heads. Yet we remained ignorant as to its true meaning and the importance of what we had just been told. All we knew was that it was bad, it had little hope of getting better and it would remain with Jordon for as long as he lived. Lisa, with a heavy heart, immediately called Brian, who was desperate to hear the news and he met it with the same perplexed shock we all now felt.

As we left, still in turmoil, I spoke quietly to Lisa, "all we can do is our very best for Jordon". Lisa, clearly still numb from the impact, slowly nodded her head.

I can honestly say we have kept that promise from that day to this.

Chapter Five - Learning Difficulties

We left the Centre clutching leaflets and a book that the doctor had loaned to us, a book that gave some explanations as to what autism was and the medical perspective, but held no information as to how one could care for and communicate with an autistic child.

Retracing our steps to the car, both of us were actually in a state of shock, emotionally stunned and without any kind of clue as to what to do next. More than anything we had questions. Most importantly, what did all this mean for Jordon? The doctor had told us that there was a National Autistic Society and that we could contact them for further information, but other than that, we had no idea as to what we should do next.

The journey back was like returning through fog. We did not know where we were headed or what direction to take. The first thing we did on returning from the Centre was to sit down and talk about what we had heard. We did not really know what was expected of us and despite having a diagnosis, in many ways it served only to make us feel initially lost.

But we needed to find a way forward and to decide upon a plan. So, we called the National Autistic Society, learning that it is a charitable organisation helping people with autism and their families and they were very helpful in sending us relevant information.

As a consequence, we made more telephone calls, furthering our research and learning as much as we could about the immediate prospects for Jordon and what forms of help were available for his education and development.

One quite shocking revelation, as we later learned, was that a diagnosis does not automatically secure help from your Local Authority. Help for autistic children at school in England is based on need, not diagnosis, and therefore you firstly need to compile a statement of special needs and then speak with your Local Authority's Special Educational Needs Co-ordinator to secure extra help for your child at school.

That means that there is no guarantee an autistic child will get the kind of schooling they need and while some local authorities provide excellent care for autistic children, others give the bare minimum. We also later learned that it meant many parents of autistic children, bringing up sons and daughters who place huge demands on the family, are constantly competing with each other for places in schools where a better standard of care is provided. Some parents even have to resort to legal battles to gain appropriate care for their children, meaning Local Authorities, their managers, solicitors and parents alike are spending time and money wrangling; resources that could be better spent serving the children themselves.

However, those were all concerns that would have to wait for the future. As luck would have it, our particular Local Authority did provide more than just the bare minimum of care and at just over two years old and having faced so many problems, Jordon's diagnosis enabled us to access, for the first time, some of the autism-specific support he so desperately needed.

Over the course of the next few months, we heard from the Local Authority's Early Intervention Team. Members of the team discussed the relevant services available for Jordon with Lisa and it transpired that there was a speech and language unit that might aid him.
There was also a service where specially trained staff came with appropriate toys and played with the child in your own

home. This served to occupy Jordon for a limited amount of time each week. They were both important, but we felt Jordon needed an intervention that was more relevant to his requirements and the services were simply not intense enough for his level of need.

What we did learn was that this intervention had all been set up by the doctor who had first broken the news of Jordon's diagnosis to us and my mind went back to that day and the big box of tissues she placed by our side, they were not merely a token gesture, she had delivered real help and we were very grateful for it. Merely having trained professionals to talk to, meant we could share our concerns and this in itself helped us in relieving some of the burden.

As time progressed and we learned more about the system, at the age of three we were able to secure Jordon a place at a special needs nursery not too far from home. This meant that a few days a week, for a couple of hours each time, we were able to get the specialist care he needed to progress.

The diagnosis also meant that we were able to push for further support. We were very lucky. At the time, Lisa was learning as much as she could about autism and part of this process was attending support groups. One such meeting was for parents of young disabled and autistic children. The group was funded by the local council and one man who attended turned out to be the head representative of Parents of Autistic Children Training and Support (PACTS), a programme that originated in the USA and was being adopted in the UK at the time. Funded by the local authority, they were able to supply home tutors to parents who qualified for support. So, we applied and were successful in securing the PACTS programme for Jordon. The added benefit was that the PACTS tutors would come and teach Jordon at home. So, from the age of four onwards in the months up until it was time for him to go to school, he received this specialist support for three mornings every week.

The PACTS programme tutors were marvellous and spent those valuable hours teaching Jordon to recognise colours, vocabulary and all the concepts he had not yet grasped. This was a revelation and would aid his development so much, setting him up for school on a much firmer footing than we could have hoped to do alone. To this day, I do not have enough praise for these magnificent people. One, in particular, was very understanding and effective in dealing with Jordon and we will remain eternally grateful for all the loving kindness, patience and tuition she and the other tutors poured into my grandson.

When the programme was up and running, Jordon would sit the other side of a very small table interacting with his tutors as best he could. Here, he learned concepts such as 'over' and 'under', the names of shapes and objects and, because the tutors were specially trained to help autistic children, Jordon actually caught on very quickly.

Even though he was still unable to talk, Jordon's ability to understand words improved immensely under the PACTS scheme and we were asked to supply materials that would help with the learning process, so Lisa and I often found ourselves on missions to search out reference tools for the programme.

The PACTS tutor would tell us what stage Jordon had got to at any one time and the next lesson would involve a particular focus. Knowing this, we might then have a day's notice to dash out and find items for reference. Sometimes, this could be a great rush for us all, but it was wonderful to be involved in doing something that we knew could help Jordon, especially as we could see daily progress as a result of the PACTS methods. So it was, that we would find ourselves dashing out to buy toy animals, cars, aeroplanes, tractors and trains; anything that could be used by the tutor to improve Jordon's vocabulary. We would be called upon to supply cups, glasses, vases, all were brought into the tuition room by us so that Jordon could learn to name and differentiate between objects, learning how to identify food, fruit, and the names of hundreds of everyday items that he had hitherto ignored.

Gradually his tuition room filled with all manner of items, toys, auditory and sensory stimulation educational tools, things that flashed, toys that beeped, everything that you could imagine that would introduce the world to Jordon and tune him into the nature of all the things around him. It soon began to look as though an eccentric hoarder had decided to assemble their collection of random objects into one small room.

As the programme progressed, so did Jordon's ability to discern. The items we were called upon to provide became more specific and we were soon supplying fabrics with different patterns so that Jordon could learn the difference between a 'stripe' and a repeated pattern, between rough and smooth, light and heavy.

The auditory stimulus included rattles and bells and the tutor even placed an alarm clock on the table so that Jordon could learn to tell the time, as well as understand the concept of it all the better; when the bell rang, the session was over.

All the while, Jordon would sit through the session and, it has to be said, he was incredibly well behaved with the PACTS programme tutor.

Initially, they could not get Jordon to sit down but they had been schooled in how to gain a response and Jordon was soon working very well with them. After a short while, Jordon could respond to a request to identify a number or object placed on the table in front of him. This, in itself, was a minor miracle and these miracles kept coming.

The programme then extended beyond everyday objects and took Jordon into the world of emotion, identifying and articulating facial expressions, so he could associate feelings (something he had great difficulty in identifying with) with the way people looked and acted.

I can honestly say that if it were not for the learning techniques and additional time and attention the PACTS programme devoted to Jordon, he simply wouldn't be where he is today. They gave him a tremendous starting point and we recognised that things were going marvellously well in his education. It provided Lisa, Brian and myself, a ray of hope to see his progress and most importantly, it showed us that he could be taught.

Further education

The PACTS programme was an intensive but short course, a few months that were essential in laying the foundations for Jordon's education. It was a breakthrough in his development yet, despite this progress, Jordon had still only spoken one word and we had many more daily challenges to face.

The autistic spectrum encompasses a wide range of difficulties and severity in all the areas that it affects in the child's life, but thankfully there is hope for many in learning how to communicate with their child. Parents, and in my case, grandparents of autistic children are used to this and the underlying and seemingly insurmountable problem you are faced with is that of communication. This is where the predominant battle lies, in establishing a connection between the child's mind, their internal landscape and the outside world.

Achieving these connections is far more easily said than done. It can take years of patience and every autistic child is at a different point on the spectrum. So, communication problems vary hugely in severity and they range from those autistic children who do not speak at all, to those whose speech is well developed and can hold conversations.

The PACTS programme showed us how essential it is to reach out to an autistic child as soon as is possible. Developing early communication skills helps them in overcoming what will otherwise develop into frustrations which boil over into rebellion and tantrums. The recognised methods for achieving this cover a broad spectrum. Communication can develop by taking as simple a course as using pictures and pointing, or using advanced techniques such as sign language.

The nature and severity of the problem differs for every child and many autistic children are greatly delayed in developing speech. So, in later life, autistic adults display a wide range of speech behaviours; some will never utter a word, some will speak barely at all, some will talk in whispers, some can only sing their words or otherwise remain silent, while others still, like Jordon are capable of speech, but their development is held back by their autism.

For Jordon, speech came slowly and we did not know at any point how far he would progress. All autistic behaviour is like this, no matter how hard you try, you have no early indications as to how successful you will be, nor when that success might come, tomorrow, or ten years from now.

The first stage in his communication development was when he learned to point to things he wanted. Although that may sound like a very small thing, for us it was huge. It meant he could at last tell us if he needed something. It didn't happen overnight, he started to learn to point at around six years of age and developed the skill gradually thereafter.

After Jordon learned to point, speech did gradually come, but it was very slow indeed. "Mum" had been his first word, uttered when he was four years old and at home in his usual class with the PACTS tutors. They had immediately told Lisa the news. Progress had been made! Yet, he was not to repeat this word outside of the classroom for a long while to come, years later when he repeated just that same word again. Then, slowly, piece by piece, individual words were added and nowadays, you can quite easily hold a short conversation with Jordon if the topic is of interest to him and provided, of course, as a typical teenager, he is in the mood to talk to you!

Even so, to some, Jordon's speech remains unintelligible, unrecognisable, slightly guttural, often overly loud, robotic language that takes a while to tune into. Sometimes, Jordon is unable to pronounce a word because of his difficulties in using his tongue to speak with. The letters 'L' and 'R' are particularly challenging and for quite some time he would avoid them and still does to a certain extent today. So often 'Robert' is said as "Wobet", 'Lauren' as "Woren" with a very soft 'r' uttered from the back of the throat. 'Train' is "Twain" and 'Lovely' is more like "Wovely" and so his sister 'Lauren' remains a rather endearing to hear "Wovely Woren"!

Even today, Jordon can say whole sentences and the meaning will elude us. This is not helped by his habit of talking very quickly. He reads very fast indeed. At school, his teachers have recognised that because reading out loud takes a lot of effort he will rush through it, going as quickly as he possibly can to get it over with. When we asked Jordon why this was, he told us that he prefers to read to himself. We know that this is because it is extra work for him to verbally express the words that are in his head.

When he is talking to me, despite continuous improvement, I will sometimes have to ask Jordon to slow down and, bless him, he does. To avoid embarrassment, I put it to him that "Nan needs you to speak slowly Jordon, I am old and cannot hear you."

"It's OK Nan. I Will Speak Slowly" and then he will slow his speech down considerably out of consideration for me.

I sometimes use this technique to see how Jordon's spelling is progressing. "I'm sorry, Jordon, I don't understand that word, could you spell it for me please". He dutifully does so, spelling the word, letter by letter.

Another complication

Even now that Jordon has learned to understand what we say and can, in turn, make himself understood, there is another layer of complication.

Language to Jordon is very much like a tool he picks up and puts down. When he addresses us or we address him, we will very often use stock phrases, triggering conditioned responses. This overcomes any need for him to think things through. However, we are careful to stretch his mind and his vocabulary.

So, Lisa and Brian will talk to him as much as possible and so will I, verbalising, communicating, opening him up to new ideas and seeking his opinion, pushing him to respond and engage with us. However, this approach can often reveal how alien language is to him as a method of communication. So, the casual enquiry, "would you like an orange juice Jordon?" could be met with the response, "No Thank You Nan, I Don't Want To Go To The Shops". His mind is associating orange juice in a familiar situation, on the shelves of a supermarket and this shows how associations in his brain do not occur naturally. He has to think hard and if he gets it wrong, when questioned further, he will think harder or he might retreat, "No More Talking". He will have recognised that he misspoke and be upset, feeling slightly awkward, we suspect.

Later on, you may receive continuous apologies for his getting the answer wrong and committing what he sees as a misdemeanour. He feels insecure if what he verbally brings into our world sounds confused. Recognising that he has not made sense triggers some feeling of awkwardness because he is unable to explain what is in his mind, as it highlights his inability to communicate as he would like to.

If Jordon feels awkward, his apologies can be constant, repeated every few minutes for quite literally hours at a time. "I'm Sorry I Said Shops" could be said so often, that it becomes like some form of mental torture. Many behaviours can trigger this, if he is disobedient, he will apologise, if he shouts, he will apologise, if he triggers his own insecurities by misspeaking, he will apologise. Sometimes it takes a truckload of reassurance before he will accept "everything is ok", while we take his hands in our own, asking him to look into our eyes, trying to get the message across and then, when we are successful, he will quieten, merely seeking our attention by tapping us on the head every now and then and telling us he loves us, a further phase in reassuring himself that we are still there for him. This is Jordon reaching out across the great divide that lies between his world and ours.

Chapter Six - Questioning Authority

The learning difficulties in autism originate within the child and therefore, of necessity, the families and carers focus wholeheartedly on their development. As Jordon's family, even as we learned about autism and overcame our own initial lack of understanding, we were at the same time facing other people's ignorance and many of the challenges that confronted us were due to a lack of understanding from those who were ignorant of autism and what it means.

It amazes me still that, even today, well over a decade after we began to confront Jordon's diagnosis, many people are unaware of autism and have no idea how to interact with those who are on the autistic spectrum. Many more people are now aware of the name, of the term autism, but far fewer understand the nature or the full extent of the difficulties it can present.

Quite often, understandably, especially when Jordon was a toddler, strangers would assume he was a naughty or rebellious child. It was plain to see that some people would leap to the conclusion that Lisa and Brian were bad parents or pandering to him in some way, when they felt a firm hand was called for. Especially when he was in a tantrum, the angry reactions around us showed that we were expected to admonish or raise our voices to him. These tactics might work with a child that was not autistic, but even if we had agreed with this approach, which we did not, we knew that it would simply make Jordon worse.

If any child and especially an autistic one, is to learn how to behave in a way that does not make them and others around them frustrated and angry, then they must be witness to the benefits of patience and cooperation. The uphill battle that ensues with many toddlers in their 'terrible twos' goes on for years with an autistic child and the learning curve is far steeper.

With all parenting, naturally the parent has to establish some level of authority and respect and when pushed beyond their ability to cope by a rebellious child, then some parents may even lose their temper and shout, forcing the child to comply. While, with us, it is a point of principle to avoid this seemingly understandable deterrent, in Jordon's case, it would have had no positive effect; in fact it would have driven him further within himself. Even though we may have sometimes felt like screaming with frustration, we never went down that route.

In general, if you try to physically control or even shout at an autistic child, they will rebel and fight back. This is because the majority of autistic children have little or no perspective on their own behaviour and they do not see any of their own actions as rebellious. It is not a battle of wills, it is a battle to breach the gap in understanding and therefore you cannot impose your will to any positive effect. While I have heard of systems where they deliberately threaten an autistic child into submission, to my mind autism is not a request for us to respond with aggression to our fellow human beings and especially not to those who have no trace of malice within them. Instead, an autistic child is a parent's ultimate test of patience, tolerance, consideration and love, a test that can perhaps last for the rest of their lives.

The "do-it-or-else" approach would only worsen Jordon's behaviour. For, it is not wilful disobedience or seeking his own way that motivates him, rather it is the huge gulf of understanding that exists between Jordon and the outside world.

For a relationship to truly develop, for a child with autism to relate to you as a human being takes years of pouring love into them, both in your words and your deeds, until they have learned to have faith in you and learned to trust.

Many of those years of relationship building can be spent without any kind of response, crying over the huge responsibility that comes with caring and loving for someone you wish to be happy. Imagine if your child were immune to your every effort to make them your friend, that they could not relate to your love and never once responded. That heartache is the daily burden of many autistic parents.

The ache for Jordon, or any autistic child, to respond can be met with indifference, rebellion or even violence. You can try and help an autistic child and yet they will only ever accept this on their terms. A devastated, sometimes distraught parent could be reaching out to their child in tears, while that child is lashing out with punches and kicks and bites. This is one of the saddest sights in the world to see, made worse by the fact that this pattern of indifference and level of separation may well continue for many years.

We took great care not to react to any of Jordon's behaviour as if it were strange and nowadays if we did, Jordon has enough self-awareness that if we felt his speech or eating habits were unacceptable, he might suppress them and then as a result we would run the risk of undoing years of hard work. If we discouraged him by making him feel odd, he might go permanently silent on us. Then, because he has to express himself somehow, negative behaviours born of his own frustration would manifest again and he might bang his head or act in any number of harmful ways that let his feelings out. These are all very real dangers with an autistic child and nothing can be taken for granted.

This is another reason why, over the many years Jordon has been with us, it is still very difficult not to become angry with the many people we find judging him. After all the effort and care we put into Jordon, the patience and understanding, we take great pains to recognise that while Jordon's behaviour is merely a symptom of his autism, theirs is born of ignorance.

Yet Lisa would never say anything in such circumstances. How can you explain to people that she had a child who could not be restrained, could not be bribed and for a long time could not be taught. I just pray they never find themselves in the same situation of having a child they love who is born so unreachable.

Another problem and a further operation

Hospitals were a recurring theme in Jordon's early years and as his grandmother, I know we all came to dread the thought of him attending, for despite their life-saving benefits, the fear and worry that accompanied each visit made each one a little dose of purgatory for us all.

One such occasion was when, at four and a half years of age, we encountered yet another medical problem with Jordon. It was just before he was due to go into school for the very first time, the doctor found at a regular check-up that his testicle had not descended properly and had gone up into his groin.

The doctor surmised that somehow the scar tissue from his kidney operation had adhered and now his testicle remained in the wrong position. This was by no means a unique situation and although the remedy was an operation, it wasn't viewed as a major one by the medical profession.

We were soon to find ourselves back in hospital and I wondered how Jordon would cope now he was older and indeed what effect it would have. We were not yet at a stage where we could explain why he was going there, nor reassure him that it would be alright.

Soon after we were allocated a date for the event and found ourselves at the hospital once more. We didn't really know what to expect and were quickly directed to a ward that was full of children. There, each bed was occupied by a young boy and sat beside them were one or two parents, holding their hands, chatting away and all obviously in the queue for similar operations.

We were told by the nurse that we were to be given a bed for Jordon, there we were to wait for our allotted time and then, upon being called, he would go in for what was a very simple procedure. They were to cut into Jordon's abdomen, do what needed to be done and his testicle should then descend normally. When he came out of the operation, if all had gone well, then he would be allowed home the same day. We kept our fingers crossed.

What surprised me, in retrospect, was that even though at this stage it was well documented that Jordon was autistic, there was absolutely no allowance made for his disorder. In fact, the hospital obviously knew nothing about it and we found ourselves where we least wanted to be, right at the end of the waiting list.

So we arrived at the hospital at 9 a.m., all three of us dutifully sat entertaining an autistic boy who was a nightmare to keep still at the best of times. We had been instructed not to allow Jordon food or drink from the night before and we were all beginning to worry how we were going to keep him occupied and quiet. Having stuck to the rules, it meant Jordon had already gone 12 hours with nothing to eat or drink. Had we known we were to face a further seven hour wait and remain in those same plastic chairs for nearly 12 hours in all, we would have raised it with the hospital, but we did not even have a hint until we saw our position on the waiting list, which was right at the very bottom, the very last child to be operated on and the one facing the longest wait.

We then knew we were to spend a good part of the day entertaining Jordon. How on earth were we supposed to keep him happy? All the while, we watched children, one by one, being taken off to their allotted surgery appointment.

It didn't take long for Jordon to become agitated and so the work began of keeping him occupied and in bed. We were well used to the difficulties by now and we laboured to keep his interest, playing little games, calling out to him and desperately trying to gain and hold his attention.

As the day progressed, after their operations, each child was returned on a trolley and would then lie in bed, still under the effects of the anaesthetic and gradually coming around into wakefulness. In their weakened states, they were comforted by attentive parents as they recovered. It was lovely to see the parents' tender loving care reflected in the eyes of their children. A mother would stroke her son's hair as he awoke and the moment his eyes opened, she would receive his undivided attention, a loving smile in response reflecting the tenderness of the moment.

That room full of children watched over by their loved ones seemed to emphasise everything we were missing out on with Jordon.

Thankfully, in the middle of the morning, Jordon was given his pre-operation medication, which had the beneficial side-effect of calming him down. It meant we had several hours where he was a little more controllable, but even so, he was still mobile and active. With no nursing staff around us and Jordon still fretting, despite the medications we decided the only thing to do was to walk him around the hospital. This was a welcome relief and so for several hours, we took turns taking him on a tour of the surrounding wards.

Despite the walking and all our other efforts, as the hours wore on, it was apparent we were losing the battle with Jordon. The pre-med was wearing off and the fact that we were unable to give him a drink or food made matters worse. He was becoming increasingly fraught. Noticing our plight, a very kind lady who was waiting for her son to return from his operation reached out to us and offered his handheld computer game for Jordon to play with. This was an instant success with Jordon and I could have raised my hands to Heaven in thanks. He was immediately taken with the game and became so engrossed with it that we didn't hear a further noise out of him. From restless and battling boy, bordering on a tantrum, he became a quiet figure in his bed, head down and so absorbed that it was like a minor miracle.

We all looked at each other and breathed a very quiet sigh of relief. Time, however, was not on our side.

The lady's son had returned from his operation and while he was still under the anaesthetic, we all knew he would soon awaken and, as she told us, want his favourite toy.

They say that computer games reduce the amount of exercise we take. Well, all I can say is that they didn't for Brian that day. We all knew what would happen if we tried to take the game from Jordon; we were facing a tantrum at best and at worst, a complete meltdown. Bearing in mind the kind of day he had already had, we were almost certain it was the latter.

Realising what was to come and the fact that we didn't know how soon, Brian was up and out of his chair and with the words "I'll get one now", he was racing to the shops to see if they had one of these new-to-the-market games in stock. The fact that they were very expensive, that they were in demand and many shops would have sold out, that car parking was very limited at the hospital and that this was, as it turned out, a two mile run there and back, didn't hold Brian back. We all knew the alternative and reached instant silent agreement. Brian was up, off and out the door within a minute and his race against time began. The boy's mother returned my smile, offering us an encouraging and knowing look.

Lisa and I then turned our attention to Jordon's intent face, his head bowed over the console, while we occasionally studied the sleeping child who owned the game for signs of awakening. It would have been comic if it weren't for the anxiety we were both feeling. Would Brian find the right game for sale, would he arrive back in time? We didn't even realise Brian had been unable to take the car as there was no guaranteeing a parking place on his return. Had we known he was running, sprinting along the pavement at that very moment, it would have been worse, as there was only one shop in the small local parade that would possibly stock the game.

Then the worst happened, the other little boy was awake and talking to his mother. He obviously wanted to play with his new toy and I could see by the look in this lady's eyes that she was loath to ask us, but felt that her priority lay with her son and returning his favourite game. The minutes ticked by and the moment was approaching, inevitably the boy asked for his game and his mother began walking towards us.

We were working out how to persuade Jordon to relinquish the game and even started talking to him, "Jordon, Jordon" while his head remained bowed. This was the moment of truth and a painful one at that.

At that very moment, the door opened and a red faced Brian appeared, bent over and breathless. In his hand was a bag with a brand new game in it. "I...got...it!" Pausing between each word to gulp in air. He looked at us wide-eyed, "and it cost a fortune!"

I nearly laughed out loud from my own relief and witnessing that so evident on Brian's face. He had obviously run as hard as he could and the fact that we were all so delighted with buying a child's toy, made it all the more funny that Jordon was still sat in bed, head down and completely oblivious to us all.

We managed the handover of the boy's game as Jordon saw the brand new one coming out of its box. I am so grateful to that lady, her act of kindness with such an expensive and beloved toy was one I will always remain thankful for and if she should ever read this book, I would like to say "thank you!"

With the arrival of the new game, we now had a solution until Jordon's turn for his operation came around and yet we were all feeling the strain. None of us had eaten or drunk anything all day and it was now well into the afternoon. Three or four boys remained recovering after their operations, while only one more was in the queue ahead of Jordon. At least there was an end in sight and the prospect of our waiting coming to an end.

Eventually, Jordon's turn came and he was wheeled into the operating theatre. So we began yet another anxious wait, for bearing in mind our previous experiences, we were always on our guard and expecting the unexpected when it came to hospitals.

Time passed, we were told the operation had been a success and Jordon was wheeled back, lifted into bed; and then we began waiting for him to wake up. It didn't take long and as expected, he did not react at all like the other boys.

There was no gradual opening of his eyes, no slow return into wakefulness. Instead, Jordon opened his eyes, sat bolt upright and immediately grabbed at the dressing over his wound, clawing at it with his hand in obvious distress.

We tried to ward his hands away from the bandage, but his distress was escalating. Jordon struggled and struggled and our fear was that by grabbing or holding him, we would aggravate his wound or split it open in some way. So we were gingerly, gently trying to hold him back, but this didn't work and he pushed his way out of the bed and started running as if his life depended on it.

Remember, this is a boy who had just come round from anaesthetic and almost immediately, we were chasing him around the hospital. Outside the large ward was a long corridor, there were no hospital staff in sight and being the last planned operation of the day, every other parent and child had gone home, apart from Jordon. So we attempted to usher him back along a long empty corridor while he shrugged us off and sought his own way.

Eventually, we managed to shepherd him back to the ward, but he absolutely refused to be put back into bed, instead he would only lay on the floor, where he promptly began to scream his head off.

At last a nurse appeared, obviously drawn by the noise, asking us what was wrong. She was plainly confused by the sight of this young boy writhing on the floor grabbing at his wound and quickly provided him with a pillow before standing still to look on.

I tried to explain that he was autistic and that this was the reason for his behaviour. I virtually had to beg for a painkiller and eventually, after getting our point across, she returned with a pill for him to swallow. For the second time that day I almost laughed out loud, this time in exasperation. I almost asked the nurse to try and administer the pill to Jordon to see how far she got. We would see the week out before she got him to swallow something like a pill. But Jordon was in pain and we couldn't afford the time to play games. I explained very gently that it would be impossible to get Jordon to take a pill and asked if there were any other alternative.

The nurse was gone for what seemed like ages and it was certainly a very long time before she returned with a painkiller in the form of a thick white liquid. Even so, Jordon still lay on the floor and we had to be very careful to ensure he did not bang his head, while we forced his mouth open to take the medicine. The important thing was that it worked and he quickly quietened down.

Word had obviously got round and soon a doctor appeared and looked Jordon over. He asked if he had urinated and I remember thinking it was pretty unlikely as he hadn't, by now, had any liquid or food for nearly 24 hours. It was nearly 8 o'clock at night but we were told that until he was able to urinate, he was not to be allowed home. So we began the wait.

We knew that we were going to have no joy in getting Jordon to take any drink or food in such unfamiliar surroundings when he was so distraught. He had an incision of about three inches long in his abdomen, he was in obvious pain and we had to get him home if he was to eat or drink.

Lisa realised we had to get the doctor to make an exception and explained Jordon's circumstances. He listened intently and then, obviously with some reluctance, agreed for Jordon to be allowed home, on the condition that if there were any unusual signs or if he failed to pass water before midnight, we were to return Jordon to the hospital immediately.

So, yet another hospital visit proved to be a traumatic experience for us all. Realising the circumstances, the hospital had provided more liquid-form painkillers for us to take home. Jordon simply didn't know how to react to pain and these helped us immensely.

Things went well for 24 hours, but then we had a further problem to deal with. On the second day at home, Jordon's dressing came loose and revealed an unhealed wound, that was thankfully not bleeding. We could see that the incision had parted under the strain of Jordon's leaping around and running. The wound had opened up completely and there was a shallow 'v' shaped hole where the two sides of the cut had not yet healed together. Concerned, we rang the hospital and they told us to call the local doctor's surgery.

We did so and the doctor advised us his schedule for that day was full and that we should come in to see the nurse. We hastened to the surgery and this lovely lady re-dressed his wound, giving Jordon yet another course of antibiotics as a precaution against possible infection, while we were left to keep him calm for the next few days to ensure the wound had a chance to heal.

The scars on Jordon's slight frame were now the only physical signs of the pain he held inside.

The naked truth

It is important to say that Jordon, at times, looks completely unaffected by any special need or disability. In repose, there is no clue or indication that there is anything unusual about him or that he has any problems. When born, he was a perfectly healthy looking baby and now he stands at around 5'10" tall, a healthy broad-shouldered young man. Yet, his mannerisms, his strange looking behaviour, his arm and hand flapping, the noises he makes - all these things are so unusual as to make him stand out amongst other children.

When still, he does not look any different, but rarely will Jordon remain immobile. When he was old enough to walk with us hand in hand along the street, we would hold him in a vice-like grip to ensure he did not run off (which he would readily do at a moment's notice). All the while, he would constantly, without letting up, pull away from you. His free arm would be flapping around, his hands and fingers twitching and writhing, behaviours that have lessened over time, but still exist in a less noticeable way to this day. When younger, periodically his eyes would roll, especially if he was nervous, but perhaps the most unusual behaviour was the very strange noises, always from the back of his throat, low moaning groans as if he were trying to drown out the noise of the world around him. To me it felt as though Jordon had developed a language all of his own and was, in his own way, talking to us and himself.

As Jordon grew, we would constantly reinforce positive behaviours, encouraging those that were beneficial and letting him know which mannerisms and actions were not acceptable. Over time, this education has paid off, gradually lowering the level of socially unacceptable habits. However, we did learn that you cannot anticipate nor control every situation or circumstance he finds himself in.

One thing to bear in mind with Jordon is that while he may now be self-conscious about his voice, he has absolutely no embarrassment about his body.

Lisa and Brian always involve Jordon as much as possible in ordering takeaway food and any activity that might help him gain independence in his adult life, integrating him with the wider community.

One particularly memorable example of this is when Lisa and Brian decided to treat themselves to a Chinese Take-Away, delivered to the door. Jordon was around twelve years old and by that stage had developed a love of Chinese food. Of course, he will only ever eat two dishes, chicken balls and chips and for him this was a great treat. Nothing else from the menu was ever sampled and as usual he was excited and very impatient for it to arrive.

So, Jordon was sent upstairs to change into his pyjamas, another part of the self-help habits we were establishing with him, getting him used to changing clothes at specific times of the day. At the time of this episode, Jordon could not put on his school uniform unaided, so it was important for him to make progress.

On this occasion, the take away food was delivered to the door very quickly. Brian went to the door to answer and handed over the payment, while behind him Jordon was excitedly shouting, "Chinese Food! Chinese Food!". Brian was smiling at his son's obvious enthusiasm as he paid and accepted the delivery, but suddenly paused, taken aback by the astonished look on the delivery man's face. The Delivery man, quite obviously shocked, was staring wide-eyed and open mouthed, fixing his gaze over Brian's shoulder.

Brian slowly turned his head, following the delivery man's gaze. There, a few feet behind him, at the foot of the stairs, a completely naked Jordon, a frantic look on his face, was excitedly hopping from foot to foot, reaching out for the packages and yelling out in his loud robotic voice "Chinese Food! Chinese Food!"

Hearing Brian's surprised shout "Jordon! Get upstairs!" Lisa stepped in and quickly ushered Jordon back up to his room to finish dressing, while a rather embarrassed Brian was left to tip an equally bemused delivery man and close the door as quickly as possible.

Brian, his back pressed against the door, met Lisa's gaze and they shared a moment of exasperated embarrassment which quickly lapsed into laughter.

Still, Jordon's behaviour had a mild effect on the local economy that day, for Lisa and Brian would never order from the same Chinese restaurant ever again!

A solitary act of kindness

Often, when we made trips to the shops, we would witness the penetrating stares that people would cast in Jordon's direction. His behaviour was very unusual and there would be audible remarks accompanied by looks of curiosity, shock, disdain or disgust, depending upon what he was doing or the person observing. We held our heads high while other parents would sometimes pull away their own inquisitive children and even add to the hurtful comments about his behaviour. We often felt as though we were walking as social pariahs, surrounded by those who could not appreciate or relate to what they were witnessing.

So it was that the stress, our near constant worry of his running away, throwing a tantrum, harming himself in some way, or being unable to tell us what he wanted, was compounded by the reaction and the rejection of people around us. It was all so very hurtful.

I know of some autistic parents who become aggressive when confronted by this seeming wall of ignorance and I can understand why, with so many people ready to treat an autistic child like an outcast. In our case, we were well aware of what was going on around us, but at the same time we knew how strange Jordon must have seemed. Generally, while we tried not to react, the potential was there to become mortified by the pattern of apprehension, approbation and avoidance.

Because we loved Jordon so much and put so much effort into improving his world, to bear this additional burden from those who knew nothing of Jordon's problems was heart-breaking. The opinions that were voiced to us, while it was ignorance on the part of others and therefore understandable, devastated us nonetheless. Yet, when we saw others recoil or judge, it strengthened our resolve.

To put all this in perspective, on one particular and very memorable occasion when Jordon was around nine or ten years old we were in a local shopping precinct, having a cup of tea in the cafeteria. A very polite older lady came up to us and enquired as to the nature of his problem. She was incredibly nice and understanding and it transpired that a relative of hers had an autistic child, a niece from memory and therefore she knew exactly how to talk to Jordon and had a lovely conversation with him, albeit one-sided!

I can honestly say that up to that point, not one single adult person had taken it upon themselves to approach us unbidden and addressed Jordon directly, then spoken to him and treated him like a normal human being. That is why it remains in my memory to this day, at that time, after nearly a decade of silence, disapproval and disdain; it was one of the few solitary acts of kindness amongst so many difficult encounters with strangers.

It's not me, it's you!

I often thought and still do, that Jordon must think of us as imbeciles because we cannot understand anything he is trying to put across. Jordon knows what he wants and early on he would often lead us to that thing or try in some way to convey his intent, but the gulf between his mannerisms, his attempts at communication, what lies in his mind and us, is often a wider gap than words can bridge.

Run run run

Despite the help we were receiving, between the ages of three and five, we experienced particularly difficult times with Jordon, not least because he was by now very mobile and loved to run around. I could get worn out just watching him!

Running, in fact, could be said to be somewhat of a full-time hobby for Jordon at this age. If you turned your back or loosened your grip on him for just one moment then he would be off, sprinting as fast as he was able and with no hesitation, nor any concept of fear or direction. If there was a road, a car, a bike in his path, none of these would perturb him. He had absolutely no understanding of traffic or danger whatsoever and I remember feeling so scared that I would cling on to him for dear life.

Pedestrian crossings were particularly trying and we would constantly reinforce to Jordon that "Green Man Means Go" and "Red Man Means Wait"! Even today, we reinforce that behaviour so that we are perhaps as conditioned as he is, to say "Green Man Means Go" and "Red Man Means Wait!"

Even now, after years of coaching on road safety, we have to keep an eye on him, as, while it has sunk in that traffic must be avoided, we cannot rely on him to know what lethal threat a moving car poses. At that earlier age, he did not have any concept whatsoever of danger, nor would he be taught without many years of effort.

For this reason, there was a long period of years when it took a lot of planning to take Jordon outside, even to somewhere as seemingly harmless and innocuous as the park. A moment's distraction and he would instantly sprint off into the distance with us in hot pursuit. This was why it was always easiest if we were out on any trip or excursion for there to be two or three of us present to look after him. It seemed like a lot of grown-ups for one little boy.

For any child who does not have autism, then you could expect their running off to have a purpose. Perhaps they might chase a ball or try to make it to the playground or the ice cream shop and you would imagine them to have at least some concept of the danger involved.

In Jordon's case, for many years, there was none. If we were in the park, he would quite happily race into the playground and stand transfixed, like a statue, in front of a child hurtling towards him on a swing. He would run with no purpose other than to run, with no concept at all of the difference between roads and pavements. We had to be constantly vigilant, for we were the only safety measure between him and the outside world and, if we failed, then he could have met with quite serious injury.

What's yours is mine

With no social skills and no sense of the consequences of his actions, Jordon behaved in ways that others found difficult to deal with. In his youth, he saw no reason whatsoever why he should not take toys from other children. Jordon never looked at people as people; if he wanted to be somewhere, there was no inhibition in pushing an adult or a child out of his way and if they did not comply, then they were merely yet another source of frustration to be reacted to.

Despite this, we tried not to allow the autism to keep us at home and we recognised just how important it was to provide Jordon with as much social interaction as possible. So, we took him out as much as we could. Whether it was to the shops, the seaside, the swimming pool, the park, we went anywhere we could go to get him involved and widen his horizons. Whenever a trip was planned, we rallied round and started out on yet another 'let's take Jordon out' mission.

Wherever we went, there were the usual things to watch out for, like making sure Jordon did not sprint away, that he did not steal from other children or behave strangely towards an adult and each destination came with its own distinct set of circumstances and situations to deal with.

When we took him to the water park, it came with its own particular set of challenges. Aside from having to look out for the danger of the water, Jordon really enjoyed the game of splashing whoever was around him in the pool. So, he would happily and repeatedly splash anyone who came near to him, adults included. With Jordon, this wouldn't be just a few quick splashes or a little game he soon tired of, he was more than capable of carrying on the behaviour without stopping at all. On several occasions, we had seen him launch a 'splash attack' on someone in the pool and keep on and on without relenting, ceaselessly splashing them, way beyond when good humoured politeness held sway, while we desperately tried to intervene. Splash, splash, splash - on and on!

The saddest thing was seeing just how absorbed Jordon was in the games he enjoyed. When he launched a 'splash attack', he was totally absorbed in splashing around, shrieking with delight and actually relating to another human being. It was one of the few times in his young life when he was totally engaged in, what was to him, a game. To witness him throwing himself about and beside himself with happiness was at the same time very distressing, for the gulf between Jordon and the world was increasingly apparent, both before and after we had a hint of the true extent of his problems. When any of us realise that those we love have emotional limitations, that they are incapable of relating to the world as fully as we would wish, that something is missing in their lives with no true hope of recovery, it is like a piece of your own life is missing too and it is this pain that is compounded and all too evident in those who care for children with autism.

This acute sadness aside, I have to be honest, our visits to the pool could be quite awkward, not because we were embarrassed by Jordon, but whoever he was splashing would feel themselves to be under attack. If he was splashing another child the parents would react protectively. We were embarrassed by the inconvenience imposed on someone who did not know us at all, especially as they might then leap to the many assumptions about Jordon that we were increasingly familiar with.

In deep water

At the same water park, there is an area with a sandpit and swings and one day, Lisa took Jordon there to play. It was sunny and there were lots of children, girls and boys playing in the sand, running around and having a lot of fun. One small boy was happily playing with his spade, engrossed in digging in the sand and filling his little bucket, having a great time. Jordon was obviously very interested and walked up to him, edging closer and closer. Lisa said you could tell that Jordon wanted so desperately to join in, intrigued by the game and quite clearly wanting to interact. For her, it was liberating to see Jordon doing something so uncharacteristic, wanting to take part and be part of this little boy's game. But without the means to communicate, he merely stood watching the boy play, wanting to get involved, but not knowing how.

Eventually, however, Jordon took action and walked right up to the boy. Without hesitation and not knowing how he should express his wish to play, Jordon took the spade from the clearly surprised boy. Lisa quickly stepped in, "no Jordon, please give the spade back" and Jordon complied, but he was still obviously very interested, wanting to be part of what was going on. So, Jordon stood watching and when Lisa sat down again, Jordon took the spade once more!

Before Lisa could step in again, there was a loud shout, "hey! Give that spade back to my son!" The boy's mother, seeing what had happened, charged over and snatched the spade away from Jordon, glaring at him. She was furious and yelled at Lisa, "can't you keep your son under control?!"

Lisa tried to explain, "I'm terribly sorry. He doesn't mean any harm, he has special needs". Now this admission in itself was a big step for Lisa; she was loath to paint a picture of Jordon as being different from any other child - her love prevented her from labelling him as limited or in any way different. She had gone beyond her own boundaries in an effort to explain.

The very sad thing was that this lady wasn't swayed by the explanation or sympathetic in the least. Lisa's attempt to create understanding was met with an icy reply "Yes, I can see that, it's obvious." When Lisa told me this woman's response, I felt her hurt. It wasn't merely the complete lack of sympathy, or the absence of empathy, it was the fact that she would so readily ignore Lisa's feelings.

So, one very angry lady promptly marched her son off, leaving Jordon standing like a socially unacceptable outcast. I wondered at the time who was most lacking in the ability to relate to our fellow humankind, Jordon who had little ability to do so, or this angry woman, who had chosen not to, setting such a bad example not only to Jordon and her own son, but the rest of the human race.

I always wonder why some people have no thought whatsoever for the effect they have on others. It would have been such a simple thing for her to invite Jordon to play, it would have been such a different story to place in our book, one with a positive outcome all round, not least for restoring our faith in other people. How telling, that a lack of any willingness to understand the feelings of others can have such a deep and lasting impact on their lives.

Lisa was distraught; what had been a moment of near normality was snatched away as quickly as the boy and his spade. So, once more, she witnessed a small ray of hope and joy in Jordon's life quickly taken away by the attitude of one single person.

Lisa vowed at that moment never again to excuse Jordon's behaviour by naming his autism, because to have done so and to have been so hurtfully dismissed cut deeper than anything else. To have to live her whole life dealing 24 hours a day with the consequences of autism and then to be confronted by someone's frank disdain, showed that some people have absolutely no thought for the burden she was living with Lisa and Brian had not asked for Jordon to be born autistic and neither has anyone who has an autistic child in their care. The ignorance of others can be one of the most hurtful parts of living with an autistic child.

Jordon's flagrant disregard for the principles of ownership weren't limited to other children's toys. In sweet shops he viewed everything as his to take. Regardless of whether it was something he would actually eat, Jordon would see something he liked and there was no hesitation, he would just take it and hold on to it. As with all his unwanted behaviours, we would gently coach him that it wasn't his and to put it back, gingerly walking the tightrope between compliance and tantrum. Of course, this would happen time and again and even though we were used to the potential for embarrassment, we were less comfortable with the potential prison sentence!

Wherever we went, there were a multitude of potential dangers, challenges and problems and it was almost enough to stop you taking him out at all. Still, it was his future that mattered and so we persevered.

Seven years of tantrums and meltdowns

An autistic child, in repose, looks like any other healthy child and this means that many people will wrongly ascribe their sometimes extreme behaviour to wilful disobedience and naughtiness, a sign of weak parents, or a lack of proper upbringing.

Even an innocent remark from a young child can be hurtful, "what's wrong with him mummy?" while people who have no clue as to the nature of the disorder are quite prepared to judge you as a parent, not knowing the reason for the child's unusual and unsocial behaviour, nor the fact that they themselves are just one of many who are willing to add insult to the daily emotional injury. Another person's judgemental attitude can increase the weight of the cross that many autistic parents bear, turning it from one of wood to stone.

Every parent will be familiar with the embarrassment of the toddler tantrums that plague the 'terrible two year olds' and one of the great difficulties with an autistic child is that, at that age especially, aside from their behaviour, there is no real sign of a disability. Autistic children have a vast range of individual problems that are collectively labelled as being on the autistic spectrum and while each autistic child manifests different behaviours, they all share a lack of the fail-safes that other children possess. So, they all have a tendency towards tantrums, unless other medical complications mean they are incapable of them. What is perhaps the hardest thing to convey is the severity of these tantrums, how unpredictable they can be and how penetrating and loud the accompanying screams are.

In addition, an autistic child's tantrum can go many stages further than the average child's. They can even go into the ultimate phase; what many parents call a 'meltdown'. If you have ever seen the full extent of one of these episodes, you will know that this is a human being who, unable to communicate with the world, is throwing their entire being into their physical reaction, compounded by a lifetime of frustration, triggered by something that the majority of us cannot understand.

Any parent will know what a tantrum looks like and many of us will have seen a child whose distress has boiled over into this extreme expression of frustration. Screaming, shouting, stamping their feet, throwing themselves down on the floor and doing everything they can to protest. It can get worse; a child who has extreme tantrums when they do not get their way can progress to holding their breath and even passing out from the effort. But that isn't the end of the scale.

With an autistic child, the tantrum progresses far beyond what we are used to seeing. Autistic children are more prone to tantrums and they are more frequent because there are so many potential causes and they have sometimes virtually no hope of communicating what it is that is frustrating them. The misunderstanding between them and the world builds and builds. The vast gap between what they are trying to express and our ability to understand them can be immense.

So the autistic tantrum can build far beyond what we might expect and last far longer than is usual, sometimes even for hours at a time and as a consequence, parents are constantly on the lookout for the first signs, desperately trying to become attuned to them. In Jordon's case, he would look increasingly anxious, his movements would become jerky and erratic, his hands starting to move around, flapping violently, as he became more agitated and visibly distressed and he would then become quickly out of control. He would verbalise his distress and then, almost immediately, erupt into screams. There was very little warning other than these signs and in almost no time he would be screaming at the top of his lungs. If any noise could shatter glass it was this.

Typically, he would throw himself on the floor, arching his back, losing all control, lashing out violently and kicking and screaming. So, a tantrum could build from seemingly nothing to being in full swing in a matter of seconds. Even though we became increasingly adept at recognising the initial signs, identifying the reason why he was agitated was often beyond us.

Obviously we would do everything we could to ensure he did not become frustrated and this is another reason why it is so important to build the ability to communicate with an autistic child, because anything that helps form a bridge between their feelings and the outside world will reduce the potential for frustration. The ability to point to what they need, picture cards that help identify what they want and the ability to verbalise; all of these offer some hope of the child being able to tell you what is troubling them. But even with all the effort in the world, an autistic child is likely to suffer tantrums and those tantrums can be more frequent, more prolonged and far more severe than any of us could imagine.

Witnessing a tantrum such as this can be soul destroying and so emotional that you could despair at why a human being has to go through such pain. The fact that this is your own child you are unable to help makes it all the worse.

While an autistic child lives in the same physical world as us, autism imposes a form of mental isolation, so there is no way of relating to what is going on outside or what is being asked of you. It is as if mentally you are locked in a box, your emotions in a strait jacket and your consciousness confined to a padded cell. Despite this, we have an expectation that autistic children should act and behave like us and our efforts are extended, encouraging them to do so.

We are used to having feelings arise within us and being able to deal with them in some way. We have options, we can work out why we feel a certain way, use reason to understand and act upon our emotions, but an autistic child does not have this ability. We can decide what to do about our emotions, bottle them up, do something to deal with the problem that caused them, talk the problem through, go for a run, punch a cushion, express them to the world; we have many ways of giving vent.

Autistic children have none of these options. They are prisoners within their own skin, all of their emotions locked up in their bodies with no outlet, therefore we are tasked with offering them any outlet we are able to, to build the communication in any way that is possible, because the situations that give rise to these problems are primarily to do with communication. It can be as simple as being unable to communicate something they want, their not understanding why they cannot have their favourite dessert, to feeling so threatened by something in the environment around them that the fear builds to simply unimaginable levels. Even the mere presence of something unfamiliar in a room can threaten an autistic child to such an extent that their senses become overloaded.

The frustration builds, the emotions wash over them and then boil over into upset, hysteria, screaming, shouting, lashing out, kicking, biting, spitting and then beyond. Some autistic children will then show extremes of self-harm, punching their own heads or battering them against any available surface. In Jordon's case, I can still remember him punching his head with so much force that we could hear each blow land before we were able to intervene.

I have heard of autistic children banging their heads repeatedly against the floor, against the walls, throwing themselves around until they could quite easily do themselves a serious and perhaps permanent injury. Also, autistic children are far more prone to seizures than other children and the accompanying convulsions and involuntary movements can be the cause of many injuries. This is why you will sometimes see an autistic child wearing head protection, because it is the only way of stopping them from concussing themselves or risking long-term damage. We consider ourselves very lucky that Jordon has never been prone to these attacks.

Sadly, some types of seizure trigger all sorts of strange sensations in the body, feelings of confusion, smells and sensory inputs that are triggered in the brain. For an autistic child, this type of input can be all the more confusing as they try to cope with the sensory assault. A vicious circle commences where seizures trigger yet more inner turmoil which can, in turn, exacerbate the problem.

Whenever Jordon was out of his comfort zone, we knew we were in a situation when a tantrum could be triggered. Yet there were also familiar situations that could upset Jordon, such as when we travelled anywhere by car. Merely placing Jordon in the car would set him off crying through upset and the danger was that we would have to stop at a red light or in traffic, when we knew he could quickly escalate into a tantrum. Merely stopping and getting out of the car to get to the shops would mean he would throw himself on the floor. Whether it was a sunny day or pouring with rain held no importance to him. Jordon would throw himself in a puddle if it happened to be there.

Jordon developed a constant cycle of tantrums, triggered whenever he encountered a situation he could not cope with, be it commonplace, strange or threatening. Most worrying and affecting was the sheer volume of the accompanying screams. Medical staff and teachers alike have all remarked upon the severity and said that they have never come across anything like it. Bear in mind, these comments come from professionals who deal with autistic children every day! When Jordon screamed, it was like he was putting every ounce of his being into it and on occasions I could feel my eardrums flutter. Sometimes you had no option other than to cover your ears against the onslaught.

In his earliest years, when he was lost in a tantrum, there was no distracting Jordon. He just did not know any better. The things that might work to calm down another child, such as walking away, talking gently or distracting them, had no effect.

It wasn't the case that these tactics rarely worked or that they were difficult to implement, they did not work - ever! There was no compromise on his part at all; the only reliable remedy we found was to physically remove Jordon from the problem if the tantrum was to have any chance of abating. Time was not a great healer in this case, Jordon did not easily cry himself to sleep when he was having a tantrum and he could quite easily go on unabated for hours. During the worst episodes he was absolutely beside himself, screaming at the top of his lungs at a pitch that would make your ears pop. What concerned us most was the very real danger that the extreme nature of these episodes would induce a fit, that he would rupture himself or injure his body. Many an autistic child's parents can attest to the injuries sustained when their child lapses into a fit.

This frequent pattern of behaviour carried on for many more years and he was seven years old before we were finally able to see a light at the end of the tunnel. In general, tantrums lasted up until he was around ten years old, when his ability to communicate reached the level where we were able to talk through situations and reason with him.

So, life with Jordon always held an edge of anxiety, not merely when we contemplated the long-term unknown that was Jordon's future, but because of the constant need for vigilance to ensure he did not lapse into another episode. Poor Lisa and Brian learned the hard way; that you had to be constantly on the lookout for the things that would set Jordon off. We learned to recognise the situations that had the potential to trigger his tantrums and the small early-warning signs that Jordon was becoming agitated. Caught early enough, we had a chance of stepping in and nipping the upcoming tsunami of sound in the bud, but there was no guarantee, despite our watchfulness, that we would be able to stop the impending tantrum or perhaps even find out what triggered it. Despite our best efforts, we would often remain totally in the dark as to why Jordon had his most recent meltdown.

This did not stop our efforts at detective work, to ensure we understood as much as we could, so that we could improve everyone's situation, Lisa and I would try to work out, often by a process of elimination, what it was that had caused the latest onslaught from Jordon. If we were able to deduce what had lead up to any given situation, that would help us remove those obstacles from his life. When he was old enough and he could communicate, then we would also take time to talk him through situations and reason with him, allowing him to move on.

One particular children's television programme was particularly distressing for Jordon because the four main characters, lovable, cuddly bear-type creatures, jumped down a hole at the end of the show. He loved the programme, but to see the characters disappear in that way was a major shock for him. Jordon simply could not understand where they had gone. In his mind, they were there, but then inexplicably, they disappeared, bringing terror to his world. How could they suddenly not be there?

His reaction would be the same every time, but then eventually, it got worse. When he realised the programme had the same ending every time, so he would become distraught from the outset, aware that the culmination of the programme was something awful. So, we had to be very careful not to allow him to see the programme at all, if we did, we knew it would upset him greatly. Bizarrely, there were other similar cartoons and children's programmes that caused him no problem at all and some of them he still watches to this very day.

On four wheels

We became very used to Jordon's tantrums, throwing himself flat onto a shop floor or into a puddle in the street, screaming at a pitch that would hurt your ears with absolutely no restraint. On shopping trips, because of our inability to get him to do anything he did not wish to and the temptation of so many appealing stores that would lead him to run off, we had to resort to taking him out in a pushchair as this was one of the few options available for us to hold him near to us without him hurting himself.

So, we took to wheeling Jordon around, sometimes with him struggling all the way I might add. Then we would face the occasional "isn't he a bit old for a push chair?" comment. One of the things you learn when it comes to an autistic child, is that you can never win!

So, we spent many years on excursions with a young boy who was getting increasingly big for a pushchair and wheeling him around on our essential shopping trips. This prevented him from running off at every opportunity and established some small level of control, but like many solutions we reached, it wasn't perfect and we maintained a constant vigilance. Even when in the pushchair, if Jordon saw a direction he wanted to go in, he would pursue it.

It went like this, he would see something appealing, a shop he wanted to go in. To reach it, he knew he had to stop the pushchair, so he would throw down his feet and struggle against the forward motion, try to stop the chair and manoeuvre it in his own chosen direction. A battle for control would then commence with Lisa, Brian or I desperately pushing one way while Jordon desperately tried to move in the other direction.

The push chair battles didn't stop there; when he was big enough, Jordon learned another tactic. He found that when he was thwarted, if he stood up, he could take control of the chair and he had a much better chance of getting where he wanted to go.

Still strapped into his pushchair, he worked out a way of struggling to his feet. Then, all of a sudden, you would have Jordon hunched over in front of you, a dummy in his mouth, a pushchair on his back, walking around like a surreal crab, determined to pursue his chosen goal! You can imagine the looks we received from even the most kind-hearted passers-by with this young boy with an upside down pushchair worn like an uncomfortable back pack, shuffling along like a hermit crab, busily sucking away on a dummy, seemingly demented in his attempt to struggle through a shop doorway.

It was nigh on impossible to stop him; Jordon has always been very strong and you can imagine what it was like, desperately trying to fight his efforts at control without inadvertently hurting him. Typically, he would want to go into a video game shop, as they were his main interest and remain so to this day, we learned to be on our guard when we were passing them!

Whenever we actually took him into a video game shop, he would be beside himself with joy, ecstatic to be confronted by so many different potential sources of entertainment, flapping his hands and roaming up and down the colourful aisles of games. Whenever we found ourselves in this situation, it was impossible to effect an exit without having bought him at least one game to forestall the tantrum that would otherwise almost certainly follow.

From the age of four years onwards, he played video games, being very adept at them, but became very upset and distressed when he completed playing all the levels in a game.

To this day, video games are a consuming passion for Jordon and over the years he has played and owned hundreds of them.

Jordon doesn't just play one game at a time, typically he will play a handheld video game, a game on the television and simultaneously watch a cartoon, perhaps the same one over and over again, dividing his attention between three or even four different electronic devices at once. He would remain happily playing for days at a time if we allowed it.

Code breaker

One of the amazing things we noticed early on about Jordon was that he has quite an uncanny ability, one that we have not as yet been able to understand. On numerous occasions, we have seen him pick up someone's mobile phone or laptop and start using it.

This, in itself, is not remarkable. The remarkable thing is that he does this even if the device is protected by a password or passcode. When we noticed this ability, we of course started changing passcodes and passwords to hide them from him. But, even if Jordon has not seen us enter the code, he seems to be able to enter it somehow. How he does this, we have no idea, but we are certain he can find the code without knowing what it is. We can only surmise that he sees the hand movement when someone is unlocking their phone, out of the corner of his eye, when his attention is seemingly focused elsewhere and knows what that movement translates into numbers.

On one memorable occasion, he managed to crack the code on Lisa's mobile phone and promptly sent all of the contacts on her phone the words "Hello Jordon!" No iPad, mobile phone, laptop or TV gaming system is safe when Jordon is around!

Gaming master

By the time Jordon was around twelve years old, it was getting a little easier to persuade him to go shopping and, as we were now more confident, one day, we took him out to a supermarket. It was a very big store and there, at the end of an aisle, two ladies were marketing a new video game.

I saw Jordon's face light up when he saw the enormous television screen and the games console beside it. He was, as he is today, very keen on computer games and striding up with his usual lack of reserve, it was clear he was intent on getting involved, Lisa tried to usher him away, but he was quite insistent, "No! No! Jordon Do It!" he happily chirped.

I was mindful of the ladies' reaction, they could see he had some form of learning difficulty as he was flapping his hands erratically and making the usual strange noises. Even though they quite obviously thought the game might be beyond the capabilities of this gangly, gesticulating child, being very kind and perhaps with an element of empathy, the slightly bemused but obviously caring, ladies humoured Jordon by handing him the controller.

What we didn't anticipate was that he would master the game almost immediately. The ladies offered to help him but it was their turn to be met with Jordon's bright and breezy reply, "Jordon Do It!"

Waving them off, he stood stock still in front of the screen and proceeded, with nothing but the smallest of hand movements, barely twitching his fingers, with flicks of his wrist, he achieved a perfect score. What made it all the more impressive was all the while, his eyes were wandering around the store and only a small part of his attention seemed to be on the game.

With the first game conquered, Jordon began switching to other games himself and each time he would achieve the highest score. One by one, switching from game to game, without being told what to do and with the same nonchalant demeanour, Jordon achieved the highest score in games of tennis, baseball, table tennis, basketball and golf.

There he stood, rooted to the spot, operating the controller with the barest of movements and with none of the intensity displayed by children or grown-ups when they play these games. There was no apparent strain or focus.

Jordon's eyes followed people as they walked past him, his hands moved, sometimes imperceptibly and all the while he got the top score in each of the games, taking the two sales ladies completely by surprise. Clearly taken aback, as his run of success continued, they looked more than bemused. They were quite clearly gobsmacked and gradually moved closer and closer, mesmerised by Jordon's immediate mastery of the console. Sometimes they would look around the store, following Jordon's gaze as it continued to rove aimlessly around, perhaps seeking some clue as to where his skill originated from.

A small group of children gathered, watching the game play and it was entertaining to witness their growing amazement, completely beguiled by the strangeness of it all. You could almost see the thoughts written on their faces, 'wasn't there something wrong with him.' How could a child who was acting so strangely be doing so well, beyond what other people, even grown-ups could achieve?'

The shock was apparent and thinking about it, I wondered if, especially in the case of the adults, it was because Jordon's performance was challenging them to compare what they thought they knew about children with special needs with what they were seeing.

Eventually, all the games were played and there was Jordon's name, at the top of the all-time high scorers list. Jordon's nonchalant, disassociated demeanour remained even when he raised his hands in the air and shouted out, "I Am The Champion!" and handed the controller back to the ladies with a polite, "Thank You Very Much!"

The expression on these two ladies' faces, who had quite obviously expected Jordon to struggle at best, was priceless and I do wish we had taken a picture. For the mental image of it all remains with me to this day, Jordon quietly wandering away, completely oblivious to the confusion he had caused and his attention already elsewhere.

Now, a few years on, Jordon has quite clearly maintained his interest in computers, however, he is much more interested in fighting games than he is mathematics or computer sciences and in this, he is not unusual, it is quite typical behaviour for a sixteen year old boy!

Nice shirt. May I try it on please?

There was always the risk of embarrassment or offending other people when we were out and about with Jordon. One such memorable situation occurred when he was about six years old. We were in a high street department store and while momentarily distracted looking at products, Jordon performed one of his favourite tricks and disappeared, suddenly running off at top speed. Immediately, we were in hot pursuit, Jordon's small form weaving in front of us through the store.

Suddenly, Jordon stopped, stock still, in front of a very stocky, short man. There was a moment of stillness and silent query as Jordon quite obviously had his attention on him. We all froze, almost as if we were all wondering what would happen next.

Then, quite suddenly and with no warning, Jordon stepped forwards, forcefully yanked up the man's T shirt and purposefully thrust his head and shoulders up into it, starting to worm and wiggle his way up inside, dragging the bemused man forwards as he busily tried to fit his entire body inside his clothing.

Within seconds, the shirt, which had been quite tight on the man already, was now occupied by two people, a puzzled man and an oblivious six year old Jordon, totally unaware of the scene he was causing or the effect of his actions.

Amazed, we got busy, apologising profusely to this stranger as he stood awkwardly leaning forwards, his hands hanging at his sides, unsure what to do, as we attempted to extricate Jordon, who was still intent on fighting his way into the t-shirt.

Thankfully, this very kind man took it all in his stride, in fact, he was a breath of fresh air at the time, laughing it off good-naturedly without taking offence as others might have. "Well, that's a first!" he exclaimed and laughed as he wandered off with a smile and a wave.

His attitude was so lovely and refreshing. By now, Lisa was constantly on her guard against feeling awkward or embarrassed and it was a revelation to meet someone who had the self-confidence to recognise that this was a child, not a threat and that not everyone will behave in the way we expect them to.

In retrospect, while we still laugh about this episode today, it was perhaps very lucky Jordon had not picked on a woman instead of a man, or it might have been a different story.

A waking nightmare

It wasn't just the daytime that held surprises and problems born of Jordon's autism. One of the added difficulties we experienced were the strange night-time behaviours. Often I would take a turn in caring for him overnight and by the time he was two or three years old, I had become familiar with the sound of his laughing or crying in his sleep.

It was always a dreadful experience when, often in the middle of the night, I would wake up to hear my grandson sobbing his heart out. There I would be, lying in bed when I would hear loud, heart wrenching sobs coming from his bed as if the worst thing in the world had happened to him.

This was a different kind of crying to when Jordon accidentally knocked himself or fell while awake; then he would cry, but when he cried while asleep, it was as though he was mourning the loss of his best friend in the world or he had heard the worst news possible. To hear this kind of heartfelt woe pouring out from such a young boy was strange; it didn't sound like a child crying. So deep and affecting was the inconsolable sobbing that poured out of him that I would often find myself too, quietly crying at his bedside.

Experience had already taught us not to interfere with the little sleep time Jordon had, especially when he was crying in his sleep. If any of us tried to awaken and console him while this was happening then it would be no use at all, typically he would wake up and continue sobbing, or immediately jump up and want to get out of his bed, shattering any hope of rest for any of us.

So, whenever this happened, I would sit at his bedside waiting patiently until the crying ceased. This could take a long time and if he did not quieten down, then eventually he would wake, usually in a state of confusion and I wanted to make sure someone was at his side in case this happened.

Whenever he woke up, Jordon would instantly leap to his feet, ever since he was a very young child and could stand; without pause or hesitation, he was straight up. There was no lying down quietly and reflecting or pausing to collect his thoughts, no slow transition from sleep to wakefulness. Instead, he would be on his feet immediately and want to be out of his bed. Any attempt to deny him this would trigger another tantrum that was hugely difficult to deal with, especially during the middle of the night when these episodes normally occurred.

This night-time outpouring of distress was worrying enough, in fact, it would affect me deeply, but it was not the full extent of the strangeness of these nocturnal episodes. One peculiarity of autism is that the child cannot readily relate to their own emotions and the further along the autistic spectrum they are, the more severe the disconnection. So, Jordon has very little connection with his feelings and he does not know how to react to them. Yet, there has been progress and after 16 years, while his own emotions are largely a mystery to him, he is now able to recognise some of the outward expression of feelings within others, telling by their tone of voice and facial expression when someone is displeased or happy with him. He also knows to cry when he is sad. Generally speaking though, he does not understand the feelings he has within him. Earlier on in life this was even more evident and happiness and sadness were so confused, so mixed up that they were interchangeable and if he was feeling either emotion, each could give rise to crying or laughter. Imagine what it is like to hear your sleeping child sobbing uncontrollably in his bed one minute and the next letting out a strange strangled laugh, one that sounds born of despair. This was a frequent occurrence with Jordon and each time it happened, it cut me to the very core.

Night terrors

This nocturnal outpouring of emotion was not the full extent of Jordon's night time troubles. Two or three times during his young life I was a sad witness to his experiencing a night terror. If you have been unlucky enough to suffer from these, or witnessed someone who is going through one, it is bad enough, but to see him endure these on top of all his other problems was heart-breaking. Jordon's episodes began when he was around two years old and continued until he was around four, which is the typical age for a child to experience them.

Any person having a night terror can appear awake, their eyes open and even moving around as if they are lucid. However, inside they are experiencing a kind of waking nightmare, that if remembered, has an awful reality to it that convinces the dreamer it is real and all the more impactful as a result. The experiences within the night terror will vary but they are often completely terrifying and appallingly, they feel real, as if they are all happening while awake.

There is no real remedy for a night terror and the recommended action is to let it pursue its course without awakening the sleeper.

In Jordon's case, the severity of any night terror was compounded because of his autism, there was absolutely no way of explaining the night terror or consoling him. Therefore, a night terror would continue to reverberate in his brain for far longer than you would expect. For him it was real, something that actually happened and as much a part of his confusing reality as we were.

When the night terrors struck, he would seemingly awaken with his usual routine of standing bolt upright in his bed. Then, he would scream and cry out, at the top of his lungs in absolute hysteria. He would be beside himself and totally inconsolable. What was also disturbing was that all the while, he would be staring high up into the corner of his room, his eyes riveted on a particular spot almost on the ceiling and if you picked him up, his gaze would not deviate from that point. It was as if he were the witness to something we could not see, but of course it was a nightmare playing out in his head and nothing we could do.

We were already familiar with tantrums and with sobbing, but the night terrors are amongst my worst memories from his childhood because he would be in such a frenzied state and there would be absolutely nothing we could do to help him. Even though he was awake, it seemed he was in a state where he could not recognise physical reality, in the grip of some awful nightmare that to him seemed real, so scared that he had become demented. The screaming would continue unabated, until eventually, he would work himself into an exhausted state and all the while we could try to distract him by singing, talking or clapping our hands; anything to bring him gently back to wakefulness and calm him down.

Never an unkind word

Jordon's world is one where love is the constant; we surround him with it. It is the only remedy that has any hope of giving him a future in his own world and in ours, for from love comes patience and understanding and, while we are all very human, we have learned these are the only effective tools to aid him in his journey. His very presence among us is a reminder that only love has the power to overcome the emotional trials that we are all subject to in some degree and yet are driven home with such force by having an autistic child in your life.

Jordon is familiar with our approach, of bringing, as many parents of autistic children strive to, love and patience to the problems he faces, meeting his worst moments with understanding. So, anything that is at odds with these calm human emotions, anything such as frustration or anger will unsettle him to the point of distraction, not least because he doesn't understand the causes of other people's distress.

From Jordon's point of view, he only bears witness to what we do and say and he doesn't understand what we do or why. He doesn't understand why we react, because he doesn't even understand his own emotions. Creating associations in his mind, instilling reason is a lifelong project and even when those associations are made, he will perhaps latch on to the entire situation rather than one element. It is one reason why, when we were feeding him in the early years, he needed the entire situation to remain constant. If he did not have the things that he was used to around him, the Yellow Pages by his side, the familiar music playing, it simply wasn't a meal time and he would not eat.

If we had not taken our loving, understanding approach; if instead we had become frustrated and interpreted his refusal to eat as wilful disobedience, if we were to have become angry and shouted at him, he wouldn't have had the first clue as to why. None of his behaviour is malicious or planned to cause hurt and so he would not have realised why anyone should get angry with him. Anything other than love would have had no positive effect whatsoever.

This is just one reason why his disorder demands that he be reasoned with, that things are constantly explained and, because of his disassociation with the world, patience is a major ally. Trying to get him to understand something new is like filling a bucket by dripping water from a great height, one drop at a time. We are so distant from his way of looking at the world, we cannot see what is getting through to him and we never know how long until the daily repetition of something as simple as asking him to clean his teeth will take hold and he will adopt the behaviour as a habit.

His inability to understand our emotions means that he cannot bear any display of anger or aggression and to him it is a reasonless eruption. It is a negative that, from his perspective, is thrust into his world unbidden and comes from nowhere, without reason or explanation. This is partly why when Jordon sees any of us becoming upset, in any way, he finds it so difficult to deal with. Because he understands the causes of our pain even less than we do, so it troubles him all the more.

Because of this inability to relate to emotions, Jordon interprets everything we do literally, so he does not understand our attempts at positive emotions, such as humour and he will never understand a joke. On the occasions that someone kids him along, lest he take them literally, we have ingrained in him that when we say, "only joking, Jordon" and because he has been told time and time again what that means, the appropriate response is to laugh. So, he will laugh mechanically, mimicking the sound, not because he understands or thinks it is funny, but because he knows he can disregard what they have said, he can dismiss it as a joke and has been schooled to do so.

However, Jordon does have a very good sense of humour. While this may seem like a contradiction, nowadays, at sixteen years old, while he will feign laughter when he knows it is called for he has also learned to appreciate things he finds funny.

One such amusement for him is when he watches his favourite programmes on the television and on his hand held games consoles. He especially likes to watch them playing backwards. He finds this immensely amusing, saying, "It Makes Me Happy!" and "It Makes Me Laugh Nan!" and then his laughter is genuine and a joy to hear.

But it wasn't always so and it took a long time to get Jordon to the point where he can at least identify with some of his emotions. For Jordon, when younger, would laugh when he should have cried and cried when he should have laughed. A happy film could reduce him to tears and a tragedy would have him laughing, as would a painful bump or cut.

I recall a very poignant incident, when Jordon was around ten years old. We were all sat as a family, watching a film on television. It was nice because everyone was settled down and enjoying a rare moment of peace and quiet. The storyline was upbeat and there was a lot of humour in it. When it reached the final happy ending we were all enjoying ourselves very much with the feel-good factor. Jordon was sitting on the sofa beside me and gradually I became aware of a noise, I turned towards him and there he was softly weeping. Quickly it escalated from little sniffles into the distinctive sobs I recognised so well.

I didn't know what to make of it. Turning to him, very softly I asked why he was crying and he replied, "Because It's A Happy Ending And It Makes Me Sad".

This was so affecting in itself, but I could not help but wonder if Jordon had said that because he had some recognition of his own limitations and the realisation that there would be no happy ending to his story. This was merely my own musing but it is true that while all our human lives are limited, we know that for autistic children, there are even greater restrictions, barriers between them and the world that create an almost impossible struggle.

The sad fact is that the very nature of their journey threatens to remove hope from their very human lives and the lives of the families around them.   This is my grandson's journey I am speaking of and the sadness that overwhelms me when I describe the facts of his life bring tears to my eyes.

Chapter Seven - Jordon's World

Being able to see past the obvious is a useful trait and it can help us in understanding ourselves and others. In the case of Jordon, seeing things from his perspective was just one way we applied this idea. The clearer the vision you have of your autistic child's situation, the more you are able to help them.

So, we regularly spent time putting ourselves, in our minds, in Jordon's shoes and identifying with what the world must feel like to him.

When any human being is born into this world, we are confronted with an overwhelming panoply of images, a crescendo of unintelligible noises, sensations and smells that threaten to overwhelm us. Even the greatest of us will cry upon our arrival into such a seemingly chaotic environment and yet today, in our minds, that same world is far more ordered and understandable. Nothing has changed about the world, but everything has changed about how we perceive it. We are able to relate to reality because we have found a way of thinking that allows us to simplify something that is so vast and complicated. So, it is our ability to rationalise that helps us to confront most situations, without dissolving into fear and panic. Without this ability we might attempt to shut reality out through self-harm when we cannot deal with its impact upon our psyche.

Sadly, this ability to form a single cohesive and unified understanding of reality is lacking in varying degrees in those with autism and it has robbed Jordon of the kind of sense of continuity that we take for granted. From an early age it was apparent to me that he was somehow walled off from us, that he only reacted to the immediate and yet even that immediate environment was to him, like a hall of mirrors.

We know that many elements of our life are routines we observe because we understand their necessity; getting up at a certain time helps us to get to work and earn money, getting into our car or boarding the train or bus means we can meet this commitment and keep a roof over our heads. Engaging in conversation can be pleasant and is seen as sociable, ensuring we wear clothes in public means we are not looked upon as strange or whisked off to jail. We have learned our necessary patterned habits and conditioned responses and most importantly, we also know that there is a rationale and a context for each and every one, even those that we perform subconsciously have a reason behind them.

So, we are not robots; everything we do has a reason and if the buses were cancelled on a particular day, we would find an alternative route. If the building where we worked burnt down, we wouldn't turn up and stay on the charred doorstep waiting to be let in. An autistic person would find it very difficult to make this kind of association. If we are at the beach, we know we wear swimwear and we know that at work, we must be fully clothed. An autistic person sees the entire pattern as one thing, they don't appreciate the reasoning behind each action. Instead, their established patterns are one of the few comforts they have in their world. In fact, to a vast degree, they are their world. They do not know that there are reasons for different clothing in different places, they just have the comfort of a routine and that is their source of stability. If an autistic child had learned that they always wear beachwear at the beach, they would in all likelihood continue to do so even in the harshest of winters, even if they were blue from cold. The patterns they learn can continue for the rest of their lives and once adopted, it is very unlikely they would question or see any aspect of them as strange.

This brings an additional aspect to the role of parenting autistic children, taking on responsibility for the growth and expansion of the child's universe, a universe that in other times and in other societies could otherwise be so small that the child would be locked away and would never see the light of day.

So the routines, the repetitive behaviour, the placing of his toys in long orderly lines from an early age - these are all an attempt by Jordon to establish order and they have all, at one time or other in some shape or form, been part of his world.

As soon as we knew that our role as a family was to be the carers for an autistic child, with Lisa and Brian bearing the brunt and me providing emotional support, we set about the work of introducing the world to Jordon, who would otherwise have remained locked in his own universe of misunderstanding.

Because everything is so strange and unfathomable to Jordon, we attempt to be his constant. We bring the set patterns of behaviour, we deliver to him a world that we desperately pray he can relate to and then we work hard to bring new things and flexibility into his life so that he isn't so afraid of that which he does not know, so that he is able to change and we do not create ruts that trap him forever. This journey is perhaps the most enlightening that any parent could have with a child, because so often there is a barrier between us and all we have to relate to in Jordon is the knowledge that there is a person trapped within, held distant from us by the nature of his disorder.

We try to open windows to his world, to let in everything we see, but to him, the majority of it remains a melange of disassociated facts. Our world to him is one where nothing interconnects. If we were to imagine what it is like to be an autistic child, it would be like watching a seething storm all around us, one where lights appear, facial expressions change, shifting for seemingly no reason and virtually everything is unfathomable and potentially frightening.

Were our brains suddenly rearranged and put together in the same way as Jordon's, it would be enough to send us mad with the strangeness of it all. We might want to do things, unaware of the consequences, try to communicate, but be totally blocked, people would talk to us in a strange language we have never heard before. We might be overwhelmed with conflicting feelings and have no idea what these feelings are and where they arise from. We might experience anger and have no idea whatsoever as to why, nor how to control how we react to that emotion. Frustrations would roll over us all the time and something as simple as ceiling lights and a moving face might strike so directly into our consciousness that it is like we are under some form of assault.

Robbed of our usual thought patterns and reasoning, we might be surrounded by people and have no idea as to who they are and their relevance to our lives. Unable to speak, with no language available to us to communicate our needs, we would only be able to express our frustrations through screaming and crying. In reaction to this walled-off existence, we might retreat, look away, try to immerse ourselves into our own world of safety, try to bring some form of sense to the world by doing the same thing over and over again or putting objects in understandable straight lines. In the face of a complete absence of order, we might try to establish our own security or block out the immense waves of confusion by creating bodily sensations that blank them out, running round and round in circles, jumping up and down, rocking backwards and forwards, rolling our eyes, vocalising our distress - anything to blank out a world that has seemingly gone mad and threatens to overwhelm us.

So every time you look into the eyes of an autistic child, try to imagine how you would bear the weight they have to carry every day of their lives and imagine if it were your son or brother, daughter or sister that shouldered that burden. How would you want those around you to behave? Can you imagine how important security and love are in that world, how important the reactions of those around you are? The burden of an autistic child's life lies with us and it shows also how blessed we are to be able to recognise that which they cannot. We need to understand that they are ignorant of our ways, appreciate how difficult just about everything is for them and recognise that inside is a beloved child.

My focus all through Jordon's early years, throughout the problem-strewn pathway he walked, was to find ways to help him and to help Lisa and Brian. Other than his parents, I was the person who knew Jordon best; I was there at his birth and virtually every day of his life and every step of the way up until he went to school. As a constant companion, I knew that the key to working with him was to gain an insight into where his problems originated within his mind, his thought patterns and to understand how he perceived the world.

Making that connection can be an extremely difficult task, especially when you are dealing with a boy whose chief problem lies in communication and is almost totally blocked from understanding himself. However, I was in a privileged position, in that I was able to interact with and observe Jordon for hours at a time, helping to care for him and helping Lisa and Brian in giving him as much love as we were able.

I found that by putting myself in his shoes, by attempting to see what life looked like from his perspective and by mentally positioning myself at his level of understanding, I was able to gain a far greater insight into Jordon's outlook. This helped all of us to understand his frustrations, why they arose and how we could work with Jordon to improve his communication skills.

Therefore, the first step in dealing with the learning difficulties around Jordon was to improve our own understanding and educate ourselves as to just what it felt like to be him and to function in a world to which he could not relate.

By appreciating what life looked like from Jordon's perspective, it was a very short journey to then identify the reasons behind many of his fears, blocks and barriers. While this insight helped us, it by no means provided us with an overall permanent solution, there were of course innumerable elements in his life and persona we needed to deal with, because the underlying problem remained.

The challenges were constant and working with an autistic child is still never easy. Even if they have the ability to develop, you may still be unable to understand their way of looking at the world and how that creates barriers and fears.

In retrospect, we were faced with one simple choice, we could either work around his obstacles, leaving him in a static state and caring for him with no hope of progress, or we could make the only choice we reasonably could and find ways to overcome them that were acceptable to Jordon and would help us, in turn, to bring him on and progress on his pathway. We took the latter course.

Open wide

Another problem we faced that was helped by seeing it from Jordon's perspective was when he visited the dentist. Before we could even attempt to do so, the first challenge was to find a dentist who would work with a child with special needs. Thankfully, this didn't take too long and after several phone calls, explaining the situation and that there was no way that Jordon could be made to sit in the dentist's chair, we found a dentist willing to work with autistic and special needs children.

Again, this was one occasion when we were called upon to both reassure and incentivise Jordon. At first, there was only one way we could coax Jordon into the dentist's chair and that was to get Brian to lay back in it and Jordon would then, in turn, lay on Brian, with the promise of some reward after the visit.

This dentist knew that Jordon needed to be familiarised and so he progressed very slowly. On the first visit, he had only the briefest of glimpses into Jordon's mouth, on the next visit, he was able to inspect for a little longer.

In between each visit, we would teach Jordon to open his mouth for the dentist, getting him to say 'aaaah' and constantly reinforcing what he would encounter at the dental surgery.
"What do you say at the dentist Jordon?"
His mouth would stretch unimaginably wide and then softly, we would hear "Aaaaaaaaah"
"Yes, that's right, Jordon. Well done!"

These tactics worked and while they may sound like quite simple steps, it is sad to say we saw even this small development as a sign of progress. I know of many autistic children who are only able to have dental work done under a general surgical anaesthetic, completely unconscious, while Jordon, by contrast, is now completely familiar with the dentist and able to accept any treatment that is needed. Jordon's progress meant one less burden on Brian, negating the need for him to take time off of work every time Jordon had an appointment and play the role of chair cushion!

We were always mindful that Jordon had to do things at his own pace and never forced him to engage in any activity, in fact, there was no way he could be pushed, lest we put him off forever. Slowly, patiently, we would allow him to become used to the world around him, knowing this was the only way he could progress.

Even deeper water

Swimming was a similar story. I knew we had to very slowly acquaint Jordon with the idea of being in the water, very slowly and gently; quite literally allowing him to test the water by putting a toe in at a time. Jordon made trips to the swimming pool either with Brian or with his school and they both let him take his time, allowing him over the course of many visits to become accustomed at his own pace. Brian would at first allow Jordon to sit on the edge of the swimming pool and dangle his feet in it before he was ready to take the plunge. Also, as a family, we took him to the seaside and walking on a sandy beach, we would stroll to the shoreline and allow the waves to lap our feet. We took him anywhere where we could slowly introduce the idea of water and gently familiarise him with it.

Introducing new things into his world was greatly helped by our gradually coming to relate to how his mind worked. Then all that we needed was saintly patience and the repetitive explanation of every new situation before he entered it. Whenever something caused him anxiety and we saw his fears rising, or we could see signs that indicated he was nervous, we would not pander to them; instead we would laugh at the situation, be it the waves lapping high enough on his legs to cause him concern, having his feet measured in a shoe shop or the strangeness of the dentist's chair. For, our role was to introduce Jordon to the world without placing fear in him, or between him and the future.

Time waits for no man

One of the idiosyncrasies we were all aware of, especially in the early years, was that Jordon did not understand the concept of things happening in the future. He thought everything happened immediately, so the moment he had some concept of language and we mentioned a trip to the shops, that we were going to eat a meal, anything at all, he thought it was to happen right now. When we made any trip, the moment we mentioned it, even before it was time to go, all his nervousness would come to the fore and he would be lost to his own trepidation.

If we said we were going shopping, even though shopping made mixed feelings arise in Jordon, he would always think we were going immediately and he would rush to the front door. Any delay and he would stand screaming at the front door. To prevent this happening we learned not to announce any activity or future event until it was actually time to do it, to get ourselves ready for any trip before mentioning anything to him. Typically we would ensure we were all dressed and ready to go before we made any mention of our plans to Jordon.

In the early years, Jordon had no interest in other people, so it didn't matter that we were all furtively getting dressed in wellington boots and winter coats for an unannounced trip to the shops. Even this would give him no clue that an excursion was imminent. We could have laid down on the floor wearing raincoats, flip-flops, ear muffs and summer hats and he would not have shown the slightest bit of interest. He found no behaviour stranger than any other.

Once this strategy of not talking about outings in advance was adopted, typically, when all our preparations were made, we would begin to dress Jordon in his outdoor clothes. When we had taken this approach as far as we could and it was obvious he was becoming bewildered at the preparations, we would then and only then, announce what it was we were doing and why.

Everything we did for him, we did to further his life and to build him so that he could have an increasing level of independence. Some autistic children, despite their family's very best efforts, can remain totally dependent on others well into adulthood and even for the rest of their lives. If you can imagine what it is like to be in his shoes, it means you are one step nearer to knowing how to find solutions that could work for him.

Slowly, little by little, we recognised that Jordon had the smallest of chances of learning and growing. We realised that he had a hope of developing and a chance of happiness and independence in his life. Knowing that there was hope far beyond the bleakness of our original expectations kept us all going.

Jordon and the beach

Determination can't be all that keeps you going; everyone needs a break now and then, but holidays with Jordon are few and far between to say the least and it is a very rare event for us to go away for anything more than a day trip as a family.

Just over ten years ago, when Jordon was around five years old, I could see that Brian and Lisa very much needed a break. The responsibility of Jordon, the stress and the lack of sleep were all taking their toll and they were getting to the point where the strain was beginning to show. So I decided to treat them to some time away, a summer break to help them recharge their batteries.

I knew the easiest solution was to find a self-catering venue, where we could give Jordon the food he was used to, somewhere that did not involve the uncertainties of putting him on a plane (none of us could imagine what would happen if we even attempted this) and not too far away so that we did not have to keep him in a car for too long.

In fact, before I decided that a car trip was preferable, I did investigate with an airline what facilities they offered autistic children and they offered to allow us to let Jordon sit on a plane and become familiar with it, which I thought was very nice of them. They had obviously had some experience of allowing children with special needs to become familiar with the surroundings and overcome their fears. However, when I considered just how much luggage we would need to take, I soon realised that travelling by car was far more practical an option.

Choosing a self-catering venue also meant that I could relieve Lisa of the burden of cooking, we would not be troubled by other guests and we would be able to keep an eye on Jordon more easily. If we were also able to get somewhere with a secure garden, then he could run around to his heart's content.

Another consideration, and a very important one if we were to have a successful trip, was that by that age, Jordon had already discovered computer games. Having found something that kept him happily occupied and absorbed, Lisa and Brian had encouraged this pastime. Brian had bought him a computer games console and his love of it and his propensity for repetitive behaviours meant it was very difficult to keep him away from the gradually growing pile of computer games. We might manage it for a day or so if we kept him busy and out of the house, but that would, in all probability, be the limit and no matter where we were in the world, without his games Jordon would want to return to the welcome familiarity of his computer and the flashing lights on his television screen.

So, I contacted a friend who lived on the coast and asked her if she knew of anywhere that might be suitable. Luckily she knew of the ideal property, just a few short minutes from the beach, with a private garden, nice big rooms and in all, not much more than an hour's drive away, in the picturesque seaside town of Broadstairs.

It was summer, we were in the middle of some beautiful weather and we soon found ourselves all booked for the trip and ready to go. We travelled in my car, loading in everything we needed, Jordon, Lisa, Brian and myself, all our luggage, Jordon's television and computer games and all the paraphernalia we needed for a week away. It was packed to the absolute limit and I doubt we could have fitted one more bag in there with us.

This was actually the first time that Jordon had come away on a proper holiday with us and we spent the weeks before the trip preparing him, constantly repeating that we were going on a holiday and that it would be really good fun, even though we knew that at that age he would have no idea what we were talking about. Indeed, he pretty much ignored us and our efforts to prepare him with constant references to "living in a new house, just for a few days" all the way up until the time of the trip.

When we arrived, the home was ideal. We busied ourselves, putting our clothes in the cupboards and checking the property over for anything that might be dangerous for Jordon; at five years old, he couldn't be trusted any more than a two year old could and so we had to ensure that the perimeter of the garden was secure, that there were no dangerous items he could lay his hands on and no rooms he could inadvertently lock himself in.

Our seven days away were beautiful. It wasn't long before we were visiting the beaches and it was so lovely to see Jordon having so much fun, ecstatic with the freedom of it all. You could almost imagine he didn't have a care in the world; he could run around with no immediate dangers. It was equally lovely to see my daughter and Brian having a bit of space and time with each other.

It was even better when my sons, who lived not too far away, decided to join us, both bringing their partners with them. I love having the family all together, Mark visited for the day and Gino stayed overnight and we had a marvellous time. The boys kept an eye on Jordon as he played on the sand and took him around the amusement arcades, which Jordon absolutely loved. It was a holiday and so we decided we didn't want to go through the trials of denying Jordon what he wanted to do and so whenever he saw a flashing machine he liked, we would give him a coin to put in the slot, witnessing his delight. Jordon was in his element, Lisa and Brian were enjoying the pleasure of having their family around them and I was so happy that the holiday was working out well for everyone. It was one of the few times when I felt that we had actually achieved something, that Jordon had a bit of happiness and everyone was able to be part of it.

Days passed with our taking a daily trip to the beach, watching Jordon play on the slot machines, running around wherever he was in sheer delight. We would sit in the sun watching him having fun, eating the ice cream he would not touch and it allowed us all to have the break we needed.

Even though it rushed by, the week could not have gone better for us all and to this day I keep a photograph on my mantelpiece to remind me of that special time.

Chapter Eight - Choices, From Lisa's Perspective

I was so happy when I heard Mum's idea to write a book about Jordon. At first Brian and I wondered who would want to know about us and our life, but seeing the book develop and seeing that we have something useful to say, I know we can get Jordon's story out to the world in a way that will help increase understanding of autism and for me, that means a great deal. It means the world to both Brian and I to know that all the love and hard work we have put into Jordon's life and now share with him, has a wider meaning and purpose.

Parents of children with autism sometimes risk losing hope. With everything that we consider to be normal in a child's development taking an age, and with no certainty that things will change and, if so, to what degree, it can actually feel like someone has taken your whole life, all your hopes, dreams, fears and aspirations and put a limit on them, encased them in a bubble of autism. It is very easy to fade gradually into apathy or despair when you see the same daily scenarios of extreme behaviour from your child, with seemingly no hope of change. I have seen these pressures mount up with many parents and sometimes I have seen them and their relationships break under the strain.

Having my mum, Carolann, as a source of assistance has helped to keep us all positive. From the time of Jordon's birth, right up until today, mum has been a rock, supporting us and helping to keep things in perspective, while we battled our way through the constant medical problems in Jordon's formative years, his confusing behaviour and through all the times when tiredness threatened to overwhelm us, such as when Jordon decided every single day started at 4 a.m. and that is when we would all get out of bed!

While nothing has come easily, as time has progressed, it is noticeable just how well Jordon is now doing compared to how bad he was all those years ago when he was first diagnosed. Of course, Jordon is autistic and while that may hold him back in so many ways, he has travelled so far from where he once was and his personality is increasingly evident every day.

Jordon is the most wonderful boy with the most endearing qualities. Every day he makes Brian and I more proud as he matures into a caring and amazing young man. Despite all his difficulties, he never ceases to amaze us with what he achieves every day of his life.

Although, given the choice, we would most definitely remove autism from his life, it would only be to make it an easier one for him, we would never change Jordon.

Jordon is our world.

School daze

Every parent will be familiar with the difficulties of getting the right school for their child, but for an autistic child as with many other things, it is all the harder. Not only are there far fewer 'special needs' schools available, but even amongst them, there is a very broad spectrum of difficulties and needs they provide for.

Some schools, as we were to later learn, provided for all types of children, meaning Jordon as an autistic boy would be taught alongside those with behavioural difficulties, those who might be aggressive and disruptive.

For an autistic child, this kind of behaviour can be upsetting, because they thrive on order and routine. Chaotic behaviour to Jordon can be unbearable and aggression is almost impossible for him to deal with. Those with behavioural difficulties are very prone to aggression and to be in an environment where children were constantly acting up and throwing things around, shouting or behaving badly, would disturb him. So, we attempted to avoid any school that mixed autistic children with those with severe behavioural difficulties.

When we were choosing the very first school that Jordon was to attend, just before he reached the age of five, there were three viable 'special needs' schools that were close enough for us to consider. I met representatives from the first choice of school at the nursery I was working in at the time and they carried out an assessment that determined Jordon was too immature for them to consider as a student at their facility. I remember that at the time, I was very upset at that judgment, it seemed bizarre to say the least to judge an autistic child on his maturity, when most autistic children are delayed in their development by the very nature of the disorder.

I was then advised to write to a mainstream school, but unfortunately, the school we contacted could not, in their view, meet his requirements. Amongst other things, there was a lack of security on site and he could have run off at any time. It is so difficult to get an autistic child into the right school to meet their needs and keep them safe.

Mum then accompanied me to visit two schools and to help me in my choice. The first school we considered, we actually rejected. On the face of it, it had looked acceptable and yet when we arrived there, we both felt it didn't feel right and then, when we began walking around it was apparent it was wrong for Jordon.

This was a school with a very successful approach, but we knew Jordon well and felt their approach was too regimented for him. While it was clear that there was very good discipline amongst the autistic children, we did not feel that walking two-by-two in imposed silence between lessons was the right way to bring Jordon out of his shell and develop the much needed social skills we wanted to engender in him. Jordon needed gentle coaxing and to be gradually introduced to the world if he was to flourish.

The next school was a different story. We discussed it and both of us knew that this was the one that Jordon should attend. It was lively, a vibrant atmosphere held sway and the children looked excited to be there. They were all obviously at ease and genuinely seemed to enjoy the environment. There was life, interaction, noise and smiling faces and yet all the children were very well behaved and wanted to talk to us about the work they were doing. It was informal and comfortable and there was a sense of pride in their work, coupled with genuine joy in their achievements.

We met with the headmistress immediately after we had looked around and it was a very strange meeting. While we were both convinced that this was the correct school for Jordon, Mum was so supremely adamant and insistent it was almost laughable. I can still remember how she stood in the headmistresses office, in front of her desk, saying "this is the school; we are not leaving until you tell us he has been accepted." Her insistence was quite comical in hindsight, especially when I recall the headmistress telling us, quite calmly in response, that we had to wait for the right procedures to be followed.

And so it was that the choice was made, events proceeded, Jordon was accepted into the school and all three of us, including the headmistress, were delighted. We could tell that she had taken our determination as a great compliment to the school.

The red shirt school

So it was that Jordon began to attend his first school when he was five years old and it was a milestone for us all. We did not call it by its name, instead it was "The Red Shirt School", named by Jordon due to its distinctive school uniform. From then on, all of his schools were named according to the colour of their shirts, because it was easier for Jordon to associate with them in this way. In order of attendance, they were "The Red Shirt School", "The First White Shirt School" and "The Second White Shirt School".

We were very fortunate, as Jordon loved The Red Shirt School and there he was to remain for the next three years, enjoying it from the very first day onwards. The teachers were superb and he came on wonderfully under their supervision.

Luckily, everything about the school was convenient, it was very local, meaning I could bundle Jordon into the car every morning and after a short, 15 minute drive, I was able to park directly outside, a very important factor considering the trouble we sometimes had hanging on to Jordon, especially near busy roads.

With little more than 70 pupils attending and almost as many staff, the Red Shirt School had its own grounds and a safe play area for the children to have fun in. The security was wonderful and it was all very safe, with no chance of the children running off. For the children's care, there were occupational therapists, speech therapists and an on-duty nurse. All these services were dearly needed, for sadly, some of the children there had very severe disabilities and were confined to wheelchairs or had to wear head protection to avoid harming themselves.

When Jordon first went to The Red Shirt School, he still needed a lot of help and development, for instance, he could not chew his food and would frequently run off whenever the whim took him. If you did not hang on to his clothes (he would not allow us to directly hold his arm at that time) he could head off with the danger that he would put himself in harm's way. However, despite his needs, Jordon did really well there. His relationships with the teachers especially were excellent and under their tutelage he gradually learnt skills that allowed him to be more independent. His computer skills, in particular, astonished his tutors and for the next two years, Jordon flourished at the school we had been so insistent he attend.

By a bizarre coincidence, many years before, our family had raised a small amount of money towards a new mini-bus for the school. We had this connection with the school because my brother's fiancée's brother went to the very same school and so we had volunteered to help with their fundraising efforts at the time. Small world!

However, despite this school being an excellent choice for Jordon's development, it was not without challenges to overcome.

Junior hacker

Even though generally, Jordon enjoyed The Red Shirt School, during one phase, he got up to all sorts of unexpected antics. Still in his first year there, he went through a period of making numerous attempts to run away and hide from everyone! Thankfully, even on the couple of occasions when he was successful in slipping away, sneaking out of the classroom when the teacher's back was turned, he could not escape the secure building and grounds. It was a very safe environment with no real dangers even when he made it out into the school's corridors.

On one such occasion, he managed to find his way into the Headmistress's office and once there, decided it was his job to test some of the office equipment.

He was obviously very interested in her answering machine and having played the messages on it, decided they were not of use and pressed the 'delete' button. During his tour of her office, he also took a turn on the Headmistress's computer. Bizarrely, he managed to access the 'delete software' function and removed some key programmes (obviously unimpressed with them).

It was not an easy function to access on the computer and no one knew how he had done it at such a young age. It wasn't an easy problem to solve either and the school had to call in a technician to fix the computer, much to our embarrassment!

After that day, whenever Jordon managed to slip away, the school staff knew where to find him as he would always return to the Headmistress's office, seeking out her office equipment.

When it came to light that Jordon had performed quite complicated actions and the school staff were amazed that he had done so, we knew this was something to follow up on. Suspecting that he had an interest and perhaps even a flair for computers, we rushed out and bought him one for his use at home, hoping it would prove to be a stimulus and that he had capabilities in this area that could be developed. This interest remains today and while he has not displayed genius with computers, he is very adept at using the internet and especially at finding games he likes - pandering to his own main interest!

Although he loved it at this school, this wasn't the only time we had an issue to deal with. After he had been at the school for some considerable time, we were very surprised that he began to become distressed about going there. Up until that point, he had been doing very well, but during this new phase, every morning he would scream, cry and try everything in his power to avoid going. His behaviour became gradually more disturbing and disruptive. It got to the stage that he would even pull at my hair while I was driving the car, anything to stop his arrival at school.

This added complication that he would not go into school without a huge protest meant that at around that time, when he was seven years old, life was becoming increasingly gruelling.

During this phase, we were discussing strategies to cope with Jordon's increasingly concerning behaviour. Mum suggested we should look at it from Jordon's point of view, for her the penny had dropped and she had an answer we could work with.

Her approach was to prepare Jordon by talking to him. This was not entirely successful, but we had to make the effort. By now he had some small understanding of language, recognising a few key words, but could not talk himself. For, Jordon, each time he left home, he was leaving his place of safety and journeying out into the great unknown. To him, the world was full of random events that were not interconnected, a great threatening place that overwhelmed him and for some reason this had recently hit home with the trips to school. So we took to talking to him every morning before we left the house and helping him to focus on the positive experiences he could expect and what he was to achieve in the day ahead at school.

That same year, mum and I attended Jordon's annual school review. Brian was in a new job and unable to get time off from work and so mum and I were discussing Jordon's progress with the headmistress and a teacher, seeking ways of improving his situation.

Our feeling was that whenever Jordon was confronted by a situation that was new to him, he would see it as a brick wall. The fear of the unknown was an obstacle that, to him, was absolute; he could not see beyond it and mentally he would be overcome. Jordon cannot see or understand consequences or outcomes that to us are obvious. So for instance, fitting his foot in a shoe measurer when he was younger could seem like the most intimidating thing in the world, because he did not know whether he was going to harm his foot, or even lose it. It was all alien to him. To get the best results we needed to prepare Jordon for what was going to happen next, just as we did when we primed him for each day at school. We discussed this at some length with his tutors and then we all agreed that this was the approach we would take.

If we had tried this approach before that time, then it simply wouldn't have worked, as he did not have an adequate grasp of language. So, from that point forward, every time Jordon was asked to do something new, to go somewhere he had not been before or encounter any situation that was alien to him, we would take some time to explain what he would encounter first.

Jordon had by that time learned to read quite well and we looked for something else that would help him progress. We thought that one of the best things we could do was to provide him with some form of visual representation of his life, something that would help him to put the past, present and future in perspective. So, we bought him a wall-calendar, a very large and clear one, the biggest we could find.

Jordon was very pleased with the calendar from the very day we bought it and it aided him in a number of ways, helping him see that there were things to look forward to, that all his life could have a structure and not everything was 'right now'.

Prior to that, if we told him a certain event was coming, he would not be able to grasp how far forward in the future it was, as he had little concept of time.

The calendar on the wall was filled with the activities of the day and every morning we would recite these activities to Jordon. We would check his schedule and if he had a swimming lesson, a physical exercise class or a computer lesson (all things he enjoyed) I would tell him so that he could look forward to it. Anything positive about his day, we would talk to him about it. This wouldn't happen just once. If he was travelling to school and there was a swimming lesson that morning, then we would tell Jordon at home, tell him as we packed his swimming kit, tell him as we put his swimming kit in the boot of the car, mention it along the way as we drove, remind him as we were arriving at the school. We had to constantly drill any positive element of his day into him, getting him to understand, to focus on recognisable situations we knew he liked.

Gradually, he learned to associate the swimming kit with swimming, to understand that if 'swimming' was written on the calendar then it was a swimming day, until eventually it sank in. In this way, the calendar helped us overcome his anxiety about school. This took a few months and then, after a few months more, Jordon made the link between all the actions and brought me his swimming gear. For the first time ever, he had spontaneously related to a future event. I was so happy that we had finally broken through.

Just this one example from Jordon's life shows the scale of the mental blocks you can face with an autistic child, the lack of ability to reason can stand like the thick towering wall of a dam, holding back all the things you want to bring into their lives, to nurture and grow within them. All that comes through are the merest trickles of understanding, dribbling through gaps in that dam wall.

Looking back and looking forward

The other outcome of the annual review, at Jordon's Red Shirt School, aside from bringing revelations about the calendar and Jordon's need for verbal preparation, was that, after attending for three years, we all recognised they could no longer meet his educational needs. The school catered for severe learning difficulties and they too now felt that, at the age of seven, Jordon had progressed beyond the academic curriculum they offered. We were once more in the position of looking for a new school. He was learning fast and it was time to move on.

For almost a year we sought out a new school for Jordon to further his education. As it turned out, having sought advice, there was really only one appropriate school available and this is the one Jordon was destined to attend from the age of eight onwards.

We visited the school and as we were shown around, we were walked into a class room and confronted by children happily sat eating chocolate Swiss Roll in celebration of a birthday. Each of them was wearing the school uniform, a white polo shirt. We just knew, we had this certainty that this would be where Jordon should next be taught and because of his habit of referring to school by the colour of the uniform we always referred to it as his 'White Shirt School.'

Strangely, years before, we had been to this school and at that time, felt it was not suitable. Now, we still had severe reservations because here they dealt with more moderate learning difficulties. In effect, this made the school a far more mainstream environment, better suited to children who had a greater level of independence and what added to our worries was that previously the oldest children in his school were eleven years old and here they were sixteen. This meant Jordon could have found himself out of his depth.

However, we were now all convinced that this school was the right option, as Jordon had progressed far enough to cope with a more challenging environment and we wanted him to move on.

We placed him here and being in this new situation with all the additional stimulus demanded more from Jordon, yet here he developed in many areas and progressed further still. This is exactly what we wanted. Though he remained generally un-talkative, he was now putting full sentences together for the first time. It was so lovely to be able to communicate with him in a meaningful way and as this next stage in his development moved him forwards, another milestone had been reached.

Two worlds

Jordon's education was not limited to his time at school. At home we worked with him all the time. One of the most profound ways in which we did so was by making a conscious effort to understand him and tuning into how he viewed the world.

We felt Jordon saw the world as if it were a distorted hall of mirrors. For, everything that he perceives is overlaid with a reflection of his own thoughts, twisting every input into a misshapen parody of what we see. This inability to discern things clearly, to distinguish his own thought process from the input of his senses, means that he is effectively blocked from directly interacting with the outside world. So, Jordon is effectively lost in his own domain, with no understanding of the reality outside his head or of his own emotions, because to him they form one single reality.

This unique insight meant we had a basis for working with Jordon and that, in turn, has helped us to bring Jordon forward to where he is today.

When we first had this insight, we put our minds to addressing it, by taking him out to very busy places, full of a variety of colours and experiences and teeming throngs of people. Open-air markets, car boot sales, parks, supermarket cafeterias, other people's homes, swimming pools, playgrounds, the seaside, shopping centres and even boating lakes. We introduced him into any situation that would stretch and challenge his boundaries, to bring the world to him so that it could break through his misperceptions. Each time we took him out, we imagined ourselves to be punching a hole in the wall between Jordon and the outside world until we were confident we had done enough work to knock that wall to the ground.

Finally, after many day trips and much hard work, we were able to take him into a restaurant environment, a massive achievement to finally put him in a place where he had to behave and could not run around as the whim took him. We had found by then that if we were able to give him foods that he viewed as a special treat, scampi, ham, egg, chips and coca cola, for instance, it would help the situation massively and offering him a choice of food and drink enabled Jordon to become active in making his own decisions, rather than remain subject to what we decided for him. Even so, we would have to distract him at the table by spinning coins and playing 'heads and tails' otherwise in the time it took for the meal to arrive, Jordon would be ready to depart the table and go for a run around the restaurant.

These situations and especially the restaurants would also help Jordon to interact, as we encouraged him to talk to the waitress directly and, on the occasions when his strange voice resulted in a difficulty in being understood, we would subtly interpret for him, remarking on his behalf, "oh! Ham, egg and chips, a wonderful choice, Jordon!" Repeating what he was trying to say, so that he would not be embarrassed, could maintain his achievement at communicating and ensure he didn't feel ostracised by his inability to be understood.

Choices, vocabulary, socialising, familiarisation with different types of travel and with busy places were all achieved through this strategy and by remaining mindful of Jordon's reaction throughout, this aided his development no end.

At the same time, we were avidly using the verbal familiarisation technique, preparing him for every impending trip by talking about it constantly prior to our departure. This background work paid off and today, as long as we are mindful of the rules, that he must be prepared verbally in advance, that he is congratulated on his successes and that we treat his lapses with love and kindness, Jordon's world has expanded way beyond what we would otherwise have expected to achieve.

Today, this progress has taken us to the point that Jordon is actively enquiring as to where we are going and when. He still maintains his underlying loathing of shopping in general for anything other than computer games or something he particularly wants, but even then, we can still persuade him to go if we explain it well enough.

So, we continue working with Jordon through the everyday ups and downs, making small steps forward every year. Perhaps one of the most important lessons I have learned in all these years, from both him and Lauren is the value of gaining an insight into how they both view the world.

All those years ago, we took the time to imagine how life must look through Jordon's eyes, observing how he acted and figuring out every step of the way what that meant for his inner life. "How must he be thinking and feeling to be acting this way?" was a question we would often ask ourselves. This way of looking at his world helped us no end.

Chapter Nine - In Perspective

Knowing that this is my daughter's story, it is so heartening that throughout the past 16 years she has remained a wonderfully down to earth and loving mother and, despite the challenges and restrictions in her life, Lisa has maintained her sense of humour throughout, remaining dedicated to her family. I know that much of the strength she has found within has emerged upon the road that she, Brian, Jordon and now little Lauren continue to travel.

The world of autism is the world of the here and now. It lacks connections, it lacks perspective and it is full of the fear of the unknown, making life a potential nightmare. This is why autistic people retreat into their own space, their own rooms, their own set patterns of behaviour, because in their worlds that is the safest place to be, far away from the confusion of our reality. To them, we speak in a strange language that connects sounds with objects, words with actions, forming the kind of associations that to them are almost meaningless, that is, unless they are taught in a concentrated way so that some kind of link can be formed. An autistic child could be six years old and still have no idea what a cup is for, the function it performs and the reason for its existence and so it is up to us to help them make these connections.

Having got Jordon to the stage where he was better prepared for outings, he was calmer and quieter as a result. Speaking to him in advance meant that he had more time to mentally process what was to come, to put it in perspective. Doing all we could to remove the fear of the unknown from his life meant that, although it remained a struggle, we even began to get him out to the shops. Doing this would entail the constant repetition of where we were going, what we were doing and why. However, we also learned that if we secured his agreement to go to the supermarket, we could not then change what supermarket we went to, that would be too much for him to cope with and we would experience all the same problems again.

Our one trump card was always Jordon's love of video games. When he was old enough, we were able to persuade him to go anywhere where there was a video game store or to any supermarket that had a video games section. Then, one of us would remain with him because the effort involved in taking him away from the games and round the shops would be too much. He would quite happily stand for ages looking at the brightly coloured boxes and then, quite carefully and deliberately, pick one from the shelf and stand studying it. Even when he was too young to read, he would pore over the words on the box as if he understood every one.

In the past, to be told that he could not have his chosen video title would not register with him. If he wanted a particular game he would simply try to walk off with the box, oblivious to any reason why he should not, nor realising that he was merely holding an empty display box. Inevitably therefore, even though we had got over the hurdle of getting Jordon to the supermarket, we would eventually still be faced with the eventual tantrum or our purses being considerably lighter, for Jordon always seemed to want the latest and most expensive games and no other kind would do!

From one perspective, being autistic is like standing behind a distorted sheet of glass, with many imperfections, trapped in the room of the 'I' with little input from the outside world. An autistic child can hear, see and feel everything, yet depending on the direction they look in, this sheet of glass will magnify, shrink, distort and twist what they see. The images are already misleading and yet there is no consistency to the garbled information they receive. In addition, they lack a way of interpreting or relating to everything that is going on.

This is a very odd place to be, looking through this glass pane and trying to translate what is coming in by associating what is going on around it. The only reliable filter you have is the input of your thoughts and yet these are limited because you find it so difficult to take on board the information from your senses as this can be amplified and distorted. The wall of glass also reflects your emotions and thoughts back to you, so you have no idea what is an image coming back to you from the outside world and what is a reflection of your own thought process.

In other words, an autistic child will see what is going on around them but have no way of telling what it means, why things are happening or what one event means in context of another. Whereas we can make connections in our mind between the sensations in our body and what is going on in the outside world, linking what is happening around us with how we feel, an autistic child exists in a kind of vacuum, which keeps them in a permanent state of not knowing. Every situation needs to be learned by establishing routines, repeatedly reinforcing every single day, sometimes for years, that a spoon is associated with food, that toothpaste is not swallowed, that we mustn't hit our own heads when frustrated. The most seemingly inconsequential things can terrify or frustrate an autistic child simply because they have no context, nor understanding to suggest whether they are witnessing the end of the world or merely an unfamiliar face.

There are many degrees of severity and a great deal depends upon the child. It is tempting for them to stay in their safe zone, to not experiment with the new lessons that are coming from their parents. For them, familiarity is a safe place to be, for the sandwich to be the same every day, for bedtime to remain constant, for the routine to continue. Any deviation from this world of safety is very frightening to the autistic child. Trying something new, even as simple as going to a place they haven't been before, even this can be threatening. The surroundings of a new room can be terrifying and there is no perspective born of experience or logic for them to rely upon. A new experience, even if it were a different restaurant, to an autistic child, even in their teens, might have the same frightening and surreal effect as leading a five year old child into a darkened room where the furniture is nailed to the ceiling and the room full of barking dogs.

So it can take years for an autistic child to relate to having their hair brushed, their teeth cleaned, their nails cut or even to get in a bath. Behaviours that are necessary to their existence may take years to reinforce. Even for the most gentle and kind parent, this can be an awful strain. An autistic child may feel that having their hair washed is a life threatening experience as the sensations are so overwhelming, having their head covered in water which they cannot see is beyond strange. It can make an autistic child feel totally out of control and they can react accordingly. Because they have very limited resources, it is only through constant daily observance of the ritual that hair washing may eventually be accepted by them.

Parents of autistic children have to face the threat of hysterical reactions to the most common place of daily events. For years, changing Jordon's bed clothes would drive him to distraction, for he could not understand why such a key element of his world would need to be altered. With no perspective or understanding that bed clothes become 'dirty' Jordon would merely see something that was constant in his life being changed and in his case it took nearly six years to acquaint him with the fact that they needed to be washed. We achieved the final breakthrough by buying duvet covers that had cartoon characters on them that he liked. Then he was far more prepared to accept the change to new bed clothes because he liked the pictures on them and it was more familiar as a result. Before then he would regularly rip them off whenever the change was made, but eventually we found this long term solution to the problem.

Jordon will readily create an association between an action and where he performs it, which is what makes him only willing to eat certain types of food in certain situations. However, forming associations can be equally difficult. He would not, for instance, know that the act of brushing his teeth is what keeps them clean, but after seven years, we managed to get him to independently pass a brush over his teeth by constant reinforcement of the action. Still in his mind, it was not to keep them clean, but it is now an accepted routine that when he wakes up and when he goes to bed, he has to clean his teeth because it is the 'done' thing. This kind of learned behaviour is indicative of how the autistic mind works. Links are not established in the same way we make them, therefore an autistic child finds it difficult even to copy the behaviour of those around them. It is like being in a sealed bubble. Sometimes the desired behaviour can be established by offering incentives such as cuddles or a favourite food or toy, so that the child will then engage. Yet, what works for one child will not work for another and Jordon would very rarely respond to any of these things when young.

Familiarity breeds expectation

Establishing patterns of behaviour in an autistic child's world can help to teach them, help them to adopt positive habits. Yet you have to remain vigilant of establishing too rigid a pattern, because familiarity is where an autistic child finds safety, security and a measure of peace within. Once an autistic child sees a pattern, he or she will cling to it and a pattern can be established as quickly as giving the same dessert at two consecutive meals.

Once established, this could mean that the same dessert is a necessity for every single meal that the child eats, which it is in Jordon's case. To maintain the equilibrium, that dessert needs to be eaten or something has gone wrong with their world. Remove this regularity, break the cycle of repetition and then there is, what is to us a massive overreaction, but to the autistic child it is them expressing their grief at their already strange and chaotic world changing once more. If the dessert he was used to eating is not available, or if a fork is offered instead of a spoon, then Jordon finds it very difficult to deal with. Breaking a well-known or recognised pattern with an autistic child can be just as difficult as establishing one, because whatever is known is familiar, whatever is familiar is safe and whatever is not familiar is a strange and scary proposition.

While Jordon has become more flexible, some patterns cannot be broken. Nowadays, we can entice him to try a dessert other than chocolate mousse, like a cake, but once he has tried it, he will still expect that chocolate mousse.

Previously, if a mousse were not available then he would become distressed and upset. Now he is sixteen, if it is not available for any reason beyond our control, then we have to make sure it is explained so that he can understand it will be bought for his next dinner, or that it was not available in the shops when we wanted to buy it for him. Day in, day out, the safe place for Jordon to be is where everything remains the same and then he is to be happy. His ability to understand why something new is happening or why things should be different, is limited. He does not understand the unfamiliar, or that a minor change in routine is not a threat to his entire existence, because changing the outside world is like changing a piece of him.

We deliberately allow Jordon to remain 'stuck' on some small behaviours, such as his choice of dessert because he needs some continuity and consistency in his world. Some patterns we observe to give him peace of mind, otherwise he can become distressed when the constants he relies upon so much, those that keep his world familiar and safe, are removed. At one point in his life, he would even check the shopping that Lisa brought back from the supermarket, making sure that the chocolate mousse was in the bags. Nowadays, after years of consistently buying the same mousses and giving them to him every day, he has abandoned the need to check the shopping bags. However, whenever I am at Lisa's home and open the refrigerator, the sheer number of chocolate mousses stacked inside it, the little rows of pots sometimes filling a whole shelf, is at once a comfort that all is right with Jordon's world and a very real and sad reminder that, in it, some things never change.

Same again

Jordon seeks continuity in the world around him in many ways and he finds safety in repetitive behaviours. By doing the same thing over and over, he creates a place that is familiar, where no other sensations intrude, gaining reassurance that our confusing world cannot penetrate every area of his life.

The things he did in his younger years were one of the first early signs of this thought process, alerting us to a potential problem. When he ran round a table for hours on end, made 'graa graa' noises all day long or span round and round in circles from waking until bedtime, these all looked like the products of a very troubled mind, yet in reality, by doing the same thing over and over, Jordon was merely reinforcing his own little world and keeping himself mentally safe, warding off the chaos outside of him and creating a familiar environment of sound and sensation to hold it at bay.

To Jordon, his repetitive behaviours weren't the problem, they were a solution to the problem, a way of finding some measure of peace. Behind the pane of glass in his mind, he was looking at a world that was seemingly incomprehensible and the spinning, the noise making and the running in circles fulfilled a dual purpose; the sensations they produced served to distract him from all the other sensory inputs, helping to cut through the overload, to wipe out all the confusing images and sounds that otherwise crowded in. Also, there was the obvious reason; that he is far more comfortable if he can merely repeat what he knows.

There are lots of other examples of this, when Jordon was a baby and had grown out of his more immediate medical issues, he loved stroking fingernails. For minutes at a time he would gently caress ours, slowly stroking each fingernail from cuticle to tip. This seemed to stem from the time he spent in hospital when very young, when all we could do was reach through the bars of the cot and comfort him with our fingers. Then, it was so sweet to see him lying there reaching out in this way, but as ever there would be no eye contact, no recognition other than this caress. When he was young I surmised that he intimately knew the feel of Lisa's fingernails, the feel of her hair and the sound of her voice but not necessarily what she looked like.

A thin line separates us

Another thing Jordon would do, which is quite common behaviour in autistic children, was to line up objects in neat little rows. This regimented lining up of objects allowed him to control, to create order in the external world, shaping it to his wishes.

He would lie on the floor and line up pieces of paper, video tape boxes, anything that was small enough for him to handle and he could place in a perfectly straight line.

Whereas his everyday life, especially when he was younger, was full of adults making seemingly nonsensical demands and doing things that he did not understand, by placing his video tapes in rows, by doing the same thing for hours on end, he was able to place some form of order in what to him was a chaotic disconnected existence.

A place for everything

There were other noticeable habits that gave away Jordon's love of the familiar and of order. When he was old enough, it became noticeable that he had a habit of replacing items exactly where he found them, such as placing a plastic tumbler he was drinking from on the table, exactly where it was left, not an inch to the right or the left. We even tested this habit, Jordon would walk out of a room and when he returned, if we had moved a mug or some thing, even if it was just an inch or so, when he walked back in he would notice it straight away and move it back to where it was. He would do it so casually, without even really showing his attention was on it, picking up the mug and moving it back to the position it had been in, his eyes barely flicking to it as he did so.

What manner of mind is this that sees everything as one whole, that includes the distorted reflections of every one of its own thoughts, that drives out the unfamiliar and yet can perceive the smallest deviation in this chaos when it occurs. What lesson are we to learn from this? Is it that our own thoughts can make the world around us a confusing place, that our mind has incredible potential? Or that we never know what efforts those around us have to make to make sense of their own lives, no matter how simple or mundane they might seem.

In my case, when I look at Jordon and I think of the life that autism has taken from him, denied before the time of his birth and how it has been replaced with one of constant confusion and seemingly strange demands, I can only surmise that there is a much bigger picture to life and while it can be seemingly cruel, the one constant that binds us all together is love and for Jordon, Lauren, Lisa and Brian; for our entire family, love has been the one thing that has held us together and seen us through what would otherwise seem the most unfair of circumstances.

Chapter Ten - Nothing Comes Naturally

If you have an autistic child, understanding the way they think is fundamental to aiding their development. Trying to imagine, to mentally put yourself in their situation, can help you appreciate why they act in what can seem quite strange or bizarre ways. It isn't easy to do this and there are many experiences we have had with Jordon where change has not come easy, even when you are lucky enough to get outside help.

Every step on your autistic child's pathway of development must be slowly and patiently trodden, but even when you have come a long way on the journey with them, you can still quite easily slip backwards. The fact that you ever succeed in changing their behaviour does not mean that it won't change again for the worse. A really good example of this is when we tried to put Jordon in a shower for the very first time.

Water world

Despite the initial problems with enticing him into the swimming pool, Jordon had always enjoyed being in the bath, loving the water pistols and ducks we brought along to enliven each bath time and keep him amused. Little wind-up frogs swam around him in his nightly bath and it was one of the very few areas of his life where we did not have to fight or worry to cope with the situation. So, knowing that we were on fairly safe territory with him in the bathroom, one day we decided that it was time to experiment and to try using the shower that was fitted above the bath.

We were aware it was a new thing for him but very confident that it wasn't so new that he would have an adverse reaction;

he was by now so relaxed at bath times that we could not foresee a problem. Even so, ever mindful of his reactions, we did it slowly. The first step we took was to talk to him about the shower and then next, to run the shower with him stood beside it, showing him the water falling and then placing our hands underneath it so he could follow suit and have an experience of the shower without actually standing in it. He knew that the whole family used the shower, so we didn't think this was such a new thing for him and we were following all the correct steps, introducing it gently and slowly. Things seemed to be going very well and we didn't see any kind of challenge looming.

Oh, how wrong we were!

All was proceeding well, the night of his first shower was upon us and we had Jordon prepared and standing in the bath under the shower. We were talking to him, he seemed relaxed and so we turned the shower on. The water rose in the pipe making the noise he was by now used to. In slow motion, the drops burst out of the shower head and fell through the air, everything was fine. Then, the moment the water hit him and burst upon his head, all hell broke loose. The split second the water hit his head, he launched into a screaming fit. He was obviously so scared by the sensation that he was beside himself, immediately jumping out of the bath, shaking in fear and bawling as if he had witnessed a horrific event.

For our part, we couldn't initially think what was wrong. We had checked that the water was lukewarm, not too cold or hot, the force of the shower was not too great and all should have been well. We surmised that it wasn't anything unusual, it was merely the sensation of having water hit his head that had caused so much fear and such an adverse reaction from Jordon and it wasn't as if he was making an unnecessary fuss, he was quite clearly terrified by the whole ordeal.

So with a sigh of resignation, we gave up on the shower for the time being and reverted to the bath once more, resolving to try the shower again at a later date.

It was then we realised that our attempt at moving Jordon on to using the shower had wider ramifications. From that point forward, he refused to sit down in the bath and was obviously very unsettled when he looked up at the showerhead. Through one tiny, well thought-out and cautious attempt to move him forwards, we had succeeded in moving him backwards. Indeed, it took the next three months of gradual, slow introduction before we were able to get him to actually relax and enjoy a bath again. Nearly 100 days of further night time bath problems, merely because Jordon had felt water falling on his head - that is how sensitive to new things an autistic child can be.

But eventually, slowly, over time, things do change, just at such a glacial pace that it threatens to drive most parents to distraction with the accumulation of frustrations, observing the same rituals and repetitious problems over and over again, always mindful that months or even years of effort can either pay off or be wiped out by a seemingly random event.

Today, with continued effort, so pronounced is the change in Jordon's attitude, that he loves showers, he loves the swimming pool and will frighten us all to death with his antics, running and jumping into the deep end without fear. Seeing him in action, it is difficult to imagine that once upon a time it was all we could do to persuade him to step back into the bath, merely because we had made one cautious effort to move him on.

Even when you feel you have overcome an autistic child's fears, you cannot make the assumption that they understand the context as you might expect. The perspective they learn is gained over years of explanation and imprinting upon them and perhaps one of the biggest mistakes you can make is to assume that because they accept one change in behaviour, they actually understand it or that they will readily accept something we see as being similar, but to them has no association whatsoever.

Knowing that Jordon accepts and likes chocolate mousse means only that. It does not mean that he will accept a strawberry mousse or a chocolate cake; the pattern is what has been accepted and it is that which provides familiarity and comfort, but nothing can change about the pattern. You cannot change the consistency, the taste, the venue, the flavour, the context, the receptacle or the sounds. Any deviation from what is known is just that, a deviation, a departure from the norm, a potential source of anxiety and fear and with it comes the risk of regression, a retreat from what little positive progress he has been able to make in the world to date.

Jordon's little sister Lauren, who is also autistic, initially had no problem at all with bathing and every time we put her in the bath to wash she was absolutely fine, sitting quietly and seemingly ambivalent to the experience. Then, when she reached the age of six months, with absolutely no change in her routine, nothing new introduced, she seemed to suddenly wake up to the situation and began to make an appalling scene every single time she was placed in the bath. There was no event or warning and neither was it a one-off reaction, it literally changed overnight.

Now, she is four years old and still Lisa's neighbours will be familiar with the sound of Lauren screaming during her six o'clock bath time.

She still wears a nappy because of her autism and so, no matter what her reaction, baths are essential. Even on the rare nights, when for no apparent reason, Lauren views the night time ritual of bathing as an acceptable activity, she will sit quietly eyeing the bath taps with suspicion, making sure they do nothing untoward.

On several such occasions when Lauren was quieter in the bath, Lisa thought she might try rinsing her hair with the shower as it would be easier to get rid of the shampoo. Big mistake! Any attempt to turn the shower on results in Lauren becoming hysterical; she is so overcome by fear that Lisa has no option but to remove her from the bath that second and get her away from the situation. It is quite usual for her to become so distraught that she will cry for at least an hour afterwards. Our suspicion is that the sensation of water in her ears, so unfamiliar to her, is a big part of the problem and gives rise to these extreme reactions.

So, nearly every bath time with Lauren remains a battle and Lisa has even gone to the lengths of removing the shower hose connected to the bathroom taps to take away the cause of any potential problem, but the old fears remain and bath times are most definitely not fun!

Mind your step

You cannot assume, even when a positive change has been achieved, that it will stick forever. Nor can you assume that an autistic child understands why that change is beneficial or necessary; you cannot rely on their seeing the bigger picture around anything you communicate to them. They will learn by example, they can develop habits and patterns of behaviour if coached patiently to do so, but they still may not know why they are being taught to do certain things. They will learn that they need to wear clothes and shoes, they will learn that unusual behaviours are not acceptable in certain situations, but still not truly understand why.

So, coaching your autistic child is a job that never ends. You can never make an assumption, nor can you slip into the trap of believing that they understand why they are doing things. You can be constantly surprised. There might be a misunderstanding lurking just around the corner that can place your child in danger or hopefully merely deliver some quite unusual and even comical situations.

Still to this day, Jordon has no idea at all that something as repugnant as dog faeces should be avoided. When he was around six years old and he was going to The Red Shirt School, he would be picked up by Lisa in their car each day. However, even though most of his journey was in a vehicle, it soon became apparent that wherever he walked, he had no concept that he should watch where he put his feet and avoid stepping in a mess on the pavement.

So, whenever Jordon walked with Lisa, he regularly returned with his shoes befouled. Worse, even though we taught him to remove his shoes when he arrived home and place them on a mat, he had no concept that he should avoid getting any kind of dirt on his hands.

This was a genuine health risk and another case for our constantly reinforcing a message that he must watch where he walks and that he must be careful what he touches on his shoes, but it is a lesson that has not yet sunk in. To this day, even at sixteen years old, Lisa has to ensure that Jordon's shoes are checked and he washes his hands immediately whenever he returns home.

What's in a name?

Autism is one problem and one diagnosis and yet it covers such a wide spectrum of behavioural problems and possibilities and every autistic child has their own particular way of acting. While behaviour can seem wildly different for each and every case, all are manifestations of the same root cause.

At the age of two, a child without autism will readily respond to their name when called and they will enjoy pleasing and sharing things with their parents. This would be unusual for an autistic child.

It took us a long time to get Jordon to respond to his name and to associate the sound 'Jordon' with him. In his mind, he knew exactly who he was, but to put a name to that identity was not only pointless, he couldn't appreciate that there were other identities other than his own. His world is the world, there isn't anything outside of that and to get him to recognise and accept anything outside of his safety zone was a major undertaking.

It was the PACTS scheme that Jordon was fortunate enough to take part in when he was four years old that kick-started his learning, putting him on the road to many future developments and it was this scheme that helped us in enabling him to recognise his own name. Even getting him to look at other people took specific schooling. The PACTS tutors introduced techniques and schooled us in those that we could subsequently use ourselves, helping to reinforce their work. So, as we saw Jordon grow with their more immediate achievements, they were also sowing the seeds for his future development.

To encourage Jordon to respond to his name, the PACTS tutors used an association technique. At that stage, getting Jordon to even make eye contact was a major task and their approach was to issue the same request over and over again, "Jordon! Look at me!" Then they would hold a toy up by their own eyes. Then, because he wanted the toy, Jordon would look around, gazing in the general direction of the tutor's eyes. Eventually, over time, the association was built up in his mind, so that when he heard, "Jordon! Look at me!" he would look at a person's eyes because he expected to see a toy or something he liked.

Eventually, this link was made and he began to respond to his name with the tutors, but even so, Jordon would take many further months to perform even this very simplest and instinctual of tasks on a regular basis. Of course, his tuition was in a room, effectively separated from us and we would learn of the breakthroughs when the excited tutors came rushing over to let us know. Sadly, what was learned in this room would often take ages to be adopted as a behaviour elsewhere, so that we might first be able to witness it for ourselves.

Not all autistic children avoid eye contact, but Jordon certainly did. I would say that he was probably around four years old before he even knew what I looked like. If you imagine every time you met someone you avoided looking directly at them, you can see that it is incredibly difficult to get an accurate picture of what they look like. You may gradually learn to recognise that person's voice, their general size and presence, but that would be about all. So we spent time coaching Jordon to look at us, otherwise he would always look past you, up at the ceiling or into the distance.

Even when you succeed in achieving eye contact, an autistic child cannot naturally read the vast array of facial expressions we use; to them they are confusing and sometimes threatening. Generally, they do not understand the subtle differences in our tone of voice, it does not provide them with any clues to how we are feeling. So, coupled with our techniques for achieving eye contact, we used to make an effort to engage him and explain our facial expressions, miming big grins and saying "happy" or frowning comically and saying, "sad."

We extended unbelievable effort in gaining my grandson's direct attention. The first time we called out to Jordon and he turned his head in response, it was a very long time after the PACTS tutors had seen him respond to the technique. When he did so in our presence, while it was at that time merely a programmed response, to us it was like all our Christmas's coming at once. For the very first time in his lifetime, this darling child, my grandson, Jordon, responded when we called his name.

He was six years old.

Traffic lights and travel nightmares

Autism is a fascinating disorder if you know how to work with it. As with everything in human life, nothing happens without a reason and in autism there is a cause behind every behaviour we witness. With an autistic child, their lack of ability to identify with the outside world means that they have no reference points, no way of finding out why things happen, seeking the security of familiarity through their repetitive behaviours, trying to make their world a stable and understandable place. They have only the past as a reference point, because their sense of security originates from association and because they have no inner compass that tells them what is usual or normal. This means that once they accept something new in their lives, they will usually only subsequently tolerate it if it remains unchanged when next they encounter it.

There is a quality to the autistic mind that finds it immensely reassuring for things to be in order. So, we see children, such as Jordon, who put their toys into long neat straight lines, like to look at long lists or to repeat the same behaviour over and over again. It is as if they are seeking their answers by creating patterns, because in the world around them they recognise none. We can understand this, because it is somehow comforting to know that things remain unchanged or that there is a routine to our own lives. We follow patterns all the time in our lives, creating our own familiar worlds, however, this need for order is greatly exaggerated in the autistic mind, where the thinking patterns can only cope with repetition and a literal understanding of life. An autistic person is also very much a potential outcast, meaning that order and familiarity may be the only source of solace in their otherwise solitary lives.

Patterns of perfection are sought because the more uniform and predictable and perfect a situation or a thing is, the more the autistic mind can relate to it. So, we see autistic children lining up their toys, repeating the same behaviours, putting things back in exactly the same spot and their rooms and all of their life being very tidy, seeking some state of static perfection, where everything's position is fixed and known. This is not true of all autistic children, but for many by creating reassuring patterns, their immediate world conforms to their wish for everything to remain the same. Anything new that is being introduced into my darling grandson's life is compared against what he already knows, checked to see if it matches those situations or things he now knows to be safe.

Inside, I am convinced Jordon originally felt very separate and apart from us all and so desperately wanted to join in, but he just didn't know how to relate. So, Jordon established his own self-imposed boundaries, the things which he knew remained inside an invisible line, a net in his mind that encompassed everything acceptable in his world. The rest, everything that was alien and therefore a potential threat, no matter what it was, nor how many times he had witnessed it, remained the other side of this line and he would refuse to let it in for fear its intrusion would somehow threaten or cause him pain. We learned our own language of autism and anything new we were introducing we referred to as the 'unknown,' for to Jordon, that was what it was. Whether it was a new food or a new set of bed-linen, we knew everything outside of his experience was a scary, potential threat and it remained on the other side of the line he had drawn in his mind. That meant even once you got him to accept something, while it came into the net of things that were acceptable, he still did not then want to move on, because each new intrusion into his world was as scary as the last. Even once we had taught him through repetition to perceive an activity or object as the norm, it became safe, but then we could not deviate where or when that object was presented to him and it became incredibly difficult to get him to change.

An example of this is when we used to take Jordon out in the car. Obviously, at some point, Jordon had associated the vehicle stopping with it being time to get out of his seat and out of the car. It had become a habitual pattern. When a car he was in stopped, he knew it was time to get out and nothing seemed to be able to change this association for him.

Every time the car stopped in traffic, for whatever reason, Jordon would immediately begin to struggle to get out of his seat and it was only the child safety lock that prevented an escape at every set of lights, or junction. So, from the age of two years old it meant that every red traffic light, every halt in traffic and every pedestrian crossing became a major threat to Lisa's sanity. To Jordon, if the car wasn't moving, it was time to disembark and within several seconds of stopping he was feeling trapped and claustrophobic. Then he would begin struggling with his safety harness, making frustrated noises and eventually screaming. The screaming wouldn't merely assault the ears of anyone within the car, it could become so loud that even with the windows shut, people outside the car could hear this awful crescendo. It sounded very much like he was being tormented in some way, when in fact it was merely that we had come to a halt in traffic and as we did so, the trouble began. Many were the times I have looked up from trying to placate a young Jordon to see passers-by on the pavement looking on curiously to see what the howling was all about. For most children, this might be an isolated occurrence, one you could quickly talk them around from, but for Jordon, it would happen every single time.

We developed coping strategies, ways of distracting him, ways of convincing him that it was ok, that we were alright to stop without disembarking. We would reassure him whenever we were at a red light that it was ok; we would count down, singing out brightly, "Five, four, three, two, one…Go!" until the light changed, trying to make a game of it. In short, anything to get Jordon to accept that it was alright to be waiting for whatever reason and that stopping without getting out of the car did not mean that the whole world was now wrong.

Another outcome of this problem was that Lisa became perhaps one of the most knowledgeable drivers in her area. In her efforts to find routes which did not involve a potential halt, she would drive every backstreet, avoid every set of lights and potential bottleneck and find the quieter longer routes that involved less stops. While she might be clocking up many extra miles through her pursuit of a route without stopping places, her knowledge of the roads would have been the envy of many a local taxi driver, had they known!

Road rage

Because we knew it was important to take every opportunity to communicate with Jordon, to stretch him and take him out of his comfort zone, to ensure he did not become too entrenched in his behaviour, we have always continued our day trips and excursions with him, taking him out into the big wide world.

One such trip was when a friend, Dean volunteered to help Lisa and I in taking Jordon out for the day. Jordon was around six or seven years old, it was a lovely sunny day and we were all really looking forward to taking my small car to the south coast, visiting a tiny seaside town with all the things you typically find in English resorts.

There was a small amusement arcade, filled with gambling machines that beeped, chimed and flashed, as well as computer games, which Jordon absolutely loved. We all had fish and chips on the seafront, except Jordon who had his own food brought from home that he would accept. We finished the day with a walk along the beach and for once, enjoyed a thoroughly incident-free day.

On the way home, we drove on dual carriageways and some of the smaller winding single lane roads, aware that the traffic was beginning to build up around us. Knowing Jordon's penchant for leaping out of stationary cars, when the flow of traffic slowed, Lisa and I began to fill with dread, especially as we too came to a complete standstill, a long line of stationary traffic stretching ahead of us and into the distance.

Dean, seeing that there was no way that the traffic was likely to move for some time, could see that he had time to leave the car for a cigarette. I desperately warned him not to, but not having seen Jordon behave negatively for the entire trip, Dean assumed I was over-dramatizing the situation and blithely ignored my advice.

Jordon, who up until that point had been convinced to stay put, knew that when someone got out of the car, he could too and he naturally began to try. Of course, we could not allow him out onto a road that could become busy again at any moment, especially as he was very likely to attempt to run off. So, there was a brief moment where he struggled with the door and his seat belt while we gently and calmly explained that he had to remain in the car, dreading what might come next.

To Jordon, it was natural to feel he could leave the car if someone else had and he was unable to relate to what we were telling him. It didn't take long before he started to vent his frustration in the only way he knew, so he thrashed in his seat, beginning to arch his back and lash out, kicking the car seats and hammering them with his fists. He was wailing and it wasn't more than a few seconds before he began to scream in a way that was quite exceptional, even for him.

His screams became so high pitched and so loud that other people in nearby cars could obviously hear them. There were people other than Dean, who had left their cars and some of them, being naturally inquisitive, wandered over to where we were.

By now, any effort to communicate or subdue Jordon was fruitless. To his mind, he wanted to leave his car seat and run around. We played music and sang to him, both things that he would usually enjoy at this age, but to no avail.

We were so concerned for him, but we could not get it across to Jordon that just because the car had stopped, he couldn't get out. To his mind, he was no longer travelling, instead he was now tied up against his will in his seat and he found this very frightening. Why should he be tethered when he knew a stationary car was one you disembarked from? But, letting him out of the car was not an option as we could not risk his running off amongst the traffic.

So we sat with our ears under assault for around half an hour and running through a whole range of emotions as we tried all the techniques we could think of to distract Jordon. We tried to offer him sweets and interest him in the world around him, all to no avail and all the while, the screaming continued until eventually and to our great relief, the traffic began to move on. Jordon gradually quietened down, still sobbing gently and clearly hugely traumatised as well as exhausted. What had been an idyllic day had been shattered by something as seemingly innocuous as a halt in traffic. Even at this age, we still had so many obstacles to overcome and even in the care of three adults, we had found ourselves powerless to help him. The aftermath left us all quite shaken and I truly did not know who I should feel more sorry for, us or Jordon.

The kindness of strangers

No matter how many day-trips and excursions we made, each one came with obstacles to face and it wasn't just the dramas of the day, it was the reverberations that might continue with Jordon for days or even weeks to come. While we carried on with our efforts, some challenges just seemed too big.

For some years, we deliberately avoided taking him to the shoe shop and getting his feet formally measured. This is because a shoe fitting involved two distinct challenges; firstly we would be taking Jordon to a shop and secondly, it involved putting his feet into a measuring device and we knew that putting his foot into a metal contraption such as this would fill him with horror. The very idea of getting an accurate reading seemed impossible and so up until that point, we had always shied away from it, knowing the mayhem that could ensue. However, we knew it had to be done and when he was three years old we decided to make the attempt. Up until that point, we had been estimating his shoe size, going to the shops without him and bringing back shoes to measure against his foot and that situation could not go on forever.

In fact, once before, we had tried to get his feet measured and because it had ended in disaster, we had virtually eradicated the memory from our minds. Just a year before, we had gone into a shoe shop in a busy shopping centre and when we placed Jordon near to the measurement machine, he quickly became hysterical, throwing himself around and becoming increasingly distressed as we gently tried to persuade him that having his feet measured was not the same as facing the electric chair! Jordon was having none of it. From placid young boy he quickly made the transformation into screaming two year old typhoon. All the while, the young shop assistant stood bemused, perplexed and obviously quite unable to know what to make of it or what to do.

In short, Jordon's reaction was as though the three of us were trying to murder him. In reality, he was facing something unknown. He had no understanding that we might be doing this merely to find out the correct measurement of his feet and he quickly escalated to the point where I was actually concerned he might injure himself. Fearful that we might see him hurt, we admitted defeat and beat as dignified a retreat as we were able. We left the shop assistant staring after us, tiny shoe in hand and probably wondering what was wrong with that little boy who saw having his feet measured as being close to the end of his world.

Now we knew it was time for Jordon to face the shoe shop once again and knowing just how awful it could turn out, we planned carefully, Lisa and I sitting down to discuss our second attempt in earnest.

For whatever reason, I had a very good feeling about a tiny children's shoe shop that was just a few minutes' walk from home and, after discussion, we decided to make this our goal. We did wonder if we should call into the shop first and warn the manager of the potential disturbance we would be bringing their way. However, we knew that would not change anything and we didn't want to overly concern the manager. So instead, we gritted our teeth and stepped out of the front door, having first strapped Jordon firmly into his pushchair and fully prepared to embark on our second 'shoe shop campaign'.

As usual, the few minutes' walk was a struggle, a battle of wills, with Jordon pushing his feet to the floor and arching his back in an effort to get us to change direction and return home. What should have been an unremarkable stroll to the shops was a fight in itself.

Eventually, however, we made it to the shoe shop, still with Jordon fighting every step. We looked inside and the shop happened to be very busy. Seeing this, we almost walked away, but decided as we had come this far to persevere nonetheless and face the crowd of parents and children.

The shop had a little old-fashioned wooden door and a bell that rang as we opened it. By this time, Jordon had got wind of the fact that we were taking him somewhere new (and therefore threatening) and so, as we took a collective breath and pushed him in, he ground his feet into the floor and reached desperately for the doorframe in an effort to hold himself back.

There was a brief moment, while we paused in the doorway with Jordon, prising his fingers off the frame and pushing onwards as he continued to writhe and lash out. We finally managed to get him inside the shop and there, he continued to struggle violently. Yet, if he were to be let loose, he would have been running around and pushing anyone he saw as being in his way, so Lisa kept him in his pushchair for the moment.

Some autistic children, but by no means all, have problems with their fine-motor skills, meaning they remain unable to button shirts, cannot use zips or perform tasks that require intricate movements and fingertip control. To this very day, despite being able to operate a mobile phone or a computer console, Jordon remains unable to grasp the intricacies of lacing his own shoes, so he has always had either Velcro fastenings or slip-on footwear.

My intuition about the shoe shop was correct, once inside, we were quickly met by the shop assistant and as it turned out, this very kind lady was quite obviously a natural at working with children with special needs. I recall she told us she had a young relative who was either autistic or had some form of disability. So, instead of sitting on the side-lines looking bewildered, she knew exactly how to gradually introduce Jordon to the idea of having his foot placed in the diabolical (to him) foot measurement machine. Lisa had no need to explain.

As soon as we had entered the shop, all eyes had fallen upon us; Jordon was already acting in a way that singled him out, overreacting beyond what most mothers would expect and his writhing and groaning made him, as always, a magnet for other people's attention. Fortunately, we knew to expect this and had mentally prepared ourselves for the curiosity we would stimulate.

Eventually, however, we had to let Jordon out of the pushchair. Immediately, he was released and quite unsurprisingly, he was off running around the shop. As lots of well-behaved children sat swinging their feet whilst they tried on new shiny shoes, Jordon ran round, making his usual repertoire of strange noises and drawing querying stares.

After a couple of minutes, we did coax him to sit down. The lady let Jordon know, at every stage, what she was doing and why. Yet, still he was creating merry hell. I remember another little boy in the shop asking his mother, "why is that little boy screaming?", because by now, despite all our best efforts, Jordon was terribly upset.

To get the measurement right, we had to hold him still and keep his foot laid flat in the machine. There we were, three adults comforting and holding a distraught little boy, trying to keep him immobile and all the while, he was attempting to pull away. Gaining control, the assistant carefully held his foot in a way that ensured his toes were splayed out rather than clawed over and after what felt like an endless struggle, she was finally able to obtain an accurate reading. Even though it had involved drastic action, we now had a good idea of Jordon's correct foot size at last.

The next step was to try on shoes until we found some that fitted him. This stage of the operation involved persuading Jordon to place yet more new and, to him, strange and unknown things on his feet. He was getting increasingly distraught and because we could not take him from the situation he worked himself up to the point he was demented. So, we decided upon a pair of shoes that fitted him as quickly as we could and hastened to get away.

There was a comical moment when we were at the till, just finishing our purchase and breathing a sigh of relief, when the assistant mentioned in an offhand way that Jordon would in all likelihood, soon outgrow these shoes. The horror at the thought of returning to go through the whole shoe fitting experience again anytime soon must have been written all over our faces and Lisa and I exchanged a look that spoke volumes. It was a fitting end to the scene.

Lisa took Jordon outside while I remained to pay for the shoes, feeling a great warmth and admiration for the shoe shop assistant for the kindness and patience she had displayed. It was so nice to be shown such warmth by a complete stranger that it made me want to hug her and express our thanks for her respectful understanding of Jordon's behaviour.

One step at a time

The aftermath was almost comical. Despite our success in getting new footwear on him, Jordon was obviously unfamiliar with the shoes; they were more formal than those he had been wearing previously and must have felt quite heavy and stiff.

Once on the street outside, we decided to allow Jordon to walk so that he could try out his new shoes. He began to take steps as though they were alien animals clinging to his feet. Walking flat-footed, with robotic strides, he held his feet as though they were blocks of wood, somehow trying to keep them at a distance from his body.

It took Jordon a while to get used to the new shoes. For several days, he would look at them with suspicion and carried on walking as though we had deliberately hobbled him or he was trying to extract himself from a field full of mud. Eventually, though, he became used to the new feeling and it was a great relief to see him walking properly once more!

Working it out

Children who are born without autism spectrum disorder generally learn and develop naturally, absorbing what is going on, gradually appreciating and relating to the world around them. For the child with autism, it is a different story. Depending upon how severe their disorder is, it is true to say that far less in life comes naturally to them. They have difficulty fathoming us or our world, they cannot necessarily comprehend why we do things and may not even understand affection or why a parent might offer a hug. Without careful nurturing and development, autistic children can remain stuck, unable to overcome their blocks and remaining that way for the rest of their lives, developing only in dribs and drabs.

Therefore, it falls upon the parents and carers of autistic children to observe, understand and interpret what is going on in the autistic child's world. An autistic parent must learn the language of autism and become a translator of every mannerism and sound. Each one is a clue as to what is going on in their world, what it is they are feeling and will help you in decoding the language of autism, one gesture and action at a time.

Once progress begins, when you start to successfully interpret behaviour and can help improve their life, no matter how small or hard fought for the achievement, it brings an immense sense of relief. Thereafter, even though the journey remains taxing and arduous, you at least have hope that there will be further revelations and growth. As a grandmother of an autistic boy, the one piece of advice I have is, even though you should maintain hope, don't hold your breath while you are waiting for your autistic child to change!

Running cold

A couple of years ago, Lisa asked Jordon to run a bath for himself; a test to see whether, at the age of fourteen, he was yet capable of this small task, of helping himself in this way. She was very pleased to see that Jordon did as he was asked, going to the bathroom, putting the plug in and turning the taps until the bath filled. Another milestone reached!

However, Lisa was shocked to see he had only run the cold tap and deliberately so. Asked why he had run a bath of freezing cold water, Jordon replied that he liked the water cold. Yet the only time Jordon had been in cold water in his life was when he had been in a paddling pool when he was younger, for the swimming pool was a lot warmer than that bath. It sparked a thought; we had both heard of children who became addicted to sensations that override their sensory input and one such example is an autistic boy who we had heard got into the habit of running himself a bath of freezing cold water every day. This kind of behaviour may seem extreme, but it would have enabled him to tune out all other sensory input and to focus on just one thing. To achieve this singular focus, this exclusion of the outside world, the water in the bath would have to be very cold. Tepid or warm water would not serve the same purpose because it would not provide an overwhelming sensory input.

This kind of behaviour can become addictive because only in this way can the autistic mind focus for so long on one set of sensations, only in this way are they able to tune out for so long all the myriad sensory inputs that might otherwise overwhelm them.

So many things make sense in the world of autism if you are able to look at them from an autistic child's perspective. From their point of view, instead of being random irrational behaviour, bathing in a bath full of cold water is a temporary fix for the massive sensory overload their brain habitually endures. Being freezing cold all over numbs the body to everything else and it is perhaps one of the most logical things an autistic child might do. The resultant clarity it brings, the freedom from all other sensory inputs, the ability to focus the mind on one overwhelming sensation that excludes all others must bring with it a massive sense of relief, just as it means they must endure the torture of icy cold water. When every nerve in your body is busy telling you that it is painfully cold, it overrides and blocks the outside world, cutting through the otherwise confusing sensory input. For someone who is normally bombarded by their own senses, being able to experience a single all-encompassing sensation would be an amazing unification, uniting the messages of the brain and the sensations of the body into one cohesive whole. All of a sudden, everything has one overriding thought, 'There is cold.'

But each autistic child is different and aside from this one incident when he drew a cold bath, Jordon has never since exhibited this kind of behaviour. In fact, he now loves the water, swimming and splashing around in paddling pools. Yet, Jordon does like the cold and is very comfortable outdoors in cold weather. Even in the depths of winter, he prefers to take off his coat and wear only a shirt and trousers, were we to allow it.

So while we didn't know whether Jordon had merely run a cold bath by mistake or whether he meant to do it, we did in fact hope he had done it on purpose. In many scenarios in his life, Jordon has to be instructed to do something to overcome the fact that he cannot interpret the evidence of his senses. Even to this day, we have to caution him that hot food can be painful and that swallowing a quarter of a sandwich whole can lead to a choking sensation. Yet still Jordon does not know what choking is, even when he is experiencing it, nor why it is happening to him. Therefore, to have a hint that he was running a cold bath in an effort to overcome all the discordant messages he normally experienced would make both perfect sense and it would actually be quite encouraging that he had taken it upon his own initiative to do so!

Chapter Eleven - The Games People Play

After joining the First White Shirt School at the age of eight, Jordon enjoyed a good few years there with some really marvellous teachers.

Initially, it had been an entirely different environment to that which he was used to, as the school was much larger and far more diverse. After about three years and without warning, he began to show signs of being unhappy. He started to say he hated the school and we could never get to the bottom of it or find out why. This was a different situation to when he was at the Red Shirt School. Then, he was reluctant to attend, now at the First White Shirt School, he seemed not reluctant, but almost angry and we just did not know why, all we had to go on were our own guesses.

The only thing we could surmise was that during the break times he was mixing with children who were more boisterous than he was used to. To give you some background, while the students were placed in separate classes according to their educational needs, typically of around 10 or 12 children, at all other times, breaks, lunchtime and at school assembly, they mixed.

The very nature of Jordon's problems meant that he could become disturbed by the slightest of things and here he was thrust into the playground rough and tumble. When the bell for playtime rang, all the children would rush out of their classrooms. While this was a natural way of organising things, it did have consequences for Jordon. He was naturally introverted and quite often preferred to play alone, wrapped up in his own little world. For Jordon to be happy, he needed everything to be perfect, no loud noises, no upsets, no confrontations, no boisterous behaviour. In short, he needed a perfect world undisturbed by other people's displays of emotion and if that world were not perfect, then he could not cope. At the Red Shirt School, he dealt with this by finding a space for himself where he could play alone, but here he had nowhere to hide and was thrust amongst children who were chaotic and disruptive. For three years he had coped here, but now for some reason, something had changed. To this day we do not know what.

We first became aware of a problem when Jordon began to show signs of not wanting to go to school. He did not tell us directly that anything was wrong, but of course the first thing we did was to ask him. When questioned, he became very quiet, "No Talking! No Talking!" was the only answer we received and this was a typical response when we broached a subject that Jordon found difficult to explain.

At that time, we had also begun to consider what would happen when Jordon reached the age of sixteen. The First White Shirt School only helped children up to that age and he was already eleven. While we had five years to wait, we knew exactly how difficult it could be finding him the right place in a school that offered further education and catered for him up to the age of nineteen.

Eventually, we decided that the school wasn't the right place for Jordon any more. He was becoming stressed and there was little that could be done about it unless we moved him on to a school that didn't challenge him in this way. This search was to take nearly a year, when we finally moved him on to the Second White Shirt School.

Hidden talents

Way before we had to consider Jordon's long term future, when he was around five years old, it became clear he enjoyed anything to do with music. We already knew he enjoyed listening to the theme tune from the Titanic movie and other types too.

Even today, he loves listening to music; anything from Abba to the most modern artists. Strangely enough, he still will not tolerate anyone singing along to the music or even singing to themselves and if you happen to burst into song near to him he does not like it at all! He will be very adamant, "No Singing! No Singing!" holding up his hand and waving it around to stop you and, if questioned why, he will merely reply, "I Don't Like It!" and that is all we can get out of him.

Back when Jordon was nine years old, his school held music lessons. These taught basic skills, the children shaking tambourines, blowing recorders and banging drums. So, while this was a very positive thing, we wanted to take it further if we could. At the time, we were seeking ways of widening Jordon's interests and this seemed like the perfect opportunity.

I happened upon the idea of an electronic keyboard. I shopped around, looking for a model that would meet his needs without involving me in purchasing a professional quality machine and found one that taught the user to play tunes by lighting up the keys in advance. This was ideal for Jordon as he could easily learn to touch each key as it lit up. It would be his present on Christmas day.

So, when 25th December came around, we presented Jordon with his gift and over Christmas he had fun playing with it until his interest waned and he went off to play his customary computer games in his bedroom. Then, my eldest son, who knows how to play, took over and we had lots of fun with the automated backing tracks, making up our own music and enjoying ourselves.

We deliberately left the keyboard set up in Jordon's bedroom and he did continue to experiment with it every now and again. Having seen this little glimmer of interest, eventually we decided that we would take Jordon for proper lessons.

We looked around for a music teacher who might take him on, visiting a local music centre and arranging for piano lessons. They accepted him at first, but after three weeks, we learned that the centre was closing as they did not have enough students and his teacher would then be accepting students at her home.

Hearing this, we booked lessons for Jordon and both Lisa and I took him for his very first one at his teacher's home. Upon arriving, it became very obvious, very quickly, that she was not now prepared to take Jordon on as a student, despite having accepted him as a client at the centre. We hoped that it was not his autism. When we enquired if there would be spaces available in the future, she was obviously very uncomfortable, especially when she saw the hurt look on my daughter's face, but even so, she remained evasive, promising to call us should anything come up. We thanked her and walked away, passing children walking in with their musical instruments, ready to attend the lesson. Holding Jordon's hand, we returned to the car, rejected but undefeated. The promised telephone call never came.

So we continued our search for a piano teacher for Jordon. Enquiring at his school, his class teacher there thought she might know someone who would work with an autistic child. She made enquiries and we were introduced to a lady who, it turned out, was perfect for teaching Jordon.

On meeting her, we realised how fortunate we were to have found such an understanding lady with a natural ability to relate to Jordon, keeping him focused on his music for the half hour lesson and establishing a strong rapport.

Initially, Jordon played nursery rhymes and very basic music, progressing well, until after attending for a while, it was obvious he had an ear for music and he was soon put on to classical pieces, one of his favourites being the Turkish March.

Whatever Jordon played, he would play remembering all the right keys and although he was not a full blown pianist, we discovered that he had learned to play by ear. With very little ability to read music, he would listen to the piece and then attempt it for himself. At that stage, despite remembering well, he had very little rhythm and although we all knew he was not a budding Beethoven, it was lovely to think he could put his hand to music and had an interest in something other than computers.

The routine developed, as did Jordon's ability. Lisa would often spend time with his teacher, chatting after the lesson and I must say that both his teacher and her husband are that rare type of person whose caring nature makes them stand out; as a result, you never forget them nor their efforts.

However, like all things, Jordon's piano lessons eventually came to an end when Lauren was born and Jordon was twelve years old and much to our regret we have not since continued Jordon's musical education. Then, a house move meant it was too far to travel, while Lisa and Brian were absorbed in the demands of raising what we later learned were not one but two autistic children.

The games Jordon plays

For many years, even while he was developing his interest in computer games and eventually being encouraged by us in his piano playing, Jordon didn't know how to play even the simplest of games. Bearing in mind that he was around eight years old before he learned to chew and even the simplest of tasks remained beyond him, the absence of game playing wasn't the biggest consideration or challenge confronting him or us.

We were, however, continually trying to get him involved. As he grew, we tried to entice him to play games in the garden, but as we kicked a ball around, he would just stand and stare at us as though we were all mad. Any activity of this sort was difficult, but gradually he did develop an interest in kicking a ball, with Brian egging him on to take part and even now he loves playing 'tag.' He can also be enticed to play Pitch Penny, throwing coins against a wall and the nearest penny to the wall earning the thrower all the pennies that are thrown. My youngest son used to arrive with a big bag full of pennies and spend his time laughing with Jordon and trying to tell him, unsuccessfully, that he was not allowed to cheat. This would amuse Jordon no-end and he would laugh as my son protested loudly and Jordon continued to cheat. Of course, it was all in fun and Jordon always ended up with a big bag full of all the pennies.

The sad thing is that aside from these occasional, yet notable exceptions, all of Jordon's game playing is carried out alone, swinging a make-believe sword and pretending to punch invisible foes or plugging in his earphones and playing multiple computer games at once.

We are always trying to widen his world and this includes visiting the biggest of events. As a family, in the last few years, we have got into the habit of taking Jordon to a huge annual fireworks display that was held not too far from my home. There, in the darkness of the park, he would stand surrounded by his family, in awe of the massive explosions of colour and noise, his face lit up by the bursting multi-coloured "Stars!", as he would call them, with one of us holding his coat in a vice-like grip in case he should decide to run off into the crowd.

Several years ago, we attended this same display and bought him a sword from one of the many stalls. It lit up when you swung it and he enjoyed himself for days afterwards, swinging the plastic sabre around and believing himself to be a superhero, albeit one fighting nothing but thin air and rejecting our advances to join in for anything but a few brief minutes.

Even today, Jordon prefers to play alone.

Park life

Part of the difficulty in getting Jordon to play with other children is that he is so different from boys of his age. In truth, the autism serves to hold him back and his options are either to play in the company of other autistic children or by himself.

One day, quite a few years ago, we had taken a trip to the seaside and Jordon was by then old enough to play on the climbing frame in the park. Being watched over by Lisa and myself as well as a friend who was present at the time, we were approached by a group of five boys of about ten years old who very politely asked if they could play with him. Their given reason was that at their own school they had a child with similar difficulties and they had been taught how to play and interact with him. We agreed and all the while, I watched them like a hawk, checking that none of them were mean to him.

As it turned out, they were genuinely kind-hearted boys and handled the situation incredibly well. We were thrilled to see Jordon enjoy what, to him, was a very rare glimpse of interaction with children of his own age.

They ran and played tag with him, which is one of the few games Jordon enjoys with other people and a favourite to this very day. The boys spent what must have been half an hour climbing on the frames and enjoying fun together.

For once, I was seeing Jordon playing alongside children with no special needs and the poignancy did not elude me, the difference between him and these other children of his own age was all the more pronounced. Seeing him in this unusual situation, we had a comparison shoved in our faces, while at the same time we could see his joy at being included. It hurt so much to see how far more advanced they were in their language and movement than Jordon. It was one of those moments in life when you do not know whether to laugh or cry, because what you are witnessing is so deeply affecting. We witnessed a bitter sweet and rare moment in his life, seeing him being accorded respect and consideration from other children who could easily have ignored or mocked him. When they went to go, we thanked them sincerely for being so good with him and for showing a maturity and generosity that many adults could well aspire to.

Leaving, I felt unexpectedly sad. Normally, we do not see Jordon's autism, we don't make comparisons or hold his development up against the example of other boys of his age. Instead, we rejoice in every achievement and are excited by every step he progresses, loving him profoundly for being who he is. Having seen him against a backdrop of boys his age, playing enthusiastically, we could not ignore how immense the distance is between him and other children.

Seeing him have fun, lost in his own personal heaven as he played, I felt the overwhelming pain of loss at what autism has deprived him of. Like a solitary meal to a starving man, we all felt the hunger of wishing this was his everyday diet. Lisa and I shared a look, but did not discuss what would only have brought forth a flood of tears; tears that are flowing as I write these words.

A loveable character

The heart can melt to an autistic child and while some children with the diagnosis can become unruly and violent when frustrated, it never stopped any one of the parents I know of from loving them.

With Jordon we have been especially fortunate. He seems to possess a quality in his personality that is at once loveable and warm hearted; he has an air of affability, a kind heartedness that makes it difficult not to love or at the very least, like him. While the greater part of who he is remains veiled by his autism, people warm to him still and he is one of those memorable personalities who, for some reason, you just cannot forget. I have noticed too, that whenever anyone who has met Jordon mentions him to me, they will begin to smile, for it is impossible to think of him without remembering those endearing qualities that his vulnerability only serves to emphasise.

Often, when I see people addressing autism, they omit one key point, that it doesn't obliterate the person who has been diagnosed and that person remains within. An autistic child is not defined by their diagnosis, they do not become their autism, rather the symptoms are something they struggle with every second of their lives. Autism doesn't change who they are, even though it damages their ability to relate to the world around them.

People with autism are exactly that, they are people, no different from us, burdened with a sometimes hellish journey that, if we pause to consider it, can reveal the true nature of what we share as human beings. Because the nature of the disorder creates so many behaviours that are strange to our experience, one of the realisations that autism offers us is that despite how the circumstances of our birth have shaped our lives and no matter how unusual we might appear, our differences can serve to highlight the common heritage and bond of humanity we all share.

Chapter Twelve - Family Fortunes

Every family has its ups and downs, pressures and strains that make life difficult, things which we find hard to cope with and would rather do without. Every parent knows that a newborn brings the potential for wrecked sleep, constant crying, pressure on the parents' relationship and stresses on siblings; how the whole family may be called upon to pull together, lest the weight fall upon one parent alone. All these things are known, but obviously with a newborn infant there is an end in sight. Each stage of their development is, in hindsight, relatively short-lived; they will grow and develop, learn language and all number of helpful habits that mean the whole family can see the fruits of their efforts, the discovery, progress, learning and joy.

It is not always so with an autistic child. Instead, the unusual demands of their upbringing mean that there is one central focus around which the entire family orbits. For many years, even decades, the pressure is unrelenting and without hope of change and this fact alone can serve to breed despair, anger and frustration. As a consequence, as the monotony of caring for an autistic child gradually seeps in, hope might die. Still having to supervise your twelve year old when they brush their teeth, for the ten thousandth time, not being able to trust anyone but a specially trained babysitter who the child will accept, sitting in a room you cannot leave while they lapse into their tenth tantrum of the week, not having the hope of an end, to see your child off making their own way in the world, not daring to allow yourself the hope of change for fear it might never happen and your dreams of your child developing being crushed by the awful minute by minute reality of their solitary road.

Even if the parents are working together and things aren't so bad because they are sharing the load, there still remains the constant stress of thinking ahead, of knowing things will only improve very slowly; that unless you follow a set routine, your child can become lost to anguish, to the extent that they self-harm, banging their heads against walls or even windows, punching their head so hard that they cause livid bruises. For, autistic children seem to instinctively know that the cause of their problems, their difficulty in relating to the world, lies somewhere in their brain, so they may bang their heads in times of frustration, seemingly targeting the root cause of their issue, the divided, obstructed, choked channel of communication.

The sad fact is that as unique and special as autistic children are, the demands they place on relationships can be immense. Even if your child develops and progresses well, it is usually the result of an intense focus on that one child, pouring love and care into them, often to the detriment of the parents' relationship.

Some surveys show that parents of autistic children have a divorce rate that is far higher than that of those who do not carry their burdens. Stress, anxiety, tiredness, lack of opportunities to socialise; all are exacerbated by the added demands and they each take their toll. For those single parents who shoulder the burden alone, it means they can sometimes remain in the company of their autistic child 24 hours a day, only getting breaks when the provision of care and education allows it. This, in turn, can restrict their ability to find a partner, for any person they share their life with must be willing to embrace the huge responsibility that comes with it.

Rarely in the early years and even today, do Brian and Lisa get the chance to be away from the children. It is so true when Lisa sometimes says, "our world is autism, it surrounds us. It is so very hard and yet that is all we know. Sometimes, I feel like I am drowning in autism."

Even if Lisa and Brian want to take a momentary break, it has to be planned meticulously, finding someone they can trust and who is qualified to look after Jordon and nowadays, Lauren, his sister, without the worry of fearing what might happen while they are away. Invariably, the only person they can truly trust is me, as I know Jordon and Lauren so well, but even the best of babysitting plans cannot be relied upon to be free of incidents and dramas.

"See you in a few days - don't burn the house down!"

When Jordon was around six years old, attending The Red Shirt School, Brian's Mum, Marj planned a special trip to give Lisa and Brian a break. It was a lovely gesture and in May 2003, when Arsenal were playing Southampton in the FA Cup Final at the Millennium Stadium in Cardiff, she arranged a weekend away for Lisa and Brian and her partner too, coinciding with the match.

The FA Cup Final is perhaps the most important match in the English football calendar. Neither Brian nor Lisa are huge football fans, but an event like this was a real treat, nonetheless. At the time, Brian and Lisa lived in South East London and the trip to Cardiff took around four hours. So, the plan was to make a weekend of it and was adjusted so everyone got the most out of it, meaning the men would go to the football match, while the girls would go shopping in Cardiff city centre; the best of both worlds for everyone.

The accommodation was booked, the route planned and arrangements made with me to stay at Lisa and Brian's home and look after my darling Jordon from Friday afternoon to Sunday morning. I was thrilled at the chance to spend some quality time with my grandson and really looking forward to the weekend. So, all of us were happy at the prospect of our respective short breaks away from home.

The day of the trip arrived, a Friday morning in May. My bags were packed for the weekend, the weather was fine and the sun was shining. I was soon in my car and travelling over to see Lisa and Brian, to pick up the keys and wave them farewell. Brian greeted me and carried my luggage upstairs and before they departed, Lisa passed me an exhaustive list of do's and don'ts for their home.

Lisa was, as usual, well prepared; the fridge was stocked with every imaginable food Jordon or I might wish for, alongside the long list of things to be mindful of, from ensuring the house was locked up at night and the windows shut when we went to bed, to what crisps Jordon liked to have (the ones that would melt in his mouth without chewing) and how many packs a day he was allowed! She left no instructions for cooking meals as she knew I was very well versed in catering for Jordon's culinary requirements and she also knew I could be trusted in the kitchen, or so we all thought!

They had dropped Jordon off in the morning and with the round trip to the school taking no more than forty minutes, I set to making dinner and getting everything ready for an evening with my grandson.

It turned out I was busier than I thought. My son, Gino, who lived locally, popped in to see me and we chatted over a cup of tea, while I prepared the dinner. Totally surprised to see him at the front door and distracted by this unexpected visit, I lost track of time and it was only when I glanced at my watch that I realised it was after half past two. I was due to pick up Jordon at 3pm and didn't want to be late.

Rushing to get ready, Gino and I were still talking away as we left the house and I drove off to the school. I knew the teachers would only release Jordon to either Lisa or me as a regular visitor, and they would be fine if I was just a few minutes late as this wouldn't be enough to make Jordon worry.

I was well on my way to the school when I was struck by the horrific realisation that I had left the dinner cooking on the hob. To make matters worse, the two dogs I owned at the time, Mindy and Gizmo were locked in the kitchen, asleep on a blanket and there was every chance that the pans would boil dry while I was out.

It was a complete dilemma. If I turned back, I would be unimaginably late for Jordon and every moment I delayed would mean he would become increasingly distraught. If I rescued the pans, he would surely be hysterical by the time I arrived and I would be burdening the school staff with an inconsolable boy. By the time I had thought it through, I was nearer to the school than home anyway so I decided to rush on and see if luck and the traffic were on my side. All the while, I was visualising the dinner going up in smoke.

Because I had rushed to the school, I arrived there a few minutes early. I waited at the main entrance, desperate to be buzzed in through the security door, then hurried to the receptionist, hastily explaining the circumstances and asking if they could find Jordon for me as quickly as possible. It all came out in a rush and quickly understanding my predicament, she dashed off to find Jordon in the assembly hall, where the school were having an end of day get-together.

Eventually, she reappeared with Jordon in tow, he was very good and taking it all in his stride, despite being slightly confused at being ushered out early.

By now, I was beside myself with worry, so we sped off and almost instantly hit a traffic jam, which meant that Jordon started to become agitated. But for once, I had found something that seemed to momentarily distract him from his own preoccupations and that was me! I was panicking! "Move! Move!" I shouted at the cars in front of me, all of them idling in the traffic jam. I don't think Jordon had ever seen me acting in this way, but then I had never set a house on fire with my dogs trapped in it before! My unusual behaviour was enough to keep him quiet. Every time we drew to a halt, I could feel the minutes ticking away and every moment longer the journey took I imagined smoke filling the kitchen. I was rocking in my car seat, gripping the wheel, pleading for the traffic to move. "Quick! Quick!"

Jordon didn't speak at that age, but the fact that he was quieter than usual suggested he knew something was not quite right. From initially worrying that the vegetables were boiling dry, I was now facing the very real fear that I could have started a fire in the kitchen where my dogs were trapped. I prayed I wasn't going to be greeted with flames when we returned.

Thankfully, when we arrived home, speeding to a halt at the kerb, there was no red glow coming from the house and no smoke pouring out of the windows, but for some reason the house burglar alarm bell was violently clanging away, adding to the drama. I knew it wasn't a fire alarm, but to this day we do not know what set it off.

Still with some trepidation, but greatly relieved, I ran with Jordon up the garden path and, gripping his hand tightly, I pushed the key into the lock and turned it.

Only the key did not turn in the lock, instead, it began to twist without the lock moving. I froze! The key was about to break in half and the dinner was still on the hob! I couldn't believe it and at that moment I could quite easily have screamed!

In my mind, I was fervently praying for the key not to break, it had bent in the lock and so, gingerly, I had to straighten it out before I firmly but gently tried to open the door. With my heart in my mouth and holding my breath, I tentatively tried again, gently jiggling the key, balancing my fear of becoming an inadvertent arsonist with the worry of irrevocably breaking the key and my concern that if I let go of Jordon's hand he would run off into the road.

Taking some deep breaths, I calmed myself down.

The lock slowly began to turn.

I could see the key bending, threatening to break at any second and all the while, the alarm bell was ringing in my ears.

A quarter turn.

I could feel the key giving in my hand.

A half turn and still I didn't know whether the door would open or whether the key would break.

"Calm, Carolann, calm!" I can't remember if I was talking to myself or merely repeating the words in my head, but either was possible.

I took another breath and put pressure on the key, "please turn! Don't break! Please turn!", I was begging the key to do its job and not to break in my hand.

The burglar alarm provided the perfect accompaniment to the panic I believe I was verging upon. All I could think was, "this can't be happening to me!", wondering how I could contact the fire brigade and whether any neighbours could help, I made one last attempt to turn the key.

Suddenly, the door gave way and opened. The relief that washed over me was indescribable, I had already been reconciling myself to explaining a burned-out kitchen and the huge guilt of two suffocated dogs.

I rushed Jordon inside, still holding his hand. I daren't shut the door behind me, so I left it slightly ajar, in case it would not open with a key jammed in the lock and we were trapped in a house that could well be on fire. Mindful that Jordon might run off, I took him quickly to the lounge and ensured he was sat on the sofa. "Stay there, Jordon!" I shouted over the sound of the alarm.

Trying to look two ways at once, I tried to keep an eye on Jordon, sat in the lounge, as I edged my way towards the kitchen, warily eyeing the blank face of the door in front of me. It looked completely normal, yet mindful of what might lie on the other side, reaching out my hand, I first tested the temperature of the door handle.

It was fairly cool to the touch and taking this as a good sign, I cautiously applied pressure and opened the door the merest crack. One inch, two inches and suddenly I was greeted by a wall of white smoke that filled the entire kitchen.

I couldn't see clearly because the smoke was so thick. Before me was a white impenetrable mist and from it, the shadowy forms of two frightened dogs came bounding, rushing past me and through the doorway, panting heavily as they emerged like animals escaping a forest fire. Looking quickly to see they were ok and that they weren't headed for the front door, I pushed my way past them, quickly turning off the incinerated vegetables and feeling my way, groping blindly to find the back door and open it.

Then I bounded back to the lounge to check Jordon was there still and called my dogs to me. Everyone was ok, although, for my part, I was just about ready to faint with relief.

The smoke in the kitchen cleared quite quickly and as the haze lifted, I could see that the dinner was ruined. However, I was merely thankful that the only damage was some incinerated vegetables and two very badly damaged pots and pans and that the kitchen had not caught fire!

Quite soon, I had things together, my heart wasn't pounding and I was calming down. Dreading making the call, I picked up the phone to call Lisa; the burglar alarm was still ringing and I needed to find out how to turn it off. Telling her the full story, there was silence the other end of the line, because the first thing she could hear was the alarm bell over my words. Quickly understanding and reassured by me, she gave me the code and I managed to silence the awful racket. Almost immediately afterwards, the police, alerted by the alarm, rang asking me if there was a problem, checking to see if I needed assistance or if there had been a burglary. Soon after that, the alarm company rang as the police had contacted them and I had exactly the same conversation as I had had with the police.

Eventually, after the calls were dealt with, I had a quiet, virtually smoke-free household. The only complication was having to cook Jordon's dinner from scratch and, the fact that we could not now leave the house for the weekend as I was afraid the key would break in the door!

A big clue as to the nature of autism, is that even though he had obviously noticed the difference in my behaviour because I had been verbalising and rushing around, since we had arrived in the house, all the while, unperturbed and not disturbed in the least, Jordon remained calmly sitting in the lounge, waiting for me to remove his coat and shoes. Although he had noticed the differences to his usual routine, none of this had made any real impact upon him and the fact that he would not react to such unusual circumstances shows just how strange he finds the everyday world. While some autistic children might react adversely, a room full of smoke and a continuous alarm bell had not upset Jordon. We later surmised this was because he had no idea what any of it meant to him anyway!

I later learned that the key I had been given was a new copy, made at the local locksmith especially for my visit. They had obviously used an inferior type of metal, for it had a fracture all the way across its width. Thank God it had not broken off completely or we would have had to call the fire brigade and smash a window to get in and then it could have been an entirely different scenario.

Despite all the drama, the weekend had happy endings all round. Jordon and I spent time together and as ever, we both enjoyed being in each other's company. All in all it was a lovely couple of days, despite being housebound and unable to take Jordon out for the walks I had planned. Two friends of mine, Helen and Jane visited and we got a chance to chat and catch up. Normality was restored.

Lisa and Brian had a lovely weekend too, despite nearly turning back on the way there with my frantic phone call, Arsenal had won 2-0 and they had both had the chance to relax.

To cap it all, I had succeeded in keeping my promise and not burning the house down, meaning I would get a chance to babysit again and I was very happy about that!

When I reflect on this entire episode, what sticks out the most for me is that this weekend is the one and only time that Lisa and Brian have been away together without their children since Jordon and Lauren were born, a total of 16 years. Autism places many restrictions on parents and Lisa and Brian are not alone in having virtually no time to themselves.

Chapter Thirteen - I'll Be There For You

Nowadays, Jordon has established himself as an affable and loving character who is always ready to please. While he is still entirely dependent upon those around him, he now has at last, a firm footing on his pathway and a very basic understanding of what is needed to function in the world. Despite all the challenges he has faced, he really has grown up into the most adorable young man.

Despite all this, taking Jordon to someone else's home can still create problems. Even at sixteen, we don't know for sure how Jordon will react nor how he will be received.

Even though Lisa and Brian receive many invitations to visit their friends, those who do not have autistic children of their own do not appreciate just how invasive it can be when they come to visit. People who do not have experience of autistic children might make an offer for them to play with their own offspring, not realising that in Jordon's case, unless there are exceptional circumstances, the likelihood of his socialising directly with other children is roughly zero with the exception that he does like playing tag and can occasionally be enticed into a game, but only if he is in the mood.

Trying to be helpful, friends might encourage Lisa and Brian to find a baby sitter, for people who have seen Lauren and Jordon at their very best may not anticipate any problems, but if they had seen them at their worst then they would understand why Lisa and Brian would only ever trust me to babysit.

For, what does the babysitter do when your child cannot accept the presence of a stranger in their home and begins hitting themselves with whatever is in their hands? What happens when they run and start banging their head against the wall? Lauren can attempt to do this on a daily basis and yet we can see it coming and nip it in the bud, stopping it or placing a cushion between her and the wall before it even happens.

What happens when the children in your babysitter's care constantly scream? And what happens when your babysitter has absolutely no idea why they won't go to bed, because in fact, they have missed one element of the required routine? Would you as a parent trust that babysitter to cope with hours of Lauren's crying? Can that babysitter handle it when Lauren is covered in blood from repetitively picking at her lip (something she is very likely to do)? What happens when her crying sets Jordon off and he becomes increasingly visibly agitated, screwing his face up, raising his hands to his own head, beginning to run around, disappearing into his bedroom, slamming the door and beyond their reach? Who would you trust to look after your children when this is quite easily a typical scenario?

On the other hand, if Lisa and Brian bring Lauren and Jordon with them to a friend's home, then they might both end up on tenterhooks. Lauren, left to her own devices, will happily charge around someone else's house and, when she arrives, no household item is safe, she will be slamming cupboard doors, smacking the front of your television, trying to push it over, shredding any paper household items, pulling cupboards over, ripping up any letters left on tables into neat strips, stretching up to flick light switches on and off, on and off, on and off, swinging and wrapping herself in the curtains and pulling the buttons off of your laptop. Lauren is the whirlwind that lands without warning, while Jordon will immediately seek to isolate himself, marching off to another room and seeming totally rude. Too much encouragement to join in and he will become unhappy and agitated, "No! No! No!" and if forced to stay in the same room with you, will sit looking downwards picking at his nails, distancing himself by withdrawing within. Even the most tolerant of people can have problems dealing with autistic children. With enough disruption to someone's home, especially those who are house-proud, it can soon become apparent that your visit creates stress in their lives.

Even once he is relatively settled, Jordon can quickly decide to leave. Lauren is another story because she can be distracted perhaps enticed into playing with our mobile phones. Yet if nothing in that friend's home is of interest to Jordon, then as soon as he feels he has had enough, he might stand up, get his shoes and head for the front door. Jordon used to do this a lot, but nowadays, through careful coaching, he does it less and yet this doesn't necessarily happen after hours of visiting, it can quite easily occur after the first five minutes! Then you have a verbal battle on your hands answering his constant assertions, "Time To Go Home Now! I Want To Play My Games! Time To Go Home Now, Mum!"

Despite this, Lisa and Brian are lucky enough to have a handful of friends who are understanding, accepting and will welcome the whole family into their homes. They don't mind when Lauren runs around and they understand that Lisa will keep a watchful eye, they aren't shocked by Jordon announcing he wants to leave and they accept Lauren and Jordon exactly the way they are.

We are so grateful to our friends, especially Sharon, Jennie, Lee, Carrie and Laura, they stand out amongst the many accepting people who welcome Lisa, Brian and their family with open arms. I can only imagine what life would be like for Lisa and Brian without these people and others I could name, who offer their support and are there when they are needed, for otherwise Lisa especially could easily feel very isolated. As other parents of autistic children know, friends like these are indispensable; they make life more bearable and we are so very grateful for their support. For any autistic parent, friends like these are definitely worth their weight in gold.

Computer networking

Even with many friends who were welcoming and knowing, especially in the earlier years, that it was important to take Jordon out, it could still be difficult. Yet, Lisa and Brian would take every opportunity to do so. Visiting other people's homes helped Jordon become used to different environments and introduced variety into his life. Still, the opportunities could be few and far between.

So, many years ago, when Jordon was around five years old, Lisa and Brian accepted an invitation to a friend's home. It was a very welcome break, catching up with old acquaintances while Lisa and Brian had a rare moment to relax as much as was possible, with one eye always on the lookout for Jordon. The day progressed and suddenly, in a gap in conversation, bemused, Lisa realised that Jordon wasn't in the room and she could no longer see him in the garden.

"Brian, where is he?!"

They were both instantly on high alert. If Jordon was not in sight, then this was not good news. Lisa and Brian did not know how secure this house was, or whether Jordon could get out through the front door and they leapt up out of their chairs, looking out on the street and then searching the house and garden. Jordon was gone and unsupervised, he could be doing anything, vulnerable and heading off to who knows where.

Panic gripping them both, they continued to search, but they could not find him. Brian quickly spoke to the other children in the house and it transpired they had seen Jordon head to the fence and climb over it into the neighbour's garden. From there, he had walked straight to the back door and into the next door neighbour's home.

Brian leapt over the fence, wondering how a five year old had made it over an obstacle that he himself found difficult. By now he was running and quickly made it to the neighbour's back door. There, he could see an elderly couple sitting watching television with the back door wide open. If Jordon made it through the neighbour's house and out onto the street, then there was no telling what could happen. He could easily get run over or lost.

Brian had to temper his natural haste, stepping through the door, his heart hammering in his chest. He tried to calm himself and, conscious that he had suddenly appeared out of their back garden, politely asked the still seated couple, "excuse me, we are visiting next door, you haven't by chance seen a young boy have you?"

The neighbours reacted as if this were the most natural occurrence in the world; quite commonplace! The husband, without batting an eyelid, held his hand aloft with his index finger straight as an arrow, glancing briefly at Brian and then back to the television so as not to break his concentration. He pointed directly upwards, "yes, he went upstairs" came the urbane reply.

They had obviously seen Jordon walk right past them, through their living room, out of the door and up their stairs without even moving once, as if it were an everyday occurrence.

Brian, slightly taken aback by their obvious nonchalance, but not pausing to consider as he was conducting a panicked search, ran up the stairs. There, to his great relief, he found Jordon, searching the rooms, obviously looking around for something. Taking him by the hand, Brian lead him back down the stairs, barely drawing a glance from the still-seated couple, who were staring fixedly at their television, briefly nodding in recognition and smiling as he thanked them profusely, but not taking their attention from the screen. An embarrassed Brian quickly made his exit with Jordon held tightly by the hand.

Brian took Jordon back out through the garden and passed him over the fence to a much-relieved Lisa. Between them, they soon worked out what had happened. Even at that age, Jordon loved computers and he had obviously decided to go in search of one. Having seen them kept upstairs in the homes of Brian and Lisa's friends, he assumed he might find one next door.

Much like the elderly neighbours who could barely tear their attention away from their television, even for a moment, Jordon is only interested in one thing - have you got a computer screen he can stare at?!

Bus stop embarrassment

Even the best of intentions when it comes to encounters with other people won't necessarily deliver friendly relationships. Even now he is much older, despite being very polite and well-mannered, Jordon's courteousness, when coupled with his distinct lack of understanding, can sometimes produce unfortunate results.

One day, quite recently, Lisa and I were walking along the pavement with Jordon and we were nearing a lady, who was probably in her fifties, waiting at a bus stop. We were about to walk past her, when Jordon, seeing this new person and ever mindful of the importance of politeness, walked straight up to her and, putting out his hand to shake hers, cheerfully said, "Hello Old Woman. My Name Is Jordon, What's Yours?"

The lady looked appropriately shocked and offended, so Lisa quickly stepped in, apologising and admonishing Jordon, quick to get to the root of the embarrassing situation "you mustn't call someone an 'old woman', Jordon, it's impolite."

Jordon quickly grasped the wrong point and having immediately misunderstood, he was quick to correct himself, "Hello Old <u>Lady</u>!"

The lady was clearly very taken aback and now looked definitely offended. Apologising profusely, we pulled Jordon along, cutting our losses as we beat a hasty retreat!

The power of words

The things we drum into Jordon have a tendency, once they are accepted by him, to stick. We also realised, quite early on, that whatever we said we were doing, we had to stick to that too. Our words had to match our deeds exactly and if we let him know we were going somewhere in the car, then we had to go there by car, there was no changing our minds.

If we had decided we were walking instead, this would be taken as yet another threat to his perception of reality and it was not therefore an option. It simply would not compute with him that we could say one thing and then subsequently do another. Today, he is far more flexible but still, any change of plan has to be carefully explained to him and he will then, quite likely, repeat the change over and over again to gain our reassurance that it is ok, "We Don't Need To Go In The Car. We Can Walk, Can't We Nan?" for repetition is one way he seeks to create stability and gain control over something that is troubling to his mind.

We are often asked about the level of Jordon's independence. The simple answer is that he remains totally dependent upon his parents for all the food he eats, for his clothes, for virtually every need and for every part of his life. So far, he has never even had to handle money, other than briefly when supervised at school visits to the shops. Here, they are introducing the idea of a transaction, but still this is all very new to Jordon and there is no way he can function in the world unaided.

Despite this, there are certain situations where Jordon is keen to prove he is grown up and mature. He does not like it when his sister cries and neither does he like it when she is admonished for her behaviour, for instance, when we tell her not to climb up onto the table, the backs of sofas or shelving units. We tell her firmly that she must not climb high up on furniture, for fear of hurting herself. Jordon, meanwhile, may step in, lifting her and placing her very gently back onto the floor, "It's OK Mum. I Am Here! I Will Look After My Little Sister! You Are Safe Now Woren."

Then Jordon will attempt to help his mum, informing her he is "Looking After My Sister". In Jordon's interpretation, this is merely referring to the fact that he is in charge of changing channels, ensuring her favourite children's cartoons and programmes are on the television.

Despite his quite limited input, Jordon is obviously very aware of the work that goes into caring for his little sister. When Lisa went to visit his school for a parents' evening earlier this year, his teacher gave her some of his written work. He is encouraged to write about the things he does at home and outside of the school and in one piece of well thought out writing, that he had obviously taken some time over, he had meticulously detailed in his school book how at home, he was the person responsible for looking after Lauren's needs; caring for her and in his own words, how he would, "Cook Dinner. Wash-Up. Look After My Little Sister Lauren."

Lisa looked at this aghast, taken aback by how Jordon had managed to construct a whole world in his mind where he did all these things. She then explained to the teacher that he did not engage in any of these activities.

What he actually did, in fact, was sit down and play his computer games and wait for his dinner to arrive in front of him while Lisa did all the cooking, serving and cleaning. It was a hilarious moment and we later laughed with Jordon over his imagined dedication to his non-existent domestic duties! He answered very truthfully that he was, "Only Joking Nan. Yes. Only Joking!"

Stubbornness

It is not unusual for any child to be strong willed or obstinate and one of the traits of autistic children is their apparent stubbornness. Jordon, especially when he was younger, would demonstrate a seemingly endless capacity for obstinate behaviour time and time again, resisting us whenever we tried to help, when we tried to persuade him to try something new, or attempted to show him a way of doing things that, to him, felt like interfering in his world.

However, Jordon's apparent obstinacy isn't him saying that he is right and we are wrong, or that his way is better. When Jordon sticks to his guns, when he will not be swayed, it is a manifestation of his fear of change, fear of anything new turning his world upside down. When he refuses to try something new, we are witnessing that same little boy who was born into a reality he has little hope of understanding, battling once more to bridge the vast gap between him and the outside world.

Introducing a new type of food is a good example, for Jordon can easily become very stuck in any eating pattern. When at school he was first offered the option of a cooked midday meal instead of his usual juice and a sandwich he started acting atrociously, waving his arms and flapping his hands, lapsing into making strange noises. This isn't rebellion, this is a classic example of Jordon becoming fearful and anxious, panic welling up inside him. How could we imagine that food could provoke such a severe reaction, that in presenting a hot meal at school, we might as well have been asking him to consume poison.

It isn't stubbornness that leads Jordon to say, "No Thank You I Am Fine!" to a new experience. In this particular case, it was that hot meals are a thing he associates with eating at home or in a restaurant. To him, the location and the meal are not separate, they are one thing, the venue and the food is inextricably linked in his mind. Eating a hot meal elsewhere is not a mere change of location, to Jordon, it is a totally new proposition.

Strangely perhaps, the exception to this is that Jordon will eat a cooked Christmas dinner at school. We have surmised that this is because for years he has seen us cook and eat this particular meal at home and the school version matches very closely what he is used to eating and perhaps the dinner is associated with the time of year rather than the location. To find the exact nature of how this particular association works would mean understanding the finest intricacies of how links are formed in Jordon's brain. Suffice to say that some of these connections are obvious, while others are as obscure as those in our own subconscious minds.

By way of example of how rigid his behaviour can become, when he was younger Lisa and I could see that he was becoming very stuck on certain types of food and we tried to introduce more variety into his diet.

One small example was ham sandwiches. At the time, if you offered Jordon any type of sandwich other than ham, he would refuse to eat it. Also, sandwiches would only be eaten at lunch time and he would eat them only at school during term time or at home during half term. There were no two ways about it, even the simplest or smallest change, such as adding mayonnaise or ketchup would trigger a complete refusal to eat that sandwich. This was not wilfulness, it was merely how his autism had enabled him to interpret the concept of a sandwich. A sandwich was only food if it was made with certain ingredients, a tiny amount of butter for instance, no more and no less. Also, sandwiches had to be prepared in a certain way and there was absolutely nothing you could do to persuade him otherwise. Later, he progressed and there had to be two sandwiches, each cut into four square pieces (triangles wouldn't do), making a total of eight pieces. Any less or any more and we would have a problem.

Still to this day, Jordon is reluctant to eat sandwiches that have not been prepared and presented in this way. He calls them his 'eight sandwiches' and I think of them as one small detail that shows just how inflexible the world of autism can be.

When Jordon first went to school, we planned to use the change as a catalyst to approach the intimidating task of adding more variety to his diet. He was then five years old and our first step was to try switching him from ham to cheese sandwiches. At that time, the only way Jordon could eat a sandwich was if Lisa cut it into tiny squares. Jordon would then flatten each square in his mouth and swallow it whole, for this was still a time when he could not chew.

On our first attempt, we tried the obvious option of packing him off to school with a cheese sandwich cut into tiny pieces, alongside the usual melt in the mouth crisps and the juice that he had every day. This first attempt at a dietary change met with the predictable response and the cheese sandwich came back uneaten, still tucked away in his lunch box, completely untouched. There was no way that Jordon would eat it. He had dutifully eaten the crisps and taken his drink, but the sandwich might as well have been a piece of wood. We couldn't allow him to go hungry at school, so we only attempted this on a few occasions and let the school know in advance that we were doing so. They were very good and worked with us on it, but to no avail. In fact, on one memorable occasion, a dinner lady who sat with Jordon every day finally persuaded him to try a very small amount of cheese sandwich, but this was as far as we got. If we tried to introduce a cheese sandwich into his diet at home, the same applied, he would simply refuse it, put it on his plate and he would ignore it. We realised that this tiny issue was becoming monumental in our lives, but it was so important that we gave him more variety in his diet.

To put all this striving in perspective and to help explain the nature of the problem, I have to explain that Jordon actually loved cheese. This can come as quite a shock to people who have no experience of autism, but it shows just how programmed autistic children can become. Jordon would happily eat cheese by itself, rolling grated pieces of it around in his mouth, enjoying it very much and in later years he even allowed us to sprinkle it on spaghetti bolognese, but when we were trying to introduce cheese as a sandwich filling, Jordon had it firmly fixed that sandwiches were always filled with ham, not cheese or jam or any other filling.

Eventually, however, we did win through. Gradually, we tried adding small amounts of cheese to his ham sandwiches and showing a lot of patience until eventually the cheese sandwiches were finally accepted. However, even today, we have to warn him in advance that it is "cheese sandwiches today Jordon!" and even then, "No!! Ham!" will come the predictable reply.

We gently repeat, "cheese today Jordon. It is good for you to have cheese."

He will consider this briefly, "OK. I Have Cheese Today. Ham Tomorrow!" for knowing that things will return to 'normal' helps him to deal with the change.

At home, we have now been able to persuade him to eat chicken and even sausage sandwiches, but not at school, we have not got there yet! Always, accompanying the school sandwiches will be exactly the same crisps and juice he has taken to school for his whole life. Some things are a step too far for Jordon. Yet, if we had not persevered with introducing cheese, then he would be eating his lunchtime ham sandwiches at school and at home for the rest of his life.

At school he has also very recently progressed to eating a cooked meal on Fridays. It is a fixed item in the scheduled menu, served to all the children every Friday. He accepts this because it is the same every time and it helps that it is a meal he loves. We have also on one occasion managed to get him to accept one meal cooked at school on a Thursday. We encouraged him by telling him that, now he is a man, he can eat cooked meals at school, but this still remains something he is very resistant to and he still very much prefers his beloved ham sandwich!

While Jordon, like any sixteen year old, wants to grow up and be an adult, inside of him dwells the little boy who sees each and every change as a threat. Changing his sandwich filling troubles him, because it disrupts his whole world and has far wider ramifications, disturbing him at some deep level where even he cannot understand why.

Not all of Jordon's actions are born from his autism. Homework is perhaps one area where he displays true stubbornness! If his mind is completely set against it and Lisa insists he sit down and answer his homework questions, Jordon has been known to write the same answer against each one. Then, despite him knowing the answers, we see a whole page with the word "No" scrawled again and again, Jordon's attempt to assert his will. Obviously, we don't show Jordon that we find this quite funny, but the temptation is there!

Living on the ceiling

One thing you learn that is common to every autistic child is their need for constant supervision. Most parents of autistic children develop the kind of watchfulness that is normally reserved for young babies or toddlers, a sixth sense as to when a sudden lack of noise means there is mischief being made or their child's behaviour warns them of impending trouble. Yet, even the most vigilant of parents can be caught off guard.

One such instance was when Brian had to go up into the loft to look for some household items he had stored there. By now, Jordon was thirteen years old and Brian had been in the loft many times before without incident; Jordon would always completely ignore him, not inquisitive in the slightest. As usual, Brian had pulled down the ladder and gone up into the loft space, however on this occasion, things did not go to plan. Brian was by now kneeling on some boards in the loft, being very careful to place his weight on the rafters and avoiding the gaps in between, knowing that if he stood directly on the ceiling he would, in all likelihood fall through it. While searching out what he was looking for, Brian suddenly heard a noise behind him.

Turning round, for a moment, Brian couldn't comprehend what he was seeing, but when it sunk in, the blood drained from his face. There, stood behind him, a dark silhouette in the dim light in the loft, looking over Brian's shoulder, was Jordon.

This, in itself, was shock enough for Brian as he had never before had to even consider that Jordon might climb the ladder; he didn't even know that Jordon could. What was causing Brian's heart to race was that he was standing squarely on the gaps between the rafters. Jordon is tall and heavy and was standing with his full weight on the plaster boards; he could have disappeared through the ceiling at any moment and if he fell, he would have gone crashing on to the bannister rail and then down the stairwell below.

Brian's heart was in his mouth and conscious not to startle Jordon into making any sudden movements, he stuttered out a warning "Jordon what are you doing here? Get off the ceiling."

But Jordon had no comprehension whatsoever of the danger he was in, that he was one step away from crashing through the ceiling and bringing it down with him. He froze at Brian's reaction, but remained stock still, not knowing that the ceiling would not bear his weight for long. "I Want To See."

"Jordon, quick! Stand on the wood! Jordon! Stand there! Stand there!" Brian was becoming frantic. The ceiling was actually bowing under Jordon's weight, a bulge appearing and Jordon was seconds from serious injury. Jordon didn't move. "I Want To See Dad."

Brian reached out, gently but urgently coaxing Jordon to put his feet onto the rafters. "I Just Want to See." Still oblivious as to why, Jordon put his feet where he was told and Brian breathed a sigh of relief, allowing himself to calm down and trying not to think about what could have happened seconds before.

The next step was to get Jordon out of the loft and Brian quietly guided him back on to the ladder, which up until that point, none of us suspected he could or would climb.

According to Lisa, Brian's face had been a picture, as he shakily returned Jordon to the safety of the carpeted floor below via the ladder, rather than the more direct route he nearly ended up taking!

Even then, Jordon could not understand why Brian was so agitated. Jordon had remained calm throughout. However, he did not want his father to feel bad.

"I'm Sorry Dad. I Won't Go Up In The Loft Again"

Brian was very glad to hear it!

Just a mouthful please

Dental health has always been a potential problem with Jordon and we are always careful to keep his regular check-up appointments with the dentist to make sure all is well. Yet, today at sixteen years old, if we leave him to his own devices, he will still quite happily swallow the toothpaste when he cleans his teeth.

When Jordon was around ten or eleven years old we went on a trip to the dentist, who was very pleased with the state of his teeth. At the end of his appointment, everything had gone very well and congratulating Jordon on keeping up his dental regimen, the dental nurse gave him the customary cup of mouthwash. Lisa knew she had to talk Jordon through how to rinse his mouth, just as she did every time he cleaned his teeth at home.

"Step one, Jordon. Rinse it round your mouth. Don't swallow!" Jordon followed Lisa's instructions.

"Step two, Jordon. Carry on rinsing. Don't swallow!" Jordon followed Lisa's instructions

"Step three. Now spit it out, Jordon. Into the bowl." Jordon followed Lisa's instructions, but sadly, not heeding her injunction to aim for the bowl. Being attentive to do as he was told, he very carefully, calmly and deliberately turned to the nurse and spat a large mouthful of mouthwash all over her, right down the front of her uniform.

Not knowing he was doing anything wrong, Jordon's face remained impassive, as if this was the most natural thing in the world for him to do. At the same time, Lisa's shock vied with her embarrassment.

Of course, this was a specially trained nurse and she took it in her stride, cleaning off her uniform as Lisa apologised and explained to Jordon that he should have spat into the bowl. "Jordon! You spit into the bowl, not on the nurse!"

Jordon quickly understood and with a breezy "OK, Mum!" and a completely empty mouth, mimicked spitting into the bowl, the matter, to his mind, completely dealt with. Lisa, aghast at the situation, returned the nurse's bemused gaze.

What could she say when the look on her face said it all "oh for goodness' sake!"

Take it or leave it

Understanding how his actions affect others is always an issue with Jordon and although he has shown much improvement, he still has many things to learn. He remains unable to appreciate that he cannot take whatever he likes from wherever or whoever he likes.

From an early age, he used to return home with objects from school, which we would then have to dutifully return. It was never the value of the object that influenced him, but whether he liked it or not and anything he liked was in danger of accompanying him home.

When he was eight years old and attending The First White Shirt School, Jordon was playing an Egyptian character. He loved dressing up in the costume, which consisted of a bed sheet, a staff and an elaborate headdress. One afternoon when he returned home from rehearsals, Lisa found Jordon playing with his bed sheet from the play and it took a while to convince him to part with it. Jordon was very eager to take part in the play and Lisa finally got the sheet from him by explaining that he could not take part in the play if he kept it at home. Taking the sheet without his cooperation would have caused a problem, so she knew she had to persuade him to return it of his own free will.

Not long thereafter, Jordon managed to greet Lisa at the gates of the school with a toy laptop hugged to his chest. We had a budding kleptomaniac on our hands!

Even now that we have explained to Jordon that he mustn't bring back things he likes that are school property, Lisa finds that he regularly returns from school with objects in his pockets which he has found in the school garden. She will typically find his clothes smeared with mud and twigs, string, bits of netting, stones, all covered with earth, jammed into his pockets or left in his bedroom drawers for her to find. Lisa and I have discussed this on more than one occasion because at first it seemed like quite strange behaviour, but everything Jordon does ultimately has a sound reason behind it. In this case, while we cannot be sure, we suspect this is his way of acting out scenes from his favourite video games, where the heroes collect special items to complete their challenges. Knowing this, when you do his washing and a handful of mud falls out of every pocket, you have no option but to laugh!

Jordon, as an autistic child, does not steal, he merely does not recognise the principle of ownership and whenever he finds something he wants, Jordon is the hero, collecting what he needs to win!

Sandwich break

To understand the way the mind that copes with autism works, we are called upon to break through a barrier of understanding.

Relating to one another's feelings is perhaps one of the deepest ways we can bond as human beings. It opens us to a level of interaction that helps us to truly share our experiences and create more from otherwise solitary lives. For what is deeper than our feelings? Sadly, an autistic child does not understand their own feelings, let alone relate to someone else's and so, this doorway rarely opens.

For this reason, most autistic children often prefer their own company, seeing us as an intrusion into their world. This sad fact alone can leave their parents feeling distanced, lonely and helpless. Even now, if left to his own devices, if we did not encourage him to socialise and put him into new situations, I can well imagine Jordon spending a whole day playing computer games in his bedroom, only leaving to go the bathroom or eat and remaining blissfully happy doing so.

But, of course, we cannot allow this kind of reclusive behaviour to become a habit and Lisa ensures she has established patterns that demand interaction. She makes sure Jordon is exposed to conversation and other people and that there is order in his life; every meal is a family affair and even snacks have to be eaten at the table. This rule is so set in Jordon's mind that it too is now a behaviour he will not break. I know this because recently I was looking after him while Lisa and Brian were out and I absent-mindedly brought Jordon a ham sandwich, cut into the customary eight pieces, while he was playing a computer game. Jordon immediately berated me, "Nan, I Don't Eat Sandwiches Here. I Eat At The Table!" He was obviously very concerned and becoming disturbed at this break from the usual pattern and so I had to apologise in case he became agitated. He was not fully reassured until I had promised several times that I would only bring him food at the table in future and then it was his turn to repeat the phrase that means he accepts the situation as it is. "That's Alright Nan! It's OK! I Forgive You!"

When you understand the extent to which the outward signs are at odds with what is going on inside Jordon, it could make you cry. From the outside, we see a boy becoming unnecessarily agitated and perhaps even disruptive because we gave him a sandwich. We could easily conclude that he is being rude, wilful and even aggressive, for no reason other than perhaps his own picky nature. Then we could take it that he is offering us forgiveness in some vaguely patronising way for our imagined mistake, when we are making the effort to bring him a meal.

In fact, a sandwich being brought to the wrong place can actually cause Jordon to feel anxious. To him it is a sign that the world is changing in some strange way that he doesn't understand and what he needs most at that point is comfort and reassurance. When he says things are "Ok!", it is a way of reassuring himself that things are 'normal' and whatever is going on at the time is not a threat. Recognising this, I wanted to hug my darling grandson to show how much I loved him and all I could say was, "thank you Jordon", to which he once more replied with his usual "That's OK, Nan!"

On this occasion, knowing that the sandwich should be eaten at the table, he immediately stood up and walked to the dining room table where he sat awaiting his sandwich. Yet, even though he had moved to the correct place, he had left the sandwich where he had been sitting. Jordon saw absolutely nothing unusual in doing this. He knew food was eaten at the table, yet he never brought his own food to the table and simply did not realise he should bring the sandwich with him. This is one of the confounding aspects of autism; with all the progress we have made, with all the hurdles we have cleared, still Jordon cannot make what to us would be the simplest of connections. Yet, if I had asked him to go and get his sandwich at that point and eat it at the table, I am sure he would have happily complied, not seeing anything unusual about the whole situation.

Sometimes, it can take something as simple as a sandwich to help us appreciate the way in which autism works to impose incredible limitations upon the child.

Party games

Throughout Jordon's childhood, we have all been very reluctant to place the responsibility of his care on anyone else and so we ensured we were always there at birthday parties he was invited to. We would keep our distance so that he wasn't over-protected, or to give the impression we were intruding, but we had to be there because at a moment's notice, Jordon would run off without giving any hint of warning; other parents or carers could not be expected to realise just how prone he was to doing this and so we never took the chance.

But despite the presence of his ever-watchful guardians Jordon loves parties, especially his own birthday. The prospect of the presents and especially the computer games he will receive as gifts excites him no end. So, we always take the opportunity to alert him to the impending day around a month in advance. Having been through so much to ensure he develops to the stage he has now reached, I cannot tell you just how special it feels when he is able to tell me what he is looking forward to and what computer games he wants to receive.

When I ask him what he wants for his birthday, he will adopt a very deep, serious tone and begin rattling off the names of computer games, sometimes long and complicated ones that I rarely understand, nor know what to ask for when I go shopping. So, Lisa and I collaborate; working between us to ensure we get the right games for him to play with and to make every birthday special.

As his writing has improved, he has taken to compiling a 'Christmas list' of computer games he really wants and the games on that list might be bought for Christmas or his birthday. Yet, once a game has been bought, he will not play it until he has taken time to study every detail of the box and the accompanying instructions. Sometimes he will spend the whole morning doing this and it is only when he is ready that he will decide to play it. Once he does and the game is switched on, then he will totally absorb himself in his gaming world.

When I visit and enter Jordon's bedroom, I am amazed to see how tidy everything is; all his computer games are lined up in alphabetical order in neat, orderly rows on shelves in his bedroom and not one of them is a hairsbreadth out of place. In fact, the actual boxes never leave the shelves and because they are all he ever wants as gifts, he had amassed a very large collection.

Around three years ago, Lisa called me. She was desperate to get rid of at least some of the video games that Jordon was collecting. There were simply too many, they were taking over his bedroom and she was running out of space. Jordon had far more than he needed and we found it impossible to persuade him to contemplate trading them in at the local games store. Instead, every new game we bought merely added to the collection.

We suggested to him that he trade his older games in for cash and replace them with a fewer number of new games, so that all of us had the best of both worlds. Jordon was adamant that he would not do this, nor let any of his precious games go and Lisa was at her wits' end. For every time she approached the subject, the answer was the same, Jordon waving his hand frantically and saying "No Thank You! No Thank You! I'm Fine!"

The deadlock continued, with the number of games growing and the space decreasing and Jordon denying any hope of change. Thankfully, our answer came when a brand new computer games console was released that Jordon was desperate to get hold of. Now we had a new bargaining chip and were finally able to persuade him that a trade-in was a great idea.

After a period of very thoughtful deliberation, Jordon chose which games he would exchange. If we hadn't allowed him to make this choice himself, taking the games from him without permission would have caused all sorts of problems. Just a single lost computer game would have caused Jordon to become distraught and so it had to be his choice.

To most of us, our personal space is important. To an autistic child, the physical layout of their bedroom can be as familiar as their own thoughts, as familiar as the presence of their own limbs. If an element is suddenly removed, they may not have any concept of the ramifications and there is a very real danger of disturbing a very intimate equilibrium. The removal or change of Jordon's personal space could be as horrifying and shocking as waking up one morning to find some of your teeth missing, inexplicably removed.

So, when we were able to progress to the point where Jordon felt he would get something back in return for his video games, for him to grasp the concept not only of a future reward for a current sacrifice, but also to gain the ability to let go of something so close to his psyche felt as if we were all entering new and unexplored territory.

Chapter Fourteen - A Mother's Fear of the Future - From Lisa's Perspective

Speaking as the mother of an autistic child, it's not like autism ever goes away, it just changes in the way it manifests as Jordon gets older. Issues that most children have overcome by the time they are toddlers are still plaguing the autistic parent, many years later and perhaps for the rest of their lives and it isn't coping with today that is the most difficult part, it is facing the future, for it is so unknown, so unpredictable.

Autism has touched us, but it has not changed who we are as people, instead it has helped us to look at life in a different way. It has made us stronger and more determined to help our children succeed in whatever way they are able.

Brian and I are very much aware that our experience of parenthood is different to many people's and even though we feel life has been tough, we are very grateful to have two healthy beautiful children. We also know that life is tougher still for many parents, whether their children are autistic or face different problems.

Some people have said to me "I bet you wouldn't change your children for the world". I have to disagree; for if I was given the chance, I would take the autism away from them both. They are beautiful souls within and it is only the autism that stands in the way of my reaching my children.

One of the main concerns that nags at me almost daily is wondering what will happen to Jordon and Lauren after Brian and I can no longer help them, when we are too old or have died. I am sure I am not alone in this worry, not knowing how much help we can get for Lauren and Jordon not only now, but in the future, makes my life one of uncertainty. For this reason alone, if I could remove the disorder from their lives, I most definitely would.

The saddest thing in my life is not that my children have suffered the consequences of autism for all of their short lives but that there is no medical answer for one of the questions autism poses. That question is, "how may my children live happy, fulfilling and independent lives?" In the absence of any answer, what we are left with is the pathway laid out for Jordon and Lauren on the days of their birth and for us all to carry on.

Yes chef!

We have always done everything in our power to secure Jordon the education he needs to gain whatever independence he is capable of. Gradually, working with his schools, we have at least sought the prospect of self-sufficiency, for his teachers are always seeking the best for the children in their care.

While we now realise that achieving full independence would be a miracle in Jordon's case, that has merely made us all the more determined to do what we can to help him fend for himself. One of the ways his schools have helped is by teaching cookery and since the age of seven, Jordon has always had some kind of regular cookery class. This means we have seen a fairly regular flow of home-made food being brought through the door and while we knew Jordon's hand had been in the making of the flapjacks, chocolate rice cakes, biscuits, scones and fairy cakes that arrived, he received a lot of help from his teachers. While Jordon showed absolutely no interest in the food he cooked, still, we encouraged him as much as we could by 'enjoying' the fruits of his labours and showing him that he was being useful. So, we would often be munching away at what was actually quite unappetising fare, demonstrably 'enjoying' dishes that were not very nice at all, in the hope of encouraging Jordon in his efforts. All the while, he would ignore us to the extent that we seemingly need not have bothered. There he was cooking food he would never eat and there we were, eating food we didn't want to, to impress a little boy who didn't care!

Today, Jordon has progressed to more complicated dishes and is now able to present us, (with a lot of help and assistance from his teachers) with a limited repertoire of main meals, such as spaghetti bolognese and tuna and pasta bake. Jordon doesn't mind cooking these dishes, but still will not eat anything he makes himself. I can't blame him!

There are, however, two exceptions; he most definitely will eat his own hand-cooked pizza, which he loves and any type of fried food. A typical young man!

Music to calm the troubled mind

After some searching, at the age of twelve, we had found a new school for Jordon, which we called The Second White Shirt School, which he still attends to this very day.

With this new school came a change of routine; he was now boarding a school bus every morning and returning in the same bus every afternoon. The journey from our home to the school was quite a few miles, involving lots of stops to pick up the children on the way into school and to drop them off one-by-one at the end of the school day. Jordon was the first to be picked up in the morning and the last to be dropped off in the evening and in all, it took over an hour door to door.

Each time he travelled on the bus, he would sit in the same seat, at the back in the corner and get very upset if someone sat in his place. Never once did he turn to wave goodbye to me when the bus departed; he would leave me smiling and waving at him from the pavement, his eyes facing forwards, for as far as he was concerned, by entering the bus he was now in a different realm, where only the carers and the bus driver were relevant.

Jordon was, by now, a lot more used to journeying by road, but there was one big difference between the car and the bus. In the car he played with his expensive hand-held games console to distract himself, but Brian and I would not risk him taking it on board the bus, where he was very likely to lose it or leave it behind. So he took the journey without a game to distract him and our ruling had an unfortunate and unpredicted side effect.

Because Jordon now had nothing to occupy his hands, he instead began to pick and worry at his fingernails, picking off the surrounding skin until they bled, sometimes so profusely that after two hours of this treatment on the journey there and back, he would return with bloody vertical stripes down his shirt where he had meticulously wiped his fingers, each stripe a testament to his inability to cope with the unoccupied hours.

We obviously had to deal with this behaviour, it couldn't be left as it was. The first step I took was to discuss it with mum, to see if she had any ideas. We agreed she would talk to him about his behaviour, as he was a little more likely to listen to his nan than me. So, she took him aside and let him know that it concerned her and in turn, he reduced the behaviour slightly in an effort to please us all. But this alone was not enough to stop the problem and we were regularly confronted with a blood stained Jordon returning from a day at school. So, we took further measures and bought Jordon an inexpensive music player to occupy his mind on the long daily journeys. The music helped him to block out the world and also as he was able to transfer music from the computer to his music player, it gave him control and allowed him to plan something positive for each journey.

The solution worked and we were thrilled that we had found a way around this problem, but an added complication was that Jordon would regularly lose or break his earphones, causing himself distress and so Brian was a regular purchaser of new earphones for the sake of Jordon's health and our sanity - which meant no more stripes on his shirt and less washing for me too!

The play's the thing

Entertainment isn't merely a passive pastime in Jordon's life. Last year in December, I found myself sat once more in the large assembly hall of Jordon's Second White Shirt School. It was nearly Christmas and there was a light-hearted atmosphere in the packed room. Mum was beside me and all around us the many parents, each of whom had a son or daughter on the stage. The children, all of them with severe, profound and complex needs were all taking part in the annual nativity play.

What struck me at the time, and always has, is just how dedicated and hard-working the staff are. Several of them were standing around the stage, their reassuring hands on the shoulders of the younger children, holding the hands of those who might otherwise throw themselves on the floor or run off, ready to usher the next child on or to prompt them with their lines. The attention they gave the children, their focus and caring attitude revealed what a vocation this is and showed the debt of gratitude owed to the people who choose to spend their lives teaching and helping children with special needs.

The play was fantastic and the amount of hard work and effort that had been put into the production by both the staff and children, despite the many challenges they face, was very clear to see.

Those in wheelchairs were pushed onto the stage to say their lines and many would call out to their parents, "HELLO MUM! HELLO DAD!" while others would not speak at all. In Jordon's case, he does not like singing, but he will happily leap around showing us his dance moves and so that was what he did. We were awash with pride watching him and all the other children take on their roles so beautifully, remembering all their lines and showing what they were capable of. Jordon and the rest of his class came on stage and did their dance routine so wonderfully. For all of the three minutes they were on stage they managed to be funny and heart-warming at the same time and there were more than a few tears in the audience.

Looking around, I was inspired at the sight of so many proud parents, so many dedicated staff and the amazing children all trying so hard, despite the difficulties they face every day of their lives. It also struck home that as the parent of an autistic child, you are never truly alone. Sitting in that hall reminded me that there are very many parents out there with children who have special needs; far more than you might suspect.

This whole scene brought to me the thought that no matter what life throws at us, it is our ability to love one another and to act upon it that is the lasting legacy of the human spirit. The true sign that we are human beings, more than our advances in learning, more than our potential to achieve, more than our ability to look into the vast reaches of space, is our capacity to love, for this brings forth our indomitable will to persevere no matter what and to do so not for ourselves but for those we hold dear.

Two of a kind

While Jordon and Lauren are both on the autistic spectrum, their behaviour can be similar yet still differ in many important ways.

One thing I learned that is common to them both is that if I drive or walk the same route to a place more than once, both children will form an association in their mind and it becomes a set routine they will not allow to change. So nowadays, I walk Lauren to school via three or four different routes to keep her flexible and open to new experiences.

Yet, there are many differences between how Lauren and Jordon's autism manifests, idiosyncrasies that mean that what worked for Jordon does not necessarily work for Lauren. A perfect example is the choice of footwear. If I allow Lauren to wear the same footwear on any particular trip, then she may refuse to allow any other type in future. With Jordon, this was never a problem, but it is definitely an issue to look out for if you have an autistic child.

Footwear is not the only type of clothing that can cause potential problems. Many autistic children do not understand the need to change their clothes or even to wear clothing at all and this can cause lots of challenges when it comes to dressing them to go out. Jordon, in particular, does not like being too warm and, if we are not careful, will quickly throw off warm jackets and jumpers in even the harshest of winters. Perhaps one of the most extreme examples of his love of freedom came when Jordon was around ten years old. We were visiting a children's indoor play centre. Jordon was delighted when we encouraged him to play in the ball pond and he quickly disappeared into the pit of brightly coloured spheres.

Playing happily, it wasn't long before he reappeared. Unfortunately for us, he had got hot with all his playing and quite logically had taken steps to cool down. So, when he did emerge, his top half was bare, his feet were bare, his legs were bare, but thankfully his boxer shorts remained and our task was merely to find his clothes, rather than chase a naked boy around the centre.

The daily trials of autism include much more than just dealing with the emotional traumas. Autistic children can take years to learn even the most basic of behaviours. In Jordon's case, this meant that he was seven years old before he learned to use a toilet and Lauren is still to learn this too. Progress in this area with Jordon was slow. Yet, thankfully, eventually we were able to firstly train him to stand up to use the toilet urinating and then gradually, by the time he was seven years old, finally to get him out of nappies. So, even if it is taking years to toilet train your child, perseverance is key.

One trait Lauren and Jordon do have in common is that which Jordon perfected in his early years. Without any prompting, Lauren can spend days in seeming misery, lapsing from audible grizzling into long-winded tantrums; crying and sometimes attempting to scream the house down. I do sometimes wonder how we are able to withstand the effects of these episodes, which are frequent occurrences in our lives. The fact that we can cope with this behaviour is more to do with the fact that we have to than a testament to our forbearance. Personally, I think my children's behaviour would sometimes test the patience of any supposed saint. I have seen friends try and smile their way through one of Lauren's tantrums, but after the first 15 minutes or so, the smiles tend to freeze on their faces and a hint of disbelief at the intensity and duration begins to creep in.

At times, firstly Jordon's and now Lauren's meltdowns have driven the whole family to distraction. Perhaps ironically, nowadays even Jordon finds it very difficult to cope with Lauren's outbursts, for, while he is in many ways locked up in his own little world, Lauren's screaming can sometimes be, in my opinion, shrill enough to break glass.

The length and severity of Lauren's outbursts has even goaded Jordon into taking action and the first time I saw him step in, it looked so incredibly funny. There we all were, having pretty much given up on our attempts at consoling Lauren and watching her run around, her face red and tear-streaked, screaming out loud. Then, Jordon stepped up to her and lifted her clean off her feet. It looked like he was handling hazardous waste, as his arms remained straight as he held her screaming form as far from his body as he possibly could. Then he promptly marched out of the back door and carried her to the bottom of the garden, calling out, "Don't Worry Woren, You Will Be Safe Here" where he deposited her as far away from the house as possible. Even Jordon obviously has his limits and he had cracked under the pressure, wanting to get his little sister completely out of earshot.

Surprisingly enough, his effort to reject Lauren had an unforeseen effect. As Jordon strode back up to the house, Lauren came running up the garden after him, her face still crimson from crying but now wreathed in smiles. She absolutely loved the sensation of being carried in that way and returned for more of the same from Jordon.

Pretty bubbles in the air

That isn't the only time Jordon has made an attempt to address Lauren's horrific tantrums.

Quite recently, Lauren was on a marathon screaming session, slowly driving Jordon and I to distraction. In desperation, I turned to Jordon who, if anyone has, possesses a unique insight into autism. "Jordon, what can I do to stop Lauren screaming. Can you help me please?"

Surprisingly, Jordon's response was, "No Problem Mum!" and he disappeared upstairs.

Several minutes later, I could hear Jordon as he carefully returned downstairs, saying, "It's OK Woren. It's Alright. I Know. You Will Be Happy Now!" and he appeared in the room clutching a bubble blowing machine I had recently bought in an attempt to distract Lauren during her bath times. In fact, I had only the day before filled the machine with liquid so it was at its full capacity.

Jordon promptly switched the machine on and the first enormous, multi-coloured bubbles started to appear. It wasn't long before the entire lounge was full of oversized rainbow globes of soap, filling the air and painting it with colour.

Now, here I have to let you know one thing about me. I am immensely house proud. It's not something I talk about, but partly because both my children have been apt to lick or even chew everything in sight, mum says she has met few people who are at such pains to keep their home so clean and tidy. You have to appreciate this if you are to imagine the look on my face when the inevitable happened.

The bubbles, as bubbles do, began to land, to collide with furniture, to burst on the ceiling to alight on the sofa and while to the casual observer, it might look as though each one promptly disappeared, the fluid of which they were made wasn't disappearing; it was leaving distinct marks wherever they landed and broke.

So, one by one, my lounge became a patterned landscape of round bubble marks, and these were not small bubbles. The machine was churning out some that were bigger than your head and leaving soapy stains that multiplied until absolutely everything was mottled with the streaky marks.

All the while, however, the machine had worked, stopping Lauren mid-scream until she quietened down and stood transfixed at the bubble filled room; and so I was loath to switch the bubble machine off, in the faint hope that the effect would be lasting. However, after several minutes of blissful bubble-filled peace, eventually the machine ran out of liquid and the moment the bubbles ceased to appear, Lauren began to sniffle, then cry and then build once more into her frequent pastime of constant screaming.

Knowing I had a good few hours of cleaning now ahead of me, but mindful of Jordon's good intentions, I was anxious to show him that his efforts to help were appreciated. I did the only thing I could and thanked him profusely for the few minutes respite we had gained. "Thank you Jordon. Thank you for helping mum."

Jordon was by now sat in his favourite chair, playing on his computer, completely oblivious to the work that lay ahead of me and quite clearly very satisfied with his efforts. He was basking in the glory of a job well done and breezily replied, "No Problem Mum. I Help Woren" and no one could deny that he had!

The Bubble machine has now disappeared and I cannot deny that my hand and the dustbin were somehow involved; Jordon now copes with Lauren's tantrums in a very pragmatic way; jamming his headphones in his ears and turning them to a high enough volume that not only can he no longer hear Lauren but it is impossible to attract his attention without tapping him on the shoulder!

Chapter Fifteen - Stranger in a Strange Land

One thing I have learned about my grandchildren is that, despite sharing the same diagnosis, while many of their behaviours are similar, in other ways they vary greatly. This is not mere blind chance or coincidence. In fact, I believe there is a very important difference between Lauren and Jordon.

I think of it like this. In Lauren's case, she is in our world, present in the same reality, but her autism walls her off within it. She has the same barriers as Jordon, but she is thrust further forward amongst us. Jordon stands in the shadow of autism, behind an invisible line, while Lauren's feet are squarely across that line, standing amongst us, questioning what we do, while Jordon at her age would have accepted everything we did that didn't involve him directly. Lauren wonders why we behave the way we do - Jordon, when he was that age could not have cared less. Lauren is inquisitive, where Jordon was reclusive and this offers hope that she will develop beyond the trappings of a safe routine, seeking out things that while they may terrify her initially, will give us something to work with in opening up her world.

While she encounters frustrations that trigger the same strange noises and repetitive behaviours, the bouts of screaming and crying, the slowness in progressing, she is not separate, she is in the same world as us and it is her inability to relate to it while she is within it that holds her back. Her screams are the frustration of not being able to relate to something that she sees yet still does not understand. Lauren will seek eye contact and look at you, showing that she wants so desperately to relate, she has a willingness to participate and tries hard to communicate, which can sadly lead her to feeling even more frustrated.

When Jordon was the age Lauren is now, his world was a million miles away from our own. He witnesses our world from his position of seclusion. To him, all of reality is alien, while with Lauren we are aliens in a world she shares with us and she is fighting hard to secure her position within it. Lauren does not accept her situation, because she can feel the differences and battles with them. With Jordon, this is not a struggle he can engage in because to him the challenges are all wrapped up in his one inability to relate. So, it is not that he does not try, he simply cannot see what it is he could struggle against. Therefore, he adopts the behaviours we constantly drill into him, while with Lauren, despite being somewhere near to Jordon on the spectrum, her struggle is to understand how to engage.

So my two grandchildren are stricken with the same diagnosis, of similar severity, with many common behaviours and yet their perception of the world differs on such a subtle but important level. While this may seem merely a question of degree in their respective states, the actual difference is where the child feels themselves to be in relation to the world around them.

They both occupy a foreign country of the mind, but Lauren has crossed our border and is seeking every day to learn our language, to understand the reasons behind our rituals, while Jordon will merely observe them and remains, to this day, a stranger in a strange land.

Hair today and gone tomorrow

Because of this inability to relate to our world, in the early years it would have been impossible to coax Jordon into a hairdressers; it was easiest to cut his hair at home. So, for many years, Brian took on the responsibility of cutting Jordon's hair himself, administering a buzzing and severe crew-cut with his clippers and revealing a nearly bald headed Jordon to the world, before he promptly did the same to himself. However, it did look to all intents and purposes as though they had both recently enlisted in the armed forces.

Eventually, however, Lisa and I couldn't stand looking at a near bald-headed Jordon and Brian and when Jordon was about nine or ten years old, we suggested that Brian took him for a proper haircut. As usual, we agreed as a family that this was the way forward and began to verbally prepare Jordon for the visit, letting him know that he was to sit quietly in the chair and have his hair cut by the barber. It would be fun and it was what men did together. For, by now, Jordon liked to feel he had grown up and was a man.

When they drove to the barbers Jordon used to get a chance to sit in the front seat of the car with dad and it was another special time for him, when he felt he was being a man by sitting 'up front' with dad. Jordon, in his own eyes, wanted to be either a man or a superhero and could be at least influenced or enticed to do something because it was "what a man would do."

Despite all our planning, when Brian first observed the manly rite of passage, taking his son to the hairdressers, it had quite catastrophic results.

Jordon knew from our preparation that upon entering the shop with Brian, he was to sit in the barber's chair. Obviously, the fact that there was someone already sat in it when they arrived didn't change this one bit for Jordon and bearing in mind he was now quite a big lad, he duly strode up to the man who was sat there and began to shove him out of it. Pushing with all his might, the first thing this poor man knew of Jordon's arrival was when he leapt on him from behind and began trying to drag him out of his seat. When Jordon's attempt failed he became more frustrated and even a little angry. Pushing all the harder, he turned on the lady hairdresser, attempting to pull her away so he could take his rightful place in the chair.

Brian had by now caught up and was profusely apologising and in turn, pulling Jordon away.

So, within seconds of arrival, there was a struggling mass of people around the barber's chair; the customer wondering what had hit him and the hairdresser concernedly holding her scissors aloft and out of harm's way, as they were pushed this way and that by an increasingly frantic Jordon who was becoming very anxious, crying out, "Nooo! Nooo!" accompanied by the customary groaning noises he still made at this age and overlooked by a previously serene queue of customers who, by now, had become extremely interested in what was going on.

I can only imagine the look on Brian's face and that he was very much regretting not having stuck to the previous routine of D.I.Y. dad and son haircuts. Thankfully, the lady hairdresser was very understanding and a very calming influence. She was able to help soothe Jordon and bring everything back to normal until he had taken on board that he must wait his turn.

To this day, Brian and Jordon return to the same hairdressers, where Jordon will joyfully greet her by name and take his place in the queue. The hairdresser will switch on the television and put on the programme Jordon wants to watch, while he quietly plays on his handheld games console until it is his turn for a haircut. When he is done, he always says, "Awesome!" and departs with a cheery wave.

Of course, even now, with the high level of dependency he has, it is very rare for Jordon to have a true taste of what independence and responsibility feel like. This does not deter him; like any boy his age he loves doing things with his dad, creating rites of passage that are an opportunity for him and Brian to bond. Having his hair cut with his dad on a Saturday once a month in the barbers is a time Jordon associates with being "A Man" and it has become an important ritual in his life.

Even as his inner need for independence grows, his relationship with his mother and his father is still a strong one and sadly, it is most evident when Jordon is in need. For who we turn to when we are in need reveals who we instinctively trust and Jordon turns naturally to Lisa, Brian and I. This is evident in many touching ways, for instance, when things break around Jordon, like a computer game, a charger or any one of his electronic devices, he does not understand the reasons and lacking perspective, he can quickly become distraught. Over the years, our only weapon to confront these potential meltdown-inducing occurrences has been the promise of Brian returning home. So, "Dad Will Fix It" became a constant in Jordon's world; something he knew as a remedy to the unexplained failure of any piece of machinery and Brian is the miracle worker when all else fails.

Merrily, merrily, merrily, merrily

With such a focus on his health, safety and well-being, I rarely get the opportunity to see Jordon away from his family and enjoying himself in the company of his friends.

One Summer's day, when Jordon was around thirteen years old, Lisa telephoned me to let me know his school were taking a day trip to my local park, just twenty minutes' walk away. The park is very large, with a boating lake and the school planned to take all the children out on the rowing boats.

I couldn't resist the chance to see him playing with his friends and so I got my two dogs and we went off in search of Jordon.

We must have walked around the park for a good half hour looking for his group, before nearing the water's edge where I heard the sound of happy laughter carrying across the lake. I stood peering out and caught sight of two boats, full of children, splashing, laughing and shouting, having the time of their lives and obviously enjoying every minute. I couldn't make Jordon out amongst them as they were too far away, but it was apparent that everyone was having a lovely time, shrill screams of excitement and giggling all mixing together and bringing a smile to my face.

The two boats slowly made their way back to shore and the children all stumbled out and on to dry land, going into the changing rooms to dry themselves off. By now, I was nearer, walking towards them but they remained a distance away and still I could not see Jordon, no matter how hard I looked.

On the point of giving up, I noticed a young boy walking towards me Head down, his arms all gangly and loose and swinging from side to side with each big lolloping step he was laughing and the boys and girls near him were chatting away;. It was Jordon, I was sure and even at this distance I could tell how happy he was.

Calling out, at first he did not hear me. I called again, louder. This time he stopped and looked around, not recognising the voice. Then he saw me standing with my two dogs and there was a further pause, while he obviously worked out what I was doing in the same park.

Then he yelled out, pure unbridled joy, his voice loud with excitement, "Naaan! It's My Nan! With Penny And Tuppence!" and with that, he came running across the grass towards me, his arms held wide. I could see he was still dripping with water and braced myself for a very wet hug. As we greeted each other, one of the Teaching Assistants noticed and came very swiftly over to investigate, while Jordon introduced me. I was very reassured by how quickly this lady appeared and with the still damp Jordon by my side, we telephoned his Mum to say hello and offer further proof of my identity, while Jordon excitedly told her of my surprise arrival, which had quite obviously thrilled him.

As Jordon returned to get changed out of his wet t-shirt and shorts, I was gradually surrounded by his class mates, all asking questions and very happy with their day out at the park.
"Who are you? Are you Jordon's friend?"
"No, I am his nan."

I marvelled at how happy and free spirited all these wonderful children seemed and as the crowd that had gathered gradually began to move away to their school bus, Jordon appeared once more from the changing rooms, waved happily to me and then abruptly disappeared once more, clearly having forgotten something he had left behind, which is just like him! As time ran out and Jordon accompanied his friends on to the bus, I stared after his retreating back and wished I could recapture that moment when he first saw me. The surprise and joy on his face had spoken volumes and the way he responded was so wonderful.

So, I stood with my dogs, so pleased to have seen him happily playing with all his friends and watching the children waving out of the bus windows as they drove off. Jordon however, stared straight ahead, as this is how he always behaves on buses.

I couldn't help but smile as I made my own way home.

Chapter Sixteen - The Guessing Game

Anticipating your child's needs is a game every parent plays. From the very earliest days of caring for a baby that needs constant supervision and attention, through the period when they become a more mobile toddler and then a lively pre-schooler, right up until their teenage years when different challenges come into play. Throughout their growing years, communication improves and once understanding and reasoning come into play, the need to guess at your child's requirements diminishes, improving as they learn to verbalise their emotions and to varying degrees, share their thoughts and feelings with you.

For the parent of any autistic child, however, this constant guessing game will never end, for even as your offspring grows into manhood or womanhood, physically becoming adults in their own right, then still the void of communication can remain unfilled. It is only your experience and the level of communication you have managed to achieve with your child that gives you clues as to what they are thinking and feeling. Even with 16 years of experience of familiarisation and learning behind us, some of Jordon's idiosyncrasies and behaviours still remain a total mystery.

Parents of autistic children endure the same kind of intense challenges that most parents experience during the battles of the 'terrible-twos', when their children are growing familiar with the world, its rules, possibilities and patterns. However, for the parent of an autistic child, this is not a brief campaign or a battle they can look forward to winning, it is not a short phase, nor a bump in the road of their child's development. From the time of the diagnosis onwards, there is a dawning realisation that the shape of the rest of your life has been set. Rather than a parent with a child and the prospect of eventually living separate lives, you have now been given a new career, one you had not asked for nor wanted. You are now and forevermore a carer and guardian to your child and you hold that responsibility for the rest of your life.

This responsibility will never leave you; as no one is likely to step in and take your place and neither do you have time in your daily work to contemplate a break from the new schedule of care that has been thrust upon you with the birth of your child. Despite the love you have for them, alongside your absolute loyalty and devotion, comes the kind of burden that some cannot bear, the kind of pain that cuts deeper than any you can imagine, the kind of pressure on your relationships that threatens to tear them in two. When relationships do break down, one of the parents usually then shoulders the responsibility for the child, taking on a 24 hour job, while the other goes on to live a life independent of the effects of autism. This is just one of the injustices, the seeming unfairness of the disorder, that one person's diagnosis can cut through the reality of so many people around them, turning lives upside down and bringing the entire focus of the family to one point, caring for the autistic child. As a parent, your entire mind-set must change; to provide the kind of environment that will meet the needs of a child with an autistic diagnosis means you have to be aware of and manage every single element of their existence, from what food they are given and how it is presented, to the programmes that are on television and to what clothes they wear. Ensuring that the meal is the right one for the right time and place, not five minutes too late and not presented in an unfamiliar way is essential and that you are looking for any sign of an ailment. Even if you do all this, putting all your love, care and attention into your child, the meal you present can, by some autistic children, be thrown across a room, judged unacceptable because you put gravy on the plate, or for some reason you will never identify. No matter what you do, you can never guarantee that what you offer will suit your child. After years, you might still be playing the same guessing game and never knowing if it will ever result in an independent and secure future for your offspring.

The earliest years of autism, before your child has developed a level of reasoning and hopefully reached a stage when they can verbalise, are amongst the hardest. It is like having a toddler going through their very worst phase and it can go on for many years. Yet knowing that this intense period will only be replaced by the slowest of developments makes it a test of patience, hope and endurance that sometimes feels like it will never end.

Up until the point reason and communication improve, you are prisoner to a routine that must be adhered to, you are the witness to a thousand tantrums, the vigilant guardian between your child and inadvertent harm from an unfamiliar world, the social pariah that bears a thousand stares, the legal counsel and political lobbyist that seeks to gain your child proper schooling, the apologist to shocked bystanders, the explainer of autism, the bearer of the responsibility for their unknown future when you eventually die, the emotional vessel for an entire family's plight, the chef of a thousand identical meals, the repetitive explainer who has to answer the same questions for years on end, the frustrated attempter who cannot explain what it is like, for who would believe you, the person who never dare spend a sick day in bed, the isolated recluse who dare not take their child out for days on end, landlord to a child that would stay in for the rest of their lives, first aider to constant self-harm, the nurse to symptoms and ailments that your child cannot name, the holder of a life's ambition unfulfilled because its demands are too great, the beggar who cannot choose what help they receive, the guesser at an uncertain future and the victim of ignorant bias and judgement and the sole bearer of a prayer for a miracle that you fervently pray will someday come, yet seemingly never does.

All the while, you may remain completely ignorant of your child's thoughts, unable to discuss even the most insignificant and trivial of things unless your child wants something for themselves. With an autistic child, you find yourself unable to meet with friends and even with their willing help, unable to entrust your child to their care, because such care needs specialist knowledge and your child's acceptance.

I know of parents in these positions who have spent days in isolation because their child will not leave the home and if they do, then mayhem ensues. Their daily routine includes preventing their child from injuring themselves or enduring blows as they vent their frustrations. They may spend hours and days asking for help from the authorities, yet be left with scant assistance and only hope to cling to. If they are not lost to anger or despair, then they are left with the empty reality of knowing that their child's life may be limited and their prospects unsure.

Sometimes a parent can wish away the days and years, hoping their child will grow up quicker because they cannot cope with the moment. Then, they feel the guilt of wishing away their child's early years and years of their own life they won't get back.

The safety catch

However, it isn't just your emotional stability that comes under threat from autism. If you ever visit the home of a family with an autistic child, especially the younger ones, you will in all probability see little physical signs as to the nature of their problem reflected in the layout of the home.

We are all familiar with the exploratory minds of your average toddler and have probably born witness to the occasional posting of a sandwich into the DVD player or a mobile phone being delicately dropped into a cup of tea, small items in danger of being swallowed, car keys being dropped down the toilet, cupboards being emptied out, books being ripped or your offspring's artistic endeavours realised in ink on your walls. With an autistic child, you can experience all of these and far more.

With Jordon, in one respect, we were lucky. Because he was initially almost totally disinterested in his outer environment, it made things a lot easier. However, when he went through his early phase of spinning round and round in circles, then we did have to be careful that he did not fall over on to something hard or sharp.

Lauren is a different story altogether; she will get into anything she can, pull over anything she is able to, bite whatever will fit into her mouth, yank at furniture until it topples, rip anything she has the strength to, climb whatever she is able to. When angry, you can depend upon her to try and bang her forehead or hit the wall with her hands.

We do not know when this behaviour will end, but it means that Lisa's home now bears witness to Lauren's behaviour. To all intents and purposes it is 'the safe house'. There are no pictures or mirrors on the walls for fear Lauren will climb a chair and pull them down. Her habit is to swing them as hard as she can until they drop. Then she might decide to bite at the pictures as she did with two portraits I painted of Lauren and Jordon. Initially, as a safeguard, Brian tried screwing mirrors and pictures to the wall, but Lauren is not deterred. If a mirror is held fast, she will pull at it with all her might and then get angry if it does not move. As a consequence, the walls are now predominantly bare and will remain so until Lauren has learned to stop or outgrows these habits. For, she has no concept of fear or danger and will pull the heaviest item down on top of herself if the opportunity presents itself.

Despite there being a mass of toys for Lauren to play with, she much prefers more dangerous and destructive pursuits. Brian soon learned that all the cupboards and shelving units in their home had to be rendered impossible for Lauren to move if she was not to try and pull them over and risk harm. So, Brian has now screwed every single unit to the wall, preventing Lauren from injuring herself or breaking the furniture.

On one occasion when she was being particularly boisterous Lisa, trying to calm her, took Lauren to her room to see if that would quieten her down. Lisa left her with her toys and a bottle of milk and thinking that there was nothing that could cause a problem, she quickly ran to the kitchen to make herself a cup of tea. There was soon some very loud banging from Lauren's bedroom and ever mindful, Lisa rushed back upstairs. Pushing at the door, she found it would not move. Something was obviously blocking it. Pushing harder, but mindful that Lauren might be behind it, it would still not budge. Lisa tried again, but to no avail.

Something heavy had been put right in front of the door. After a while of pushing and shoving and being careful not to topple whatever was on the other side, Lisa managed to make it into the bedroom, squeezing through a narrow gap. Lauren had evidently been very busy; she had decided to pull out every drawer from her chest of drawers and to pull them out far enough that they blocked her bedroom door. Lisa could hardly believe it. The strength it must have taken to do this was amazing from so small a child.

After this worrying incident, Lisa and Brian moved the chest of drawers to prevent it happening again.

Brian has suffered Lauren's destructive tendencies and his prized DVD collection now remains securely under lock and key, some of them bearing evidence to Lauren's habit of merrily pulling out the DVDs, biting at them, ripping the covers open and tearing the paper inserts to shreds. Lauren will happily sit for hours tearing up paper and so Brian's pride and joy has to be kept well away from her grasping hands in two units that are firmly screwed to the walls against which they stand.

Books will easily share the same fate as the DVD collection and will quickly become confetti under Lauren's ministrations.

When you enter Lisa and Brian's home, you will notice these small signs. All of the electrical sockets in the wall have been replaced with the type that do not have switches on them, evidence of Lauren's constant habit of playing with the switches. The furniture units are flat against the blank walls, screwed into place. There are no DVDs or books other than those under lock and key and the laptop has half the buttons missing; the scarred evidence of Lauren quickly sneaking up when Lisa's back is turned and meticulously picking the buttons off one by one as each opportunity presents itself.

The settee has no cushions upon it, for most of the time, Lauren has a strange obsession with pulling the seat and back cushions off of the settee. There is no rhyme or reason to this behaviour, they are not removed so that Lauren can play with them, they are not used for any purpose, it is merely that Lauren has a strong aversion to there being any cushions on it and Lisa will constantly battle with her for them to remain on the settee. It takes a lot of strength to remove all the cushions and to see Lauren exerting so much effort in removing them can be quite comical, she will be red faced and breathing heavily, furiously focused on her goal. When her task is complete, then Lauren will sit on a bare sofa, in front of her big pile of cushions, sometimes higher than her head, where she has managed to throw them directly from the sofa. It looks for all the world as though she is a queen commanding her cushion subjects to fall into line, rather than a little autistic girl with a strange obsession and this behaviour happens virtually every time Lisa leaves the room.

The television is now mounted high up on the wall in an attempt to evade Lauren's habit of continually switching it on and off. However, despite Brian's hard work, it transpires it is not high enough, for Lauren is now tall enough to drag a chair up to the television, climb onto it and happily engage in button pressing once more. At four years old, Lauren is very tall for her age.

The physical signs don't merely appear at home. Recently I met Lisa and Lauren and was taken aback at just how many holes she had bitten in her new winter coat. On the walks to and from school she will gnaw at her clothes whenever she is able. Lauren had managed to bite holes in the front and lapels, making it look as though some deranged moth had decided to attack her clothes. Anything she wears, dresses, t-shirts, and the paper from the nappies she sadly still has to wear will be torn apart, chewed, ripped and thrown everywhere. Today, we see small signs of this habit abating, but none of us are holding our breath! I believe that the action of chewing provides Lauren with the same comfort Jordon derived from his dummy and Lauren's new coat now hangs in the cupboard, the old one discarded.

Biting doesn't stop with clothes; much of the furniture in Lisa's home has a subtle motif around the edges where Lauren continuously bites at any edge she can find. All of these subtle signs are a reminder to me just how seemingly impossible it is to change the behaviours of an autistic child, that is, until they are ready and able to do so. While we try to assist, to encourage and to constantly repeat, we are now effectively in Lauren's hands until she is ready to change.

A world of hope

An autistic child's life is a lesson. Even as adults, we can spend our entire lives reacting in ways that are not sane. We confront everyday situations with unnecessary frustration, even though we will encounter them time and time again, showing that we live our lives with a very basic misunderstanding of what approach works best. How many of us become angry at traffic queues and waiting in supermarkets and allow these small things to spoil our days? So it is not that we are sane and autistic children are odd, they can, in many ways, show us the strangeness of our own ways. One lesson an autistic child teaches us is to hammer home uncompromisingly that patience can often be the only way forwards, lest we become lost to negative feelings of frustration and anger. Another valuable lesson is that they may not initially reflect our love and through witnessing this complete absence of response, is to appreciate how difficult it is to get a child of this nature to respond with a hug or any display of affection. It feels like you are here to serve this child with no emotional reward at all and the heart wrenching effects show us just how important love and affection are in our lives.

Hope is where the heart is

In writing this book, I wanted to bring a message to the world, to shed light on the plight of autistic children and their parents everywhere. I wanted to bring insight into the world of autism and illuminate the emotional hardships that the families endure. In doing so, I realise just how hard it might seem for those parents whose autistic children have just recently been born into their lives and how steep the mountain is that they have yet to climb.

While we all know how tough life is for parents of autistic children, for the children themselves and their wider families, this isn't the whole story. I want to say one thing loud and clear, there is hope. There is a future for your child and they will develop, they will experience life and they will progress in the way they are able. For they show us that love does not depend on what the other person does for us, it does not depend on the career they are able to grow for themselves or the power and wealth they amass. Autistic children show us that it is what we are able to share, despite life's adversities, despite our own limitations, that is of the ultimate importance. Every parent knows the joy of watching their child take their first step, of witnessing their moments of unbridled happiness. These moments exist for parents of autistic children too and eventually your child will grow and prosper, despite their unending need for attention and care. It is, in fact, this very same need that draws you into such a close relationship with your child.

It is all too easy to hear an autistic child's voice when they are frustrated with the isolation their autism lays upon them. Yet they also bring us a message, letting us know that our inner selves are the most important part of us, telling us that we may take pride in our children no matter what their potential.

Their message is that each of us has a huge capacity for patience if we choose to develop it, that if we look beyond the obvious we will find reasons for every strange behaviour and that when we take this viewpoint, we can develop seemingly limitless depths of understanding, merely because we have chosen to look for the cause rather than react to the behaviour. With understanding we lay a fertile ground for love, unearthing the limitless capacity that lies buried within us. Autistic children help us to look above competitive rivalries while they themselves rarely think about how others view them. No longer is our child in a race to be better than all other children in their group, but rather we are thankful for each new discovery they make. This seeming defencelessness, this inability to stick up for themselves also shows us the strength we might find in standing up for our children, for fighting for their rights as much as we are willing to take up their cause.

Perhaps the most exciting news is that Jordon just recently sat his very first school examination. His tutor decided to put him forward, along with other members of his class, to be assessed in Land Based Studies; the study of plants and animals. Yes, this is the most basic of exams by our usual standards, yet when I look back to all those years ago when he was a little boy turning in circles and making the weirdest of noises, the boy who looked as though he would never even speak, let alone write, my heart could burst with pride.

But even his new-found status as a beginner at botany didn't seem to influence Jordon when he visited the famous Hampton Court flower show this year. When he returned home, I was expecting some description of the wonderful flowers but when I asked him what he saw, the reply came promptly back, "Dandelions!" and I couldn't get another word out of him!

Jordon has now passed his Land Based Studies exam with flying colours, gaining a B grade, a very exciting development, as sitting an exam, let alone passing one, is something we never envisaged Jordon attaining in his lifetime.

So, there is hope, regardless of what interventions and medical changes happen in the world. An autistic child brings one of the hardest lessons of all, how we can love someone who is born with a limited capacity to demonstrate their own feelings, who might as a consequence only offer us the merest glimpse of affection in their formative years. An autistic child shows us how to love despite our own faults and failings, to cherish a child that may be walled off from us. They help us to become better versions of ourselves, help us see beyond the obvious and as a consequence, take our own pathway to a more enlightened future; one where we have all grown stronger.

If I have one hope for this book, other than to help those whose lives are directly affected by autism, it is that those who do not have autism in their lives will take up the message too and help stand up for autistic children and their families. For in standing up for those who cannot help themselves, we all have a chance of becoming better people as a result. There lies much of the hope for autistic children, not that they will change, but that the world will.

Chapter Seventeen - Discovering What Works for Your Autistic Child

Jordon and Lauren have both given us an insight into life that could not be had on any other journey and what we have learned from them about the nature of love and the value of patience and encouragement is immense. Autistic children are beautiful human beings, often defined by the vulnerability autism places upon them. Now at last, autism is in the public eye, offering beleaguered parents a glimmer of hope, that recognition will promote understanding and perhaps a shared acceptance for the children who were once merely thought of as odd.

The sad thing is that, like all children, they do not come into this world with a handbook or manual that explains how you might cope, how you can meet their needs and understand their mysteries. Even when you do figure out how to work with your autistic child, it is difficult to share knowledge that is useful to other parents of autistic children. Autism manifests in so many different ways and with such a vast difference in severity, that what works for one child will not necessarily work for another. Yet, despite the differences, there are many common traits in autistic behaviour and many experiences that parents can relate to.

When we began writing this book, we wanted to reach out to parents of autistic children everywhere and as best as we were able, through Jordon's story, to show that they are not alone in their journey. Perhaps most importantly, we wanted to share some of the lessons we have learned on Jordon's pathway, to illustrate some of the limitations and possibilities and to put these in context, for while every autistic child shares a common heritage, each one is unique.

Puzzling thoughts

Perhaps the most important perspective I have gained from Jordon over all these years is an understanding of how he thinks. While he sees our world through a warped pane of glass, his sensory input distorted, clearly it is not just his perception that is affected, there are other differences, distinct contrasts in how he is able to process the information that filters through to his mind from his five senses. Gaining a perspective on this is immensely important because it helps a parent to appreciate how to introduce new elements to their child's life and even to some extent anticipate what the likely reactions are when they do so.

Jordon's thought process is born of his efforts to understand the world around him and to work around his own limitations, to function without the ability to make the kind of associations we take for granted. Instead of the background of reasoning and emotional reactions we employ, Jordon has to create a map of the world without the aid of intuition and with very limited communication and so, the thoughts in Jordon's mind have, to him, the same importance and solidity as the distorted input of his five senses. When I think of his mind, I see it as a maze that is choked with information, crammed with dense thoughts in an effort to cope.

Each situation Jordon encounters has to be understood before he will accept it and to understand that it is not a threat or source of anxiety, he has to relate it to what he already knows. Integrating all this information, getting him to accept any given situation for the first time, is like solving one side of a Rubik's cube™, lining up the squares until that situation is in effect, all one colour and therefore coherent in his mind. Yet, if you take one element of the situation and change it, to move one square, then nothing makes sense to him anymore and the situation becomes a threat again.

This is why, even when he was eating cheese, we had such a hard time in getting him to accept the thought of eating a cheese sandwich, because he cannot intuitively recognise associations. He did not know cheese in that context. We had already solved one side of the cube and he had accepted ham sandwiches, to then have that same sandwich filled with cheese, he would have to scramble the perfectly constructed side of the cube that he had lined up in his mind, the one that associated the square of ham with the square of bread and the square of butter and instead, introduce the yellow square of cheese. To do this, at each turn, he would have to question one of the associations he had made, effectively scrambling his entire world. He would have to turn the cube in his mind to associate ham with bread, to turn it again to associate it with a sandwich cut into four, turn it again to associate eating that sandwich on a plate, then turn it again to associate them in context of being served at the table. Only once this association had been made, would another square fall into place in the puzzle of his mind. To then change the association of where he ate the sandwich would mean starting all over again from the beginning.

So, everything is categorised and mapped out and Jordon cannot differentiate between what is relevant and what is not. Each step of the way in any change is an exercise in his thinking it through, working it out and being led by us. Even the simplest of changes will involve many turns of the cube in Jordon's mind, as he changes the relationship of every element around a particular action and that is why it often takes so long to do so.

The thoughts in Jordon's brain have the same importance and solidity as the outside world because they are his only way of relating to it and the map in his mind has become the territory he is willing to occupy.

You can appreciate then, why autistic children avoid the things that are strange to them and why, before they become more familiar with our world, they would choose to ignore it as much as they can. Because the unfamiliar is so frightening, anything that is strange to their experience will often be tuned out and avoided.

This is why it is so important to bridge the gap between our two worlds, introducing language and pictures to your child as soon as you are able, anything that can promote familiarity and understanding. Language, be it picture cards, sign language or verbal, is perhaps the most important route to accelerating the development of any autistic child; it is the key to communication and even those who have yet to learn to speak may understand far more than we suspect. For this reason, we have spent hours with Jordon, reinforcing the phrases that become verbal keys to help him feel secure and to help us introduce new ideas. This then opens the door for the slow, methodical introduction of ideas and situations and behaviours. Meanwhile, time passes as you wait for the moment your child is ready to progress.

Even with the ability to communicate established, autistic children will often lean on routine as a place to hide in safety. Routine lets them know where they stand and what to expect next, for this makes their world more secure. This is why it is so important to introduce and help them understand the concept of time. Once they have developed this ability, you can introduce set times for set activities. A bed time, bath time and meal times help them to feel secure during their day. However, we had to be cautious not to make Jordon's day too regimented and rigid, otherwise he would have expected every element of his days for evermore to conform to his timetable.

Jordon currently has three timetables, each one of them different; the one he has at his own home, the one he has at school and the one he has when he visits my home. It is very important to maintain this flexibility and in the case of when he visits me at home, we change his daily timetable deliberately, in a distinct effort to keep him flexible, to understand that changes are acceptable and that each one does not herald the end of the world!

Routine aside, encouraging an autistic child to participate in our world is another key to their development, otherwise many of them would prefer to remain locked in their own world forever. This is why meal times, family parties, socialising at school, all of these play a very important role in Jordon's development. Yet, Jordon will only come into our world when we encourage or, on occasion, push him to do so. Even though he chooses to stay in his safe haven because our world is so confusing to him, still part of him wants to be engaged with us. Though he has to make a conscious effort to translate what we are saying or doing, he will instantly relate to that which is of natural interest to him, suddenly on high alert. So, his ears prick up when we mention shopping for a new video game or buying food he likes, but the rest of the time, even now he is older, we have to metaphorically take his hand and pull him into our reality, all the while reassuring and reasoning with him as he crosses the divide, providing verbal encouragement to help him understand and feel safe. For Jordon is selective as to what he allows in, be it a new food or a new piece of clothing and even when he makes the effort, he still does not understand every situation he finds himself in or why we ask him to participate. The danger, as with all autistic children, is that he stays stuck, for his interpretation of the world is so hard fought for, that changing any one element is like scrambling that Rubik's Cube™ once more.

Before autistic children can match up all six sides of their cube and become accustomed to life, their parents have to help them solve one situation at a time, effectively marrying up one side of the cube on a daily or hourly basis. Each new element, each food and situation has to be brought into acceptance before they move on to the next.

Showing them that the yellow of a cheese sandwich can fit into the green of their school day is therefore a monumental undertaking. But once this is accepted, then the puzzle of their life is one turn nearer being solved and you can then turn to the next challenge!

This is one reason why autistic children prefer to avoid interacting with us, especially when we are seeking to introduce change, because each and every one of our efforts to bring in something new is a threat to the situations they already understand. Solving the whole cube may take an entire lifetime and even then all you have done is equip them to function to the degree they are able. In the meantime, often they will focus on one subject, perhaps mastering it until they become savants that specialise in one side of their cube. This is why perseverance, reassurance and a measured approach will serve you well in combatting the limitations autism seeks to impose.

No man is an island

Many autistic children enter life as silent observers, seeing everything, but not appreciating what it is they are witnessing or what relevance it has for them. They view our world devoid of conscious need, compassion, familiarity or understanding of their relationship to it. Irrelevant and unexamined, without our intervention, life might otherwise pass them by and they would remain lost on their own individual islands, cocooned in their repetitive behaviours.

Like looking at the world through a borrowed pair of binoculars, sights, sounds and smells all compete for equal priority in Jordon's narrow focus and nothing is in perspective. If your eyes lied to you, if you could not interpret what they told you, if you could not work out what was relevant, wouldn't you seek to run and hide in your own private world?

This is yet another reason why the commonality of a shared experience is almost entirely missing from the autistic world and every parent of an autistic child knows this is why communication, the one element that is most difficult and elusive is also the most essential component in their child's progression.

Too much of a good thing

This gap in understanding is partly why Jordon loves playing his computer games so much. Any new situations that are outside of his understanding are immensely scary, nightmare intrusions, while, with his computer games he can wrap himself in them, become absorbed in a reality that does not demand his physical interaction and is controllable and safe.

With all the trials he has been through to progress to the lovable man he is fast becoming, it is lovely that he has something in his life that he enjoys so much. However, Lisa, Brian and I often find ourselves wondering whether we should be allowing Jordon to be so lost in the world of gaming.

Ours is not an unusual dilemma; many parents will be familiar with the sight of their teenage children hunched over their phones, tablets, laptops or consoles. The danger for Jordon, is that his teenage preoccupations could easily extend into the rest of his life.

In the meantime, gaming helps Jordon live in the world and there are a lot of games he enjoys, but for the last eight years Pokemon™ has remained his favourite. Each year the Pokemon™ Annual appears on his Christmas list alongside a Pokemon™ game and all the while, he will watch his favourite Pokemon™ video clips over and over again.

Thankfully, Jordon is developing in many ways and his increasing realisation of the relevance of time helps us to put the length of time he spends at his laptop and gaming consoles into perspective for him. Yet, like most boys his age, he likes things his way and very much prefers to spend his time on his own terms.

So, for now, our attempts to limit Jordon's time on computer games are very much a work in progress!

I am Jordon, Jordon I am

One quirk of Jordon's speech is, that up until the time he was around fifteen years old, generally he referred to himself in the third person. From the time he was able to talk he would do this and when he was older and more compliant, "Jordon Do It" or "Jordon Get It" would be a typical reply if we asked him to do something for us. Typically, if an adult displays this behaviour, then they are seen as being narcissistic, while in Jordon's case it shows that initially, at least, he was merely copying exactly what we said to him, word for word. Very occasionally, he reverts to this habit, which is a common one amongst autistic children, but generally speaking, it is something he has grown out of as he gains a greater grasp on his own identity.

To observe and protect

The best advice to autistic parents is to spend time observing their children, to watch and learn the things that make them respond well and those that send them into a downward spiral. There is normally a trigger, something that provokes the response. In Jordon's case, while we do not know everything about him, we do know that any sign of an argument or somebody singing out loud causes him a lot of disquiet. We know that this is so, we know not to argue or sing in his presence, but we still do not know why. We know that loud computer games or music do not bother him in the least as he will contentedly sit listening to them for hours at a time. So, while observation may help you understand more, it does not necessarily grant you all the answers.

The phrase that pays

For an autistic child, where understanding is so plainly elusive, you can partly hope to bridge this gap through constant repetition. Repeating phrases helps your autistic child understand what to expect next, creates familiarity with the world around them and can, in turn, help bring security that would otherwise be absent.

Repetition, saying the same thing to him over and over again, was perhaps one of the most important techniques we used to help Jordon adopt desirable behaviours. It was the most important key to improving his communication and unlocking his life. Repetition is especially important when you are introducing a routine. While Jordon has progressed beyond this stage, Lauren is a work in progress and we use exactly the same basic naming techniques with her. So, "dinner" with the action of putting the plate on the table prepares Lauren for the change from not eating to eating, "coat" while we present her with her coat, helps her to realise it is time to go out and puts meaning to the words, while allowing her time to mentally prepare. "TV" while we hand her the remote control means it is time for her favourite programme.

We still use repetition with Jordon daily; it serves to create familiarity and reassures him that whatever situation he is in is an acceptable one. The irony does not escape us; that the key to unlocking Jordon's world and helping him overcome his own repetitive behaviours is to adopt our own!

Even though this technique works, teaching even the simplest of things, such as the names of objects, can take years and yet this patient effort is worth it, because the more words Jordon understands, the more he can relate to us directly and the more we can explain the world to him.

So we say, "well done Jordon", "you are being a good man" and "I am so proud of you!" to reinforce positive behaviour and encourage him and we have key words for bad behaviour too. Things we say to deter Jordon from acting in ways that are not helpful, such as, "you must not do that Jordon. It is not appropriate" and we have key words for reassurance, "it's ok!" repeated over and over again, as many times as he needs to hear it to feel secure. We have used these phrases since his childhood and we develop new ones to meet new situations.

Repetition is not the only answer, because while it has helped Jordon to learn, it only goes so far and even though he has learnt many phrases from us as a consequence, he does not necessarily fully understand their meaning. So, when he does not want to eat a certain food because he does not like the taste, he will use the only appropriate phrase he knows and say his "Tummy Is Full." And he will often answer inappropriately in amusing ways. If we say to him "I am sorry that you hurt yourself" he will inevitably reply "That's OK I Forgive You" and we will laugh good-naturedly as we explain that "sorry" can be a simple expression of regret as well as an apology. Still, he does not yet understand this and the same response comes back time and again.

Of course, that is not the only phrase Jordon does not understand. Generally, if he is unsure about what I mean and doesn't know how to respond, he says, "Don't Be Silly Nan. You're Only Joking" which I think is a lovely way of putting it. To Jordon, even today, English remains a foreign language.

Superhero or superhomebody?

Even when Jordon does pick up on the literal meaning of words and phrases, it can sometimes create quite amusing circumstances. A few years ago, for a while he went through a phase of telling everyone, "My Name Is Spirit Boy!", the name of one of his favourite gaming characters. For months, Jordon was adamant that we address him by his new title and he would often approach bemused shop assistants and passers-by to tell them, "Hi! My Name Is Spirit Boy!" while they tried to work out what to do with this information.

Even today, Jordon maintains high aspirations for his future career as a hero. Recently, he approached Lisa, his face serious as you can imagine with such a momentous decision, "Mum! I Want To Join The Army."
Lisa was quick to explain, "you realise you won't be able to stay at home Jordon. Are you going to cope with that?" Jordon was quiet, then slowly he responded, thinking it through "Yeeess."
"You won't be sleeping in your own bed at home anymore. Are you going to cope with that?"
He thought some more "Yeeess".
"And you won't see Mum, Dad, Nan and Lauren and you won't be able to have the food you like."
Silence, then another slowly spoken "Yeeess".
"And you won't be able to play computer games."

This final blow was obviously far too much and this time, Jordon's response was a lot quicker; his new career chosen!
"OK. I Don't Join The Army Now. I Change My Mind. I Be A Super Hero".

Lisa gently explained that superheroes had to leave home too and couldn't play computer games as they would be far too busy. Jordon quickly decided that perhaps, after all, staying at home was the best option.

Chapter Eighteen - A Visit to Nan's

I have written this book out of love for my grandson Jordon, so that his legacy to the world might be more than just the memory of one more autistic child born to a family desperately trying to cope.

Jordon's life already has meaning, both for him and for our family, but on the pathway we are walking together, there is so much we have learned and I did not want this knowledge to be wasted, nor my grandson to be overlooked.

As a family, we have learned never to give up on an autistic child and that by understanding the reasons behind their behaviours, we can discover that we are all created equal, that autistic children grow up to become autistic adults and they need our understanding and acceptance too, for all of us are human beings. Through the eyes of others, I have learned not to judge that which we do not understand. Most importantly, the meaning of Jordon's life, the one I wanted to share through his story, is that no matter what faces us, love conquers all.

I have walked with Jordon, Lisa, Brian and Lauren on every step of their pathway and I wanted to tell the world what a wonderful young man Jordon is. There are many autistic children in this world and this book is their voice.

Now that Lisa, Jordon and the family live further away from me, I only see Jordon for any length of time when he is able to stay overnight at my home, typically for a weekend or when he has a holiday, encouraging his visits because I love his company.

Now, a pattern has been established and every school holiday he expects to come and see me, it is a treat he looks forward to, away from his usual routine, but in the familiar surroundings of my home.

Lisa and I plan well in advance and in the time leading up to each trip, Jordon counts the days on his calendar and mentions it whenever we speak on the phone, which is a regular occurrence. For reassurance, he uses the phrase that means something we have said is going to happen, will happen, "A Promise Is A Promise Is A Promise, Nan! Just You, Me, Penny, Tuppence", he will say, his voice rising with excitement, then he names the time and day he is to visit.

I will reply, "I am so excited, Jordon."

And invariably his response, "Me Too, Nan. Bye!"

On the allotted day, Lisa telephones me to say they are on their way, letting me know what clothes she has packed for Jordon. Meanwhile, Brian gathers together all of his gaming equipment, filling bags with handheld games, a portable television, laptop and a gaming console, together with a bag of cables and chargers. No matter whether he is staying for a few days or a week, all of his equipment must come with him.

The preparation that goes into each trip seems to take as much planning as a full-blown holiday! For, while Lisa and Brian are gathering all the necessary items, I will be on a major shopping trip, double checking that my fridge has an adequate supply of chocolate mousse and that my cupboards are full.

Jordon's sole contribution is to choose the games he wants to bring and we have to limit him to his favourite twenty or so, otherwise he would bring his entire collection! Everything else he needs must be remembered by Lisa and Brian and bitter experience has taught Brian that leaving just one charger or cable is not allowed and he would have to make the whole hour-long trip again.

When Brian parks his car outside my home, I go to the window and watch Jordon walking ahead of him, both of them laden down with bags. I cannot help but smile as I see just how much they are carrying between them. Brian's arms are full to the brim and I cannot imagine Jordon has actually left anything behind in his bedroom!

As I open the door, every single time, the first thing I see is Jordon's smiling face beaming back at me, his eyes wide with excitement.

"Naaan! I've come To Stay Monday 'Till Saturday Just You, Me Penny Tuppence!" Jordon will always name the exact number of days he is staying.

Every time he returns, I greet him the same way, so that he knows this place is one where he is loved, welcome and safe. I throw my arms open and tell him "Oh Jordon, I have been waiting all morning for you. I am so pleased you are here."

We hug and he will kiss me on the cheek, greeting my two Yorkshire Terriers, Penny and Tuppence with the words "Hello Penny! Hello Tuppence!" and from that point on, he will totally ignore them for his entire stay, for him, they hold no relevance, nor interest, whatsoever.

Jordon then makes himself at home in my spare bedroom while Brian sets up all of his games for him. This is all part of his ritual and when everything is set-up, Jordon will tell Brian to go.

"You Can Go Now. Bye Dad. Look After My Little Sister, Woren. See You In Five Days!" Once more, Jordon names the specific period of time he will be staying, reassured by knowing when Brian will return. From that point onwards, for the entire stay, he never once mentions his mum or dad, he will not even talk to them on the phone when they call each day.

For, just like when he boards the bus to school and does not look back to wave goodbye, Jordon relates far more readily to the here and now and the future than he does the past. Relating to what has happened already and his role within it is very difficult for Jordon. When I ask him about his week at school, I can see him making an effort to articulate what happened, but most of the time he will abandon the attempt. I suspect this is because to him, his school is one solid thing in his memories. I am sure he can picture his classroom, but separating out a period of time, such as last week, remains an impossible task.

Jordon will then happily play his computer games until I choose to interrupt, knocking on his bedroom door "Jordon, what are you doing?"

"Playing Fighting Games Naan! I Am The Champion!" and without any pause whatsoever, in the same breezy tone "Bye, See You Soon! You Go Downstairs. I Will Stay Here And Play My Game!" From outside the bedroom door, I can hear Jordon leaping around, acting out the sword fighting or martial arts moves he sees on the screen.

Despite his keenness not to be interrupted, when friends call he always leaps to his feet, rushes out of his room, a whirlwind presence, promptly greeting them with the same formula of words that rush out in quick succession, "Hello. What's Your Name? My Name is Jordon. Welcome To My Nan's Home. Make Yourself Comfortable!"

Then he will shake hands, as he has been taught, before immediately disappearing again. "I Must Go To Play My Games! Bye!"

Still, Jordon is always eager to please and it is endearing to see how spontaneous and completely unreserved he can be in expressing himself. You can make him happy with the smallest of gestures, even something as small as giving him a biscuit can prompt a beaming smile and he is so polite he will thank you profusely for whatever is given. What adds to my delight is that conversely, he is totally unembarrassed by refusing any offer. If we invite him out and he does not wish to go he will happily say, "No!" without the slightest reserve or regret. Yet, everything is an adventure to him and to see how eager he is to visit the pizza restaurant or spend time with me in my home can serve to remind me that every human life is full of daily surprises that we might otherwise take for granted.

Not all of Jordon's responses are verbal and when I ask him, "How much do you love Nan, Jordon?" He will throw his arms wide, stretching out into his fingertips and showing the measure of how deeply he cares, just as he answers me with his stock answer, "A Big Much!"

Despite his natural expressiveness, Jordon wants so desperately to be seen as a grown up, just like any typical teenager, to be accepted in the adult world he does not understand. He tries very hard to be a man and if I remind him to behave like one, he will stand like a soldier at attention. For some reason, he believes that real men stand at attention! Yet, it is the vulnerable boy within him that is making this effort to conform and that boy will never truly go away. At these times, my heart feels like it could burst with love; he is such a sweet and innocent child and yet his personality comes through loud and clear even when he is trying so hard to live by our rules.

Yet, many of the rules he follows are not imposed. Jordon's waking and sleeping hours are very regimented, partly because he likes it that way. What initially started as an effort to bring a recognisable pattern to his life has resulted in him following a routine he finds it very difficult to deviate from. At 9 p.m. every night, without fail, he will announce to me that he is going to bed and he will not listen if I say he can stay up later or to wait a little while; 9 p.m. is his bedtime and that is that!

So, I have to ensure he has washed and cleaned his teeth before he disappears to bed. If he has gone just a few minutes past the allotted time, then he will lapse into exaggerated yawns and sighs, "Time For Bed!"

At 5 a.m. Jordon will wake up and at 7 a.m. he knows it is time to come down for his wash and breakfast, all of which are fixed points in our day. He will always greet me with the words, "7 o'clock, Nan, Time To Get Up!" shouted through my bedroom door before he goes downstairs. Sometimes, it feels like I am sharing my home with a soldier, so regimented are his hours!

I often go with Jordon for walks and the occasional trip to the shops. Crossing the road used to be a great concern, for I cannot control him physically if there is imminent danger and I must secure his cooperation in all things. Even up to the age of ten years old, if we grabbed Jordon's hand, he would do everything he could to escape and we would be forced to drag a struggling child across the road. Not a very comfortable position to be in when there are cars whizzing past. Yet, now he is sixteen it is increasingly possible to reason with him and I use the ploy of appealing for help. This works well as it offers Jordon a choice and makes him feel grown up and useful.

So, we approach the kerb and I will address him softly "Nan needs you to help her cross the road please, Jordon. Will you help me?"

His reply is nowadays always, "No Problem, Nan!" and he will dutifully put his arm in mine before we step out. The moment our feet hit the opposite pavement, his arm disappears from mine with no hesitation whatsoever.

With this reassuring pattern established, I feel more relaxed taking Jordon out and when the time comes for us to shop, rather sweetly, Jordon will pull my shopping trolley for me. When we return from the shops, it can be quite heavy, stuffed full of yet more of his favourite foods, for his appetite is now very well developed. Whenever Jordon does this for me, it can be quite comic, as he is always on a mission, walking as quickly as possible, racing ahead of me to return home, while I am on a mission of my own; to keep up with his fast pace!

At meal times, we always sit down to eat at my dinner table. Despite enjoying every moment of his time with me, one sad aspect of his visit is that, unless I ask him questions, Jordon does not talk and so if I do not talk, we sit in silence.

As I look at Jordon across the dining table, knowing that this is my grandson, I recognise that there is so much missing from our relationship; the everyday conversations, getting to know each other, laughing and playing, sharing my life experiences with him. Instead, if I ask him questions, I will often receive that same response, "No Talking Nan. No Talking!" and he is extremely reluctant to talk about the past. So, if I ask him what happened at school last week, he will reply, "I Don't Want To Talk About It Today!" If pushed, he will say "It Is In My Memories" but that is all you can get out of him. Talk about a film or something separate from him and Jordon will be happy to chat about it, but anything that happened before this day and involved him directly will always elicit the same response. This means Jordon won't discuss what he ate for dinner yesterday but he will always remember his favourite food.

It is at times like these that I feel so aware of what autism truly denies us and it is that which many of us take for granted, the everyday laughter, the interaction and the ability to talk things through. I gaze at my grandson, taking in every detail of his face and I wonder how other grandparents of autistic children feel, do they wonder as I do how to fill the silence, how far they can go in establishing a relationship? All of us must worry, all of us must fret at our inability to do anything more than constantly encourage our grandchildren. Instead of sob with the frustration of it all, do they stay positive and battle every day to bring their child further into the world? Looking into Jordon's eyes it is like gazing across a vast plateau, one that we hope to cross in this lifetime. I could crush him in my arms, such is the depth of my feelings, but what is it we can do, how far can we go in letting our grandchildren know we are there for them?

I put every effort into communicating with Jordon and yet I know the answers will never be instant. Asking him the most basic of questions, I receive the answers he knows, but these are stock phrases and when I probe deeper, asking him how he feels or "why" he is doing something, I am asking him to embark on a journey that only he can make and it is not a pathway I can walk for him. If I ask, "Jordon, why are you doing that?" the effort he makes to answer is clear. He will stand still, gazing off into the distance, immobile, his arms at his sides, even the concept of "why" is almost alien to him, yet I will not allow him to remain alien to us and so I persevere. The struggle to answer is evident in the look of concentration on his face, his features serious and taught. When he finally speaks, articulating what he finds within himself, he falters and even stutters, just as I struggle with my own stuttering emotions, hoping that one day he might successfully make that journey into self-understanding and bridge the gap between us. Inevitably, he gives up on this impossible task and his words are almost too quiet to hear. It is when he answers that I struggle the most, for it is then that the isolation that autism imposes is most clear, "I Don't Know!" or "No Questions!" is always the end of our conversation. As a family we only move forwards when Jordon is able to take his next step.

As the years have passed, our love for Jordon has never ceased, only grown, and I believe he now knows we all love him "A Big Much!"

Jordon will often play in my back garden, which typically involves pretending he is a hero in one of his computer games, fighting imaginary foes with a stick he pretends is a sword.

Because he has been taught to be polite, if he sees one of my neighbours, he will say hello. On one such occasion, I could see Jordon swinging his stick, totally absorbed in an imaginary fight. Then, over the fence, he saw my neighbour Marie, earnestly working away in her garden. Jordon paused and walked to the fence.

"Hello, My Name's Jordon! What's Your Name?"

"Hello, Jordon, I am Marie."

Jordon took a moment to consider this. "What Are You Doing, Marie?"

"I am gardening, Jordon."

Again, a moment to consider. "Why Are You Gardening, Marie?"

"Because I have to cut my grass and make my garden tidy."

Again, Jordon took a moment to consider. Nothing in Marie's reply had any impact in his world. He had done his duty in addressing our neighbour.

Ever since that day, they always have a similar conversation over the garden fence and inevitably these brief interludes end in the same way, "OK Marie I Have Got To Go And Play My Fighting Games Now."

Jordon returns to battling his imaginary attackers, chatting away to himself as he cuts the air in wide arcs with his stick, while Marie returns to her gardening; a lot more than a fence separating their two worlds.

Much as I love his company, Jordon's visits are still a full time job. I ensure he has a cooked meal for breakfast, lunch and dinner, as his appetite is growing and I marvel at just how much he can eat without becoming overweight and yet still be ready for the next meal.

We are always trying to gently introduce new things to Jordon and every time he visits, I am mindful that it is an opportunity to try some new food or introduce him to new people. His reaction can sometimes add a touch of humour to our lives. On one memorable occasion, I decided to introduce cauliflower cheese to his diet to see if it was something he would enjoy. Cauliflower wasn't a problem, he had eaten it before, but I knew serving it with a sauce, putting something new on his plate, ran the very real risk of Jordon rejecting it forever.

So, I served the meal, placing a tiny piece of cauliflower cheese with it. Jordon, well aware of the new addition observed me closely as I ate the cauliflower cheese. His intense stare told me he was thinking hard about the possible ramifications of putting this alien substance in his mouth. He did not say anything, but he was obviously watching my reaction, waiting to see if I keeled over at the table or ran from the room, for in his mind he has no context to tell him what this new food stuff might do. With no obvious signs of distress on my part, he set to his meal.

As is his custom, he ate one type of food at a time, first the green vegetables, then the meat, then the potatoes. I watched intently, wondering what reaction we would get when he got to the cauliflower cheese. Eventually it was time. Smiling at the small island of cauliflower cheese on his plate, I knew what a big thing this was for him. Jordon's fork hovered in his hand as he stared at it. The next moment would be a telling one!

His attention lingered on the creamy yellow sauce, obviously considering what this new intrusion into his life might mean. He could see that I had already tried some. The fork remained poised, "come on, Jordon, eat your cauliflower cheese!"

Abruptly, Jordon's decision was made. Shaking his head earnestly, his reply was decisive and final. "No Thank You Nan. I Don't Like Salad Cream On My Cauliflower."

Trying to reassure Jordon that this was not actually salad cream, I exchanged a glance with Roland, who was eating with us at the time, but the fork was back down on the table. Jordon had given his verdict and there would be no moving him, nor changing his mind. He had surmised that a yellowy white sauce on his plate must be salad cream, the only other similar foodstuff he had seen.

Now he had made the connection, no matter how much I coaxed him, there was only one reply forthcoming.

"No Thank You, Nan. I Don't Like Salad Cream On My Cauliflower."

Roland and I stared at the lonely cauliflower cheese, recognising how strange it must appear to Jordon and we nodded to each other smiling. After all, who would eat cauliflower when it was so completely covered with salad cream?

The same thing happened recently when I offered Jordon what was to him, a new type of sweet. He does not have a particularly sweet tooth and we find ourselves in the unusual position of having to persuade him to try new sweet things every now and then, to ensure he stays flexible and open to new experiences.

So, I offered him the brightly coloured pack. "Jordon would you like a jelly baby?"

Earnestly, he eyed the bag and after a brief moment of solemn contemplation, he addressed me, his face completely serious with no hint of irony, for he meant none, "No Thank You Nan, I Don't Eat Babies."

Jordon had surmised that I was inviting him to eat something very strange indeed and was at pains to explain to me that he would not. He didn't see anything strange in my offering him one. Nor was he phased at all as I burst out laughing, he merely shook his head repeating earnestly, "No Thank You Nan, I Don't Eat Babies"

To this day, his answer remains the same and he will not be tempted to eat a single jelly baby, yet his response fills me with delight. It is a sign of how sweet his nature is, that he should react so sublimely to what to him is such a horrific invitation and yet remain unmoved by it. The mind boggles!

So for now, the many things that remain off of Jordon's menu, these failed additions to his world are telling signs of the nature of the disorder that permeates his reality. It shows just how careful we must be in how we approach change. We learn about Jordon every day and I now know that he doesn't eat cauliflower with salad cream and he doesn't eat babies, but he does make me laugh!

A favourite food Jordon can eat in great quantity is pizza and I will take him on a trip to our local restaurant whenever I am able. However, the very first time Jordon ever visited a pizza restaurant, he wore his red baseball cap and of course, he now has to wear that same hat every time we return. We travel by bus, Jordon sitting very still with his baseball cap squarely on his head. He has been taught not to make strange noises or movements on public transport especially and he interprets this as a need to sit rigidly immobile, his eyes staring straight ahead, his hands held in tight fists, his eyes half closed to prevent them twitching, all in an effort not to draw attention to himself.

When we reach the restaurant, I know to opt for the all you can eat buffet option and, as this is a treat, I do not try and get Jordon to eat salad, instead he concentrates on consuming as many pizza slices as I have seen any human being eat at one sitting. I sit watching him contentedly eating and wonder what he will do when his bright red baseball cap, which is still sitting squarely on his head, becomes too worn and frayed to wear.

Throughout Jordon's visits to my home, every aspect of his day has to be looked after for him, ensuring he bathes each night, that he cleans his teeth, changes into his pyjamas, even ensuring he goes to the toilet, for he still has a habit of only going once a day if we aren't careful, because he seems to have an idea that this is the right thing to do. If I was not on hand to supervise and look after him, then he would quite happily spend the entire day or even the week in his pyjamas, without cleaning his teeth or washing. The only reliable routine he has established in this respect is spraying his deodorant on every morning. It is a reminder to me just how hard Lisa has to work now that she has not only Jordon but his sister Lauren to look after too.

So, our time together is a busy one for me and sometimes I feel like Jordon's personal chef! Yet I enjoy every moment of having my grandson with me and this enjoyable time is like a ray of sunshine for us both, because I know just how important it is for Jordon to have this closeness and continuity, while it gives me an opportunity to bond with my grandson.

When the allotted day arrives for his departure and I am gathering up his possessions, packing his bags and getting him ready, Jordon will constantly repeat, "Don't Be Upset Nan, I Will Ask Mum When I Visit Again." He does not like to think that any of his family are unhappy and I once mentioned I would miss him when he was gone. To set his own mind at rest, he repeats the same reassuring phrase over and over again, reassuring himself and feeling both grown up and useful too. Because he is missed when he is away, he knows he is important in my life.

Inevitably, Brian will arrive and Jordon will take my hand to say goodbye. His mind is now set on returning home and I have to remind him to kiss me on the cheek. Dutifully and rather sweetly he does so, because Jordon does not know how to make the noise of a kiss, he will merely place his cheek upon mine. He turns away from me and as he does so he calls out his final words.

"Love You, Nan. It's OK. A Promise Is A Promise Is A Promise. I'll Be Back!"

Only You Can Help Me

Born into your world
Yet still trapped in my own
The box of my senses
Remains my true home

Autism casts me
Into an alien nation
Who are you
What is our relation

I am the stranger
In your strange land
How can I join you
I don't recognise your hand

You believe I am with you
And yet I am not
I live in the confusion
Your mind has forgot

This nightmare world
Crowds closing in
I remain in a void
And will not join in

My own thoughts
More than I can bear
Please do not wake me
I will not go there

Cold alone
Carried moved about

Please do not touch me
I beg you stay out

Someone is crying
The voice is quite near
These are not your cries
But my own that I hear

Wrapped up restricted
I don't want to escape
My mind has evicted
The world you have shaped

The last port of call
The place I call home
Is the haven within me
Only that is my own

Light dark sound touch
Everything you take for granted so much
The rocking and running
Are my only crutch

Learning to accept
Parts of the world more familiar
I can cope all the better
When everything is similar

Repetition and rocking
They both work a charm
Your gentle touch
And light music all calm

Show me now let me touch
Let me look around
I have discovered your world

But it is yet to be found

At two years old
Only you can help me

I wake up to voices
My choices made clearer
I still cannot talk
But somehow we're nearer

I seem very good
Staying put I sit quietly
But it is fear not good manners
Making me act so mildly

I wake up to voices
Every now and every then
You say the same thing
Again and again

Your words trickle in
Their meanings not caught
The understanding is thin
And yet still I am taught

Cross legged and rocking
I cry not knowing why
My behaviour not shocking
For now you get by

My thoughts run their circles
Round and round in my head
To drive out the world
I spin round instead

Run run

And run yet again
There's nothing I'm chasing
I run from my pain

At four years old
Only you can help me

Four years old
And a lot more open
To your world
And the words you have spoken

Yet the things I say
You do not hear
My words aren't formed
My meanings not clear

I fight and I struggle
And fall into rage
To be understood
We're not on the same page!

My anger and frustration
Always overwhelm
We're now on a voyage
But who's at the helm

At six years old
Only you can help me

You are placing restrictions
On all that I do
I like my way my order
Who's in charge me or you

I like things

To be as they are
It's you who bring changes
And seek to take me so far

Go away! I lash out
Go Away! I said
Let me play in my safe place
Let me live in my head

I'm alone in here
Lost not understanding
The gap in my thoughts
Is where you put your hand in

Your way isn't best
Why are you talking
And what do you want
It's my world please don't walk in

At eight years old
Only you can help me

Closer now
Yet the world feels so wrong
I don't want to join
I'm not feeling that strong

The effort the fear
The pain in my head
Should I hurt you
Or myself instead

At ten years old
Only you can help me

The world now has a shape

The routines are known
The strangers are family
And I recognise home

Two places I know
Where I feel secure
My room my computer
Of these I am sure

Your world is a classroom
You ask me to conform
But why should I follow
What you say is the norm

"Do it this way, Jordon
Don't say that
Not appropriate, darling
Why can't we chat?"

Stand my ground push your blocks
My way is best
Everything you say
Puts me to the test

At fourteen years old
Only you can help me

Change comes quicker
I am a man
I know I am different
And don't understand

The words are there
But the meanings unclear
I now trust my family
Only they have stayed near

You shape my life's purpose
Full of love and respect
I give back what you share now
No longer reject

The pathway I'm treading
Is a rocky road
You've smoothed it out for me
And we've shared my load

I struggle to grasp
All that you offer
Turn away from the hard things
Because why should I suffer

Change comes more easy
But always in bounds
Defined by the rules
I place on my own grounds

The box I was born in
Has lost some of its walls
It may still confine me
But not all in all

You're looking for hope
But I am not
It's something I don't relate to
And it's you that forgot

My family understand me
Most of the time
I know them much more now
What's theirs is mine

The future is brighter

Because my hand is held
By a family that love me
And want to grant me the world

At sixteen years old
Only you can help me

Contact the Authors

For more information on Jordon's Pathway and to find other books by Carolann Frankie and Roland Bush-Cavell please visit
www.jordonspathway.co.uk
Or email info@carolannspathway.co.uk

We are very grateful for your feedback and if you have the time, then please do find our book on Amazon. Each and every review is so very valuable to us and helps us spread the word about Jordon's Pathway. We cannot thank you enough for your support.

With very best wishes

Carolann and Roland

London, England
January 2014

Made in the USA
Charleston, SC
16 April 2014